INDUSTRIAL RELATIONS AND
NEW TECHNOLOGY

THE UWIST/CROOM HELM SERIES ON MANAGEMENT
AND NEW INFORMATION TECHNOLOGY

*THE MANAGEMENT IMPLICATIONS OF NEW
INFORMATION TECHNOLOGY*
Nigel Piercy

INDUSTRIAL RELATIONS & NEW TECHNOLOGY

ANNETTE DAVIES

CROOM HELM
London • Sydney • Dover, New Hampshire

© 1986 Annette Davies
Croom Helm Ltd, Provident House, Burrell Row,
Beckenham, Kent BR3 1AT

Croom Helm Australia Pty Ltd, Suite 4, 6th Floor,
64-76 Kippax Street, Surry Hills, NSW 2010, Australia

British Library Cataloguing in Publication Data

Davies, Annette
    Industrial relations and new technology. — (UWIST/
    Croom-Helm management and new technology series)
    1. Technological innovations — Great Britain
    2. Industrial relations — Great Britain
    I. Title
    338'.06   HC260.T4
    ISBN 0-7099-0882-2

Croom Helm, 51 Washington Street, Dover,
New Hampshire 03820, USA

Library of Congress Cataloging in Publication Data
applied for:

Printed and bound in Great Britain by Mackays of Chatham Ltd, Kent

CONTENTS

TABLES AND FIGURES

Tables

Figures

Key

BM – Brewery Managers
GM – General Managers
M   – Total Management Sample
BU – Brewery Unionists
GU – General Unionists
U   – Total Union Sample

People do not resist change but they do resent being changed.

Kurt R. Student.

INTRODUCTION

The problem of introducing and assimilating new technologies into organisations dates back to the beginnings of industrialisation. Solutions to this problem are important because firms which are able to make effective use of technological advances may increase their efficiency markedly. Those which fail to adjust to changing technology may find themselves outpaced and outclassed by their more innovative competitors. Failure to implement change swiftly and efficiently may prove fatal. Yet there are dangers and difficulties in the process of incorporating technological advances. Over-eagerness or too much haste may lead to a premature acceptance of a technology which proves, ultimately, not to live up to its initial promise. Innovation may prove too costly in human or financial terms. There is an optimum time for innovation, an optimum pace for innovation and an optimum mode for innovation. There are difficult decisions to be made. Who should be involved in such decision-making, and what if their their interests differ?

Such issues have recently taken on a new immediacy and a new level of significance. The reason for this is the 'microelectronics revolution' and an increasing awareness of the potential of microtechnology. At the most basic level of definition, microelectronics constitutes the miniaturisation of electronic circuitry, enabling the entire circuitry for a computer to be built onto a single chip of silicon less than a centimetre square. This technology has possible applications across a wide spectrum of industry and the continuing reduction in the size and cost of components, together with constant improvements in performance and reliability, would seem to make it certain that British industry can benefit from its use. But such imple-

1

mentation may have considerable problems. Some of
these problems will be technical. Others will be
related to manpower adjustment. This book examines
these manpower problems of the implementation of
microtechnology as well as the relationships which
develop between management and union in an attempt
to overcome them.

But what are the implications of microtechnological change for people at work? There is currently
a great deal of speculation in this area, and fears
of a major displacement of labour and deskilling
have aroused considerable debate and anxiety.
However, very little empirical research is available, and arguments in favour of such research have
two main justifications. Firstly, it is important
that any anxiety concerning the adoption of microtechnology should be allayed if it is unwarranted;
and secondly, if there are indications of current or
future manpower problems resulting from the
implementation of this technology, additional information may permit effective solutions to be found.

There are two major schools of thought concerning the likely manpower implications of a technological change project. One of these, firmly
embedded in the socio-technical approach to organisations, emphasises the 'indeterministic' quality of
technological change, and the possibility of a
number of different outcomes resulting from any
given technology. It is argued that 'outcome' will
be the result of an optimisation process involving
the various economic, technical and social factors
of a particular situation, and that decision-makers
are especially influential because of the degree of
'choice' that exists in both the design of new
technologies and their implementation. A possible
consequence of such discretion is the ability to
avoid the negative consequences of technological
change, ensuring that the quality of working life is
improved as a result of the change. The second
school of thought, however, strongly refutes any
suggestion that managerial discretion during technological change will be concerned with improvements
in the quality of working life and the retention of
'surplus' labour. It is argued that under a
capitalist system of production, technological
change has a built-in 'social bias', favouring the
owners of industry and their representatives. The
development of new machinery is shaped by a desire
to increase managerial control over production,
thereby increasing productivity and reducing the
strength of the labour force.

A critique of the above schools provides the theoretical framework of the present volume. While in many respects they are very different, a major limitation of both is that they tend to ignore the role of labour as an important variable in the technological change process. They therefore treat such change in an unproblematic way, assuming the decisions made to be the prerogative of management, unhindered by the forces of the labour movement. An historical analysis of technological change in industry shows it to be a process which is very much one of conflict, struggle and cooperation between management and trade union interest groups. It is therefore unjustifiable to ignore or undervalue the actual or potential role of the unions in any theoretical formulation of the process and outcome of such change. Indeed, the trade union movement has since the early 1950s shown a great deal of interest in issues concerning automation and the implementation of increasingly sophisticated technologies. Their argument has always been that increased union involvement in the process will ensure that the 'costs' of technological change will be reduced, and that the benefits will be equally distributed between capital and labour. Therefore, technological change in the present framework is viewed as a political, and potentially problematic, process, with different interest groups in the organisation attempting to achieve their preferred outcomes. Within the constraints of various socio-economic factors (such as the investment situation of the industry and its constituent firms, the nature of the market for the product and the rate of introduction), the outcome of change will be partly dependent on the relative influence of management and trade union negotiators, and the relationship which forms between them.

It is certainly the case that the repercussions of technological change tend to spread across many traditional subject areas of collective bargaining, such as manning levels, payment and working conditions, and it may thus be assumed that a number of the problems induced by technological change are likely to become a focus for management and trade union concern and/or conflict. However, an interesting feature of present trade union interest in microtechnological change is a desire, at least at the national level, for involvement beyond that of traditional collective bargaining. The Trade Union Congress (TUC) has argued that the union response should seek to widen the debate about new technology into the area of industrial democracy, the latter being achieved by an extension of collective bargaining into such areas as the initial investment decision and the type and extent of technology to be implemented. The feasibility of achieving this degree of involvement provides the main focus of this book.

A recent criticism of much of the research work in the area of participation or industrial democracy suggests that many studies may be over optimistic in investigating the topic. They tend to assume that employees or their representatives wish to attain high levels of awareness and involvement in organisations (Loveridge 1980). It is argued that it may be more realistic to assume that participants may have a more instrumental approach to industrial democracy, with high institutional awareness and commitment being based on a temporary consciousness of personal and sectional interest, usually achieved through a realisation of threats to that interest. This is what Loveridge terms 'constitutional pluralism', a concept which fits in well with the theoretical framework adopted, and with the assumption of a high trade union demand for involvement in the issue of technological change. A review of the participation literature highlights a strong need for the study of management-union participation as it relates to 'specific situations', much of the previous research being too general to be directly relevant to the specific problem under consideration.

The type of management-union participation studied in the present context is one which is achieved through an extension of the collective bargaining system. It is argued that the 'bargaining' likely to occur during technological change may contain both cooperative and conflictual elements. There are at present only a few empirical studies, most of them carried out in the United States, which examine the potential for a collaborative management-union relationship in settings where power and conflict are an inherent feature (Kochan and Dyer 1976). However, where such 'integrative bargaining' (Walton and McKersie 1965) is observed, the outcome is perceived to be of greater 'mutual benefit' to the parties, and a greater degree of satisfaction is expressed with the bargaining process. In a time of rapid technological change, it is important to conduct empirical investigations which examine the effectiveness of alternative types of change strategies in situations characterised by

conflicts of interests, shared power, and a high
potential for conflict. Such studies may provide
models for understanding the process by which the
competing interests of management and workers are
resolved in the context of fewer jobs and management's determination to change the mode of production. In the face of the pressure of such change
what functions do trade unions serve? In what ways
are their functions being redefined and what impact
does this have on management decision-making?

PART I

PERSPECTIVES ON TECHNOLOGICAL CHANGE

Chapter One

THE TECHNOLOGICAL DEBATE

CURRENT DEVELOPMENTS AND CONCERNS

While the full potential of computer technology is
only now beginning to be realised, excitement
concerning automation via computerisation dates back
to the 1950s. A publication in 1956 by the UK
Department of Scientific and Industrial Research
referred to developments then as 'something new,
beckoning us toward the electronic office and automatic factory'. However, the implications of this
first generation of computer technology were not so
dramatic. It was a technology which was essentially
inflexible, and linked systems of machines, whether
controlled by computers or not, could generally
produce only one kind of product (Marsh 1982). Only
with the introduction of microelectronics has the
blueprint for the automatic factory been transformed
into a possible reality.

Since the late 1970s the advent of microtechnology has aroused considerable debate and has
succeeded in capturing the minds of academics,
employers, trade unionists and governments alike.
The result to date is a literature which is diverse
and contradictory, with many predictions and specu-
lations but little solid empirical evidence. It
abounds with differing opinions concerning likely
impact. Short term and long term perspectives are
discussed with scenarios for working life as well as
society at large. For some, microtechnology represents the dawning of a 'new industrial revolution'
(Forester 1980), and has been described as the 'most
remarkable new technology ever to confront mankind'
(Maddock 1978). There are indications from others
that the revolution will be rapid, with applications
of microelectronics in commerce and industry
proceeding apace, and the rate of diffusion and

innovation being extremely high (Curnow 1979). However, it has also been argued that the process of change will be much more 'evolutionary' (Department of Employment 1979).

Despite these many disagreements, most of those involved in the debate are united in their recognition of the importance of adopting microtechnology. In September 1978 the Department of Industry set up a new Electronics Application Division with 'the task of stimulating awareness of the competitive advantages offered by microelectronic techniques, and encouraging their adoption by companies in all sectors of British industry and commerce where they can be of benefit'. The Trade Union Congress (T.U.C.), in its report 'Employment and Technology' (1979), also argued that a large part of Britain's trading and economic future will be determined in no small measure by its success in creating the skills and investment needed to exploit microelectronic technology. Similarly, the Confederation of British Industry (C.B.I.), at its national conference in 1979, unanimously resolved that 'prosperity in the 1980s will depend upon investment in, and acceptance of, new technology which will promote competitiveness'. It has always been recognised that technological change plays a crucial role in economic growth. Is microtechnology so different that it merits such special attention?

A number of characteristics of microtechnology make it a special and interesting case of technical innovation. The first important feature of this technology is that it is one which can be mass produced and sold very cheaply. While it has long been possible to apply computers to perform some of the functions of microtechnology, expense and bulk have always been deterrents. For example, the first computer marketed in Europe in 1950, based on valves, cost nearly a million pounds and filled a room. By 1980 it had become possible to buy a microcomputer much more powerful, much faster, which is 30,000 times smaller, consumes 5 million times less electrical power and costs £200 (Green, Coombs and Holroyd 1980). The result is that microtechnology has brought computing power within the scope of much smaller sized businesses and organisations.

Secondly, not only has cost been drastically reduced, but the performance of the present technology is also significantly superior. It enables the extension or even the displacement of human thinking and judgement, and the field of 'artificial intelligence' has benefited greatly by its utilisation. In

10

terms of reliability, it far exceeds any engineering
device to date, and also has the flexibility which
enables swift and inexpensive changes in performance
to be programmed. But, perhaps more significant
than its present high performance rate is the fact
that its development rate is much higher than for
any previous electronic technologies. The speed of
obsolescence not only of the 'micro-chips'
themselves but also of the many systems which employ
them is so great that there is hardly time to adapt
to one stage of innovation before another emerges
(Maddock 1978).

A third distinguishing feature of this technology concerns its wide range of applications.
Microelectronics is capable of dealing with a great
variety of tasks involving the reception, manipulation and transmission of information, and it can be
used in any situation that currently employs some
form of information processing technology, whether
electronic, mechanical, pneumatic or hydraulic in
nature (Lamborghini and Antonelli 1981). The use of
the microprocessor ranges from consumer products to
capital goods and to the automation and control of
office procedures and industrial processes. Robotic
devices have in recent years excited a great deal of
interest, and observers believe that the number of
'robots' employed in factories will increase by
something like 25% per year during the 1980s. The
system designer's dream of using computers to moni-
tor production as a whole is slowly becoming
reality. The result would be to turn complex non-
routine production (like batch engineering) into a
sophisticated process type industry - so called
Computer Aided Manufacture (C.A.M.). Thus microtechnology, by reducing the size and cost of
computers and increasing their power will give
impetus to the diffusion of C.A.M. techniques
(including robotic devices, numerically controlled
machine tools, and new transfer and machine loading
devices). The development of such systems could in
theory result in an entirely unmanned machine shop,
or at least unmanned areas. There are also visions
of the 'electronic' or 'paperless' office with the
convergence of such developments as word processors,
data retrieval systems, 'intelligent' reprographic
equipment and telecommunications facilities for
electronic conveyancing of information (Department
of Employment 1979). Such varied and impressive
applications have all the indications of having an
unprecedented impact.

11

Therefore, it can be argued that the above characteristics justify the consideration of micro-technology as a totally new and qualitatively different innovation. Most large companies are already applying some aspects of this new technology or making plans to do so, and they are being encouraged by large amounts of state investment. Since 1979 the U.K. government has made available substantial sums of money to publicise the potential of microtechnology through the Microprocessor Application Programme. The government also subsidises private companies directly in two ways. The electronics industry itself receives money from the Microelectronic Industry Support Programme, and for companies wishing to use microprocessors in their production methods, or in their products, there is money from the Microprocessor Application Project. In addition, all semiconductor companies are vitally interested in the expansion of the application market, and many have now set up application divisions. Also, many are closely associated with or part of equipment manufacturing organisations. Thus, given its unique characteristics and the incredible drive towards adoption, the eventual widespread application of microtechnology would seem to be assured.

Potential Problems
It has already been stated that there is no shortage of speculation concerning the implications this technology will have for both employment and society. Some argue that by being aware of the potential benefits of the microelectronics revolution, industrial society can be made qualitatively better than ever before. It can become a society in which people enjoy great leisure, realise their full potential in terms of creative talent, and enjoy the high quality low cost goods produced by the automated processes of the world's industries (Forte 1979). However, others accuse the 'new technology' of bringing deskilling, fragmentation and increased monitoring of the work process. Unlike previous periods of rapid technological innovation, every sector of the economy is being affected at once, and there is job loss everywhere. It is argued that workers whose jobs are destroyed by rationalisation, and those entering the labour force for the first time, will have nowhere to go (Counter Information Services report 1979).

While history may provide evidence of the long term success of technological progress in raising wages and general standards of living (Musson 1980), it would be misleading on that basis to overlook many of the short term problems which may arise. Jenkins and Sherman (1979) suggested that:

> The person made unemployed in a provincial town does not care whether or not it is in Britain's interest to adopt new technologies overall nor about the macro-economic effects of doing so, for two reasons. The first is that the national economy means nothing real to that person, or indeed to any individual; the second is that any benefits that accrue will not immediately benefit that person.

Whatever the eventual impact, a number of manpower issues are likely to emerge as areas of concern during the implementation of any technology, and because of the special characteristics of micro-technology it is argued that such issues are now of extreme concern. Two particular manpower problems which have received considerable attention are job loss and skill changes.

The Impact on Jobs.
The potential for substantial savings in labour input with microelectronics has caused much concern and anxiety. Predictions of how much work will be lost range from those of mass unemployment to more conservative estimates of labour displacement. Many examples of job loss or reduction in job opportunities resulting from microtechnology are already evident in many industries (Thornton and Routledge 1980; Department of Employment 1979). It has been argued that in such areas as telecommunications, assembly, warehousing, printing and publishing, there is sufficient evidence available in Europe, Japan and the United States to conclude that labour displacement consequences may be very severe indeed. There are cases on record of the labour force being halved in spite of substantial increases in production (Freeman 1980). Products which incorporate microtechnology have also resulted in job loss. Cash registers, for example, have led to the reduction of that industry's manufacturing workforce by 50%; and rationalisation of the office, especially through the introduction of word processors, is now a real and economic possibility (Downing 1980). A

13

major problem in this area, however, is to identify whether job loss has resulted from microelectronics or from an increase in unemployment linked to quite different factors. For example, Francis and Willman (1980) have suggested that an unemployment figure of 4.5 million is likely to come about by the end of the decade regardless of the impact of new technology and mainly as a result of the gap between the rate of economic growth and the rate of growth in the number of those seeking employment. Due mainly to bulges in the birth rate 10 to 15 years ago, it is suggested that there will be an extra 2.5 million workers entering the labour market up to 1991. It is also feasible that job loss will result if Britain fails to innovate at a rate similar to those of her overseas competitors.

Even those who adopt more conservative estimates of the employment effects recognise the possibility of severe transitional unemployment. It is argued that while the overall demand for labour may remain high, there might be, at least temporarily, high levels of unemployment as jobs are lost from traditional sectors and potential new jobs take time to emerge. If this occurs against a background of already high unemployment, it is possible that these transitional effects could have serious implications (Francis and Willman 1980). As a final point it should be emphasised that the job reduction argument is not a simple one. Technological change must be viewed within the context of economic, social and political factors which are influential in directing 'technological impact'. These factors will be discussed in the next chapter.

New Skills and Retraining.
Two quite different scenarios may also be found depicting the effects of microtechnology on skills. On the one hand, microtechnology has been accused of removing much of the skill associated with some jobs, making them less satisfying (Cooley 1979; Noble 1980). On the other, it is argued that the skill level in certain jobs has been increased with the new technology, or that there has simply been retraining, much of the change being from mechanical to electronics skill (Sorge 1979). Such changes in skills, whether an upgrading or a deskilling, have already led to industrial relations problems and demands for increases in pay to either compensate for the monotony or to reward the acquisition of new skills. Changes in skill requirements are also

14

likely to raise questions of union jurisdiction (Bamber 1980), as members of one union are redeployed to another area of work represented by a different union.

At present the type of occupation most at risk from microelectronics is characterised by being repetitive, routine and relatively simple (Jenkins and Sherman 1979). The occupations in which job opportunities will be created are mainly technology related, and prominent among these will be those involving computer specialists (including both hardware engineers and programers). A number of studies have outlined the mismatch in Britain between the skills currently available and these future requirements (Bessant et al 1981; Pavitt and Soete 1980; Rothwell 1979). Provisions for the selection and training of those to be retrained are further issues of concern.

Another potential problem is the polarisation of the workforce, producing a relatively small technological elite, able to move with and enjoy the advancing technologies, and a much larger proportion of work people whose skills have become outmoded, and who lack the education or motivation to adapt to change (Maddock 1979). It is feared that if such a two-tier society should emerge, with work and the fruits of work not uniformly shared as a result of technological change, some form of social breakdown may occur (Curnow 1979).

With the likelihood that microtechnology will lead to a number of manpower problems, the satisfactory resolution of these problems will require much discussion and negotiation. It has often been stated that manpower adjustment is the most difficult and important element of technological change (Lawrence 1969; Mumford and Pettigrew 1975), and one which is all too often ignored in the pursuit of organisational goals such as financial and technical efficiency. Workers who operate the new technology must at least be willing to work with the technology, and in some cases must want to work with it. If such an attitude is missing, the technology, however advanced, will become inefficient.

TECHNOLOGY, CHOICE AND THE QUALITY OF WORKING LIFE

During the past 20 years a great deal of literature has been generated around the topic of individual and organisational responses to increased automation and other forms of technological change. A main debate in this area concerns the existence of a technological imperative within organisations and society. Studies which demonstrate a variable technological impact are usually cited in support of the position that the technology itself is largely indeterministic. On this assumption the socio-technical approach to organisations and the concept of 'organisational choice' was founded.

The concept was formulated as a result of several field projects undertaken by the Tavistock Institute for the British coal mining industry (Trist and Bamforth 1951). The research was instigated because of the negative effects which had resulted from the introduction of automated coal mining equipment at that time. There had been a failure to yield the anticipated increase in productivity, and since the change men had left the mines in large numbers for more attractive opportunities in the factory world. Among those who remained absenteeism averaged 20% and labour disputes were frequent despite improved conditions of employment (Trist 1981). The research indicated that technological change had destroyed the traditional structure of small self-regulating teams responsible for the whole coal-mining task.

However, in a few of the mines a conscious change of 'work organisation' had occurred in response to the new technology and the negative effects outlined above had been avoided. In these cases the miners, in order to adapt with best advantage to the technical conditions of the new seam, had evolved a form of autonomous work groups which had been common in the days before mechanisation. Resulting from this rejection of oppressive and bureaucratic work procedures, it was argued that organisations could 'choose' to disobey the technological imperative with positive economic, as well as human, results. There emerged a new paradigm of work (Emery 1978), in which the best match would be sought between the requirements of the social and technical systems, as opposed to the old paradigm which had led to an increase in bureaucratisation with each increase in scale and level of mechanisation.

Thus, according to this socio-technical approach, work could be meaningfully arranged, resulting in a higher quality of product and, not infrequently, in greater productivity (Taylor 1975). It differed from other approaches to the problem by attending simultaneously to the technical and production requirements of the work, and to the psychological and social aspects of individual and group needs. It operated to jointly optimise the requirements of the social system, as well as the technical one, regarding man as complementary to the machine and valuing his unique capabilities for appreciative and evaluative judgement. Therefore, the main argument of this movement is that fragmentation and deskilling of work, perhaps introduced for reasons of apparent efficiency, are not in the long term interests of either managers or workers. Corresponding reductions in the quality of work life and reduced motivation will inevitably increase conflict at work and so negate gains in technical efficiency (Davis and Cherns 1975).

Thus it is concluded that individuals and organisations alike can 'choose' different consequences of technological change. This raises a series of questions. What exactly is the scope of such choice, and how may discretion be used to improve the quality of working life? An important variable is the discretion of decision-makers both in the design of technologies and in the organisation of jobs (Davis and Cherns 1975; Child 1972; Cooper 1972). A number of studies have provided evidence of how the impact of sophisticated technologies can be mediated by managerial actions or attitudes. Wedderburn and Crompton (1972), studying continuous process technology in three plants owned by the same organisation, highlighted the strong effects of individual management within the plants on the resulting skill demands of the jobs. Similarly, Hazelhurst, Bradbury, and Corlett (1969) studied relationships between numerically controlled machines and job characteristics, and concluded that policy decisions on the part of management affect the skill demanded of the operators as much, if not more, than the technology itself.

It is therefore suggested that in analysing technological change and its contribution to the quality of working life, three factors relating to discretion and choice must be looked at separately:

Firstly, there are the assumptions about human behaviour which are built into the technological

17

design; this is the responsibility of the design engineer.

Secondly, there are strategies of work and job re-design, as well as various manpower adjustment policies, which may be utilised during the process of implementing the technology.

Thirdly, there are restrictions on 'choice', result-ing from social, economic and political factors, which dictate certain consequences of technological change rather than others.

The first two issues will be dealt with in the final section of this chapter. The third, restrictions on 'choice', will be the subject matter of the next chapter. One factor not dealt with in this book is the influence of the individual worker in techno-logical change. While these individual reactions of workers are important at the implementation stage of introducing new technology (Wilkinson 1981), any input from the workforce into the decision-making process at earlier stages will normally be through trade union representatives. The aim here is to investigate the roles of the key decision-makers representing capital and labour.

THE DISCRETION OF DECISION-MAKERS

Designing the Technology

The importance of looking at the design process of production technology is advocated by a number of authors. Davis and Taylor (1975) for example maintain that the shape of technology is not prede-termined by its own developmental 'laws', but also substantially reflects the psycho-social assumptions of the systems designers. Once certain requirements are built into the system, behaviour may follow the only path available amply fulfilling the prophecy implied in the design. Thus, in part, the observed effects of technology on workers and organisations reflect the assumptions about men and social systems held by the designers of the technological system. As Davis (1971) points out - 'Engineers must recog-nise that in designing technical systems, they are also designing social systems, and that the assump-tions about man which underlie their designs are often horrific'.

However, it would be wrong to assume that such psycho-social intentions are always explicit, and as Davis and Taylor (1975) point out, it is not known to what extent engineers are unaware of the assumptions they make in the design or choice of a technical system. There are now a number of studies which have sought to highlight the social principles which should underlie technological design in order that the quality of working life may be improved. Mumford (1977) believes that engineers should consciously provide individual workers with opportunities for skill development, problem-solving, control, personal development and social relationships. Machines should certainly not prevent such activities taking place. The principles she outlined may be described in more detail as follows:

1. Technology should enable the development of a skill which provides the worker with job interest, a sense of challenge, a feeling of competence and a desire to learn more.

2. Following on from 1, it should enable the development of a progression of skills ranging from comparatively simple to complex. If possible the technology should assist the operator to train himself so that he can learn as a result of his own interaction with the machine.

3. The operator should be able to start, stop, control the speed of the machine and make necessary adjustments to it. Machines which control the operator because they are pre-programmed in some way, should be regarded as ethically unacceptable.

4. The operator should work as a member of a small supportive social group. Isolated individual tasks should be regarded as unacceptable. Similarly, machines which require routine work from the operator but also concentration should be regarded as unacceptable for social reasons as well as contravening principles 1 and 2 above.

5. Machines and machine systems should be flexible enough to be adjusted if the operator develops new methods and techniques which he/she considers to be more effective in the sense that they produce a higher quality of

product or help avoid the occurrence of work problems.

These principles embody the notion that the operator should control the technology and not vice versa. Technological change should lead to an increase in skill and not a decrease, and the whole potential of the human operator used. The situation should not be allowed to develop in such a way that the operator becomes employed as an appendage of the machine. While it is possible for the technological design to be so inflexible that it is the most dominant factor of the work organisation that emerges, it is by no means the only factor that needs to be taken into account. It has already been argued that technology itself need not reduce the quality of working life, but may provide a new opportunity or challenge in which choices can be made.

Work Design
Most work design strategies are closely linked to the socio-technical approach to organisations, their success being dependent on finding a compromise between the demands of the organisation and the needs and the desires of its members, so that the needs of both are jointly maximised (Davis 1966). Those who advocate the benefits of 'new technologies' in improving the quality of working life lay great emphasis on the conscious process of work design in bringing about such improvements. It is argued that more sophisticated technology is able to provide a whole new work definition as the worker's role shifts from the tool and its guidance to the system and its maintenance, regulation and control (Davis and Taylor 1972). The International Labour Organization (1972) suggested that the 'unique opportunity that automation and other advanced technologies offer for progress in the social field resides in the humanisation of work.'
      Basic to the process of work design is some knowledge of the psychological requirements individuals have of their work. These have been termed 'intrinsic characteristics' and a number have been identified. For example, Emery (1964) describes six such needs:

-     the need for the content of a job to be reasonably demanding in terms other than sheer endurance, and to provide some variety.

- the need to be able to learn on the job and to go on learning.

- the need for an area of decision-making that the individual can call his/her own.

- the need for a certain degree of social support and recognition in the workplace of the value of what he or she does.

- the need to be able to relate what he/she does and produces to his/her social life, for it to have meaning and to afford dignity.

- the need to feel that the job leads to some sort of desirable future.

In order to improve work design so that the ideal of joint optimisation can be approached, a set of principles are needed based on the above requirements. These would link the needs of people at work to the objective characteristics of industrial jobs (Trist 1981). Fig. 1.1 outlines the set of principles which have been identified by Trist (1981). Similar principles and core dimensions of jobs may also be found in the work of other writers (Hackman and Lawler 1971; Herrick and Maccoby 1975; Oldham et al. 1975; Walton 1975).

Over the years many strategies of work design have been formulated, the most popular being job enrichment and autonomous working groups. The aim has been to conceptualise the consequences of reversing existing divisions of labour, and it has been claimed that such reversals need not reduce, but can actually increase, productivity. With job enrichment, the worker's role is enlarged vertically as the worker is given responsibility for 'higher' level tasks previously done by supervisors, or involved in quality control. The other approach to improving the quality of work, the formation of autonomous work groups, is also based on the general model of responsible, autonomous behaviour as a key element in productive organisations. However, here the emphasis is on group rather than individual behaviour, with each group becoming multi-skilled and taking increased responsibility for a substantial area of production.

Autonomous work groups was the approach adopted in the coal mining studies of the Tavistock school in the 1950s. The work group in that instance was responsible for all the activities associated with

Figure 1.1:   Principles of Work Design

At the level of the individual	At group level – interlocking where:
Optimum variety of tasks within the job.	There is a necessary interdependence of jobs for technical or psychological reasons.
A meaningful pattern of tasks that gives to each job a semi-balance of a single, overall task.	The individual jobs entail a relatively high degree of stress.
Optimum length of the work cycle.	The individual jobs do not make a perceivable contribution to the utility of the end product.
Some scope for setting standards of quantity and quality of production and a suitable feedback of knowledge of results.	The linkages create some semblance of an overall task.
The inclusion in the job of some of the auxiliary and preparatory tasks.	There is some scope for setting standards and receiving knowledge of results.
The inclusion of some degree of care, skill, knowledge or effort that is worthy of respect in the community.	Some control can be exercised over the 'boundary taks'.
The inclusions of some perceivable contribution to the utility of the product for the consumer.	Channels of communications are such that the minimum requirements of the workers can be fed into the design of new jobs at an early stage.
	Channels of promotion to foreman rank exist which are sanctioned by the workers.

Source: Trist (1981)

mining coal from a particular section of the coal face. These activities had normally been carried out by three different groups of miners, each group carrying out different tasks on different shifts. The autonomous group concept required each group to assume responsibility for the management of their own piece of the coal face. This involved the allocation of tasks and shifts on the basis of mutual agreement together with a joint problem-solving approach by the team when difficulties were encountered. Communication with management principally concerned arriving at an agreement on how much coal the work group would produce and how much they would be paid for doing the job. The most publicised recent experiment in this area was one carried out in the Scandinavian firms Volvo and Saab Scania (1976). As the President of the Volvo company stated:

> This is a factory that, without any sacrifices of efficiency or financial results, will give employees the opportunity to work in groups, to communicate freely, to shift among work assign-ments, to vary their pace, to identify themsel-ves with the product, to be conscious of res-ponsibility for quality and to influence their own work environment.

While there are no studies which show a causal link between the above strategies, individual performance and organisational performance (Lupton 1975), a number of correlational studies have found an asso-ciation between increased productivity and product quality for the employer and higher levels of employee intrinsic motivation (Butteriss, Margaret and Murdoch 1975; Paul and Robertson 1969; Trist 1963; Herzberg 1959).

Manpower Policies
Various types of personnel policies may be implemented to aid the labour transition from one technical system to another, and to make the change more acceptable to the workers. It may be argued that where some reduction of labour is clearly necessary with a technological change, redundancies can be avoided through well developed manpower policies. In a recent survey it was concluded that where managers did resort to enforced redundancies, 'they had frequently failed to take any steps to avoid redundancy or had taken measures of the type

that tended to be less effective' (Daniel and Stilgoe 1978). The Department of Employment (1979) in a paper on the employment effects of microtechnology, emphasised the availability of alternatives to labour reduction, and like others (e.g Dey 1980) cited Japanese companies as providing notable example of how maximum exploitation of new technology can be combined with reasonable guarantees of continuing employment for the labour force. A number of existing policy options lend adequate support to the argument that the 'resort to redundancy by management may be neither so necessary nor so avoidable as first might appear' (Dey 1980).

Manpower Planning

Manpower planning would seem to an essential element of any future integrated personnel policy dealing with the types of changes likely to be produced by microprocessors. Four important facets of such planning have been outlined by Thornton and Routledge (1980) and will be briefly summarised here. Firstly, they indicated the need for long planning horizons so that companies faced with technological change are not restricted in their options by the pressure of time. It is argued that in a situation in which the application of new technology is hurried, companies can be forced into unsatisfactory compromise solutions, which will over time erode the potential benefits to be derived from microelectronic technology. Secondly, they highlight natural wastage as one of the least costly methods of reducing staff levels. By using labour turnover records most companies could predict the level of turnover in the near future and thus should be able to estimate the potential for reducing manpower by this method over a particular period. For this to be effective however, a detailed analysis of the manpower in the organisation (by age, skill, qualification, length of service etc.) is required, so that potential problems such as skill shortages and differential wastage across functions can be identified in advance and the maximum benefits gained from natural wastage. Thirdly, the appropriate use of part-time labour, sub-contract labour and overtime can be of immense use in the planning for the manpower requirements of the new technology and avoiding compulsory redundancies. Finally, the authors point to increased 'flexibility' in personnel specification and selection criteria as a means of reducing future problems in this area. Management can encourage this flexibility by designing more flexible job descriptions, placing more emphasis on broad skills rather than on specific task orientated skills and focusing on systems rather than on particular work methods.

There is ample evidence in the literature of the importance of manpower planning for organisations. A study by Sciberras (1979) concluded that effective manpower policies contribute greatly to the success of those Japanese companies in the television industry which are in competition with firms in Europe and the U.S.A. Also, in a cross-cultural study carried out by Senker et al. (1980), it was concluded that 'the U.K firms did not take manpower planning seriously, nor did they integrate it well into company planning'. Similarly a comparative study between British and German companies outlined the 'crisis' model of change which seems to have been adopted by many British companies. They had been accustomed to letting things drift until the accumulation of years of neglect forced drastic change that could be implemented only after direct confrontation with the workforce (Jacobs, Orwell, Paterson and Weltz 1978).

Training.
The retraining of existing employees can serve two useful functions in the adjustment of manpower to technological change. Firstly, it can reduce the number of employees surplus to requirements by preparing them for redeployment into other jobs and situations. Secondly, it can reduce the need for outside specialists. The recruitment of specialists to operate the new system can be both costly, as the appropriate skills are in short supply, and also a source of conflict, when the company is in an overall labour surplus situation. Therefore, many studies advocate that companies may need to become less conservative in its selection of workers for retraining, in order to adapt existing workforces to the needs of new technologies (Senker et al. 1980).

Work-Sharing, Reduction of Hours and Overtime.
Work-sharing schemes may represent a key element in future employment strategies, when the prospect of a massive introduction of new technology is likely to demand fundamental changes to the organisation of work. A number of work-sharing schemes are

available including a shorter working week, longer
holidays, sabbaticals, job sharing and earlier
retirement. These have been viewed as examples of
workers' solidarity with the acceptance of reduced
hours and maybe lower wages so that no worker, or
small group of workers, will suffer serious economic
hardship as a result of redundancy (International
Labour Organisation 1972). Research has already
shown that the option of working fewer hours, even
at the cost of reduced incomes, would attract widespread interest. Once a satisfactory income level
is approached, reductions in hours were found to be
relatively more appealing than an equivalent further
increase in incomes. This could yield a large
number of unworked hours which in turn could form
the basis of new employment opportunities (Blyton
and Hill 1978). Such schemes also enable the
creation of a more flexible working time framework,
so that organisations and individuals can devise
working arrangements to suit the needs and
preferences of both.

However, despite these obvious attractions of
worksharing many studies have stressed negative
aspects. The Manpower Services Commission and the
Department of Employment have both outlined the
problems of costs and efficiency as apparently
insuperable obstacles to any significant reduction
to the working week. In 1978, the Department of
Employment estimated that a general reduction to a
35 hour week might create anything between 100,000
and 500,000 jobs depending on assumptions about
overtime, output and employment effects. It was
predicted that if wages were to be maintained,
labour costs could be expected to increase by some 6
to 8 per cent. It is believed that while this might
be offset in the public sector through the reduction
of unemployment benefit and tax gains, the private
sector would bear the brunt of a substantial
increase in costs, with obvious implications for
industrial competitiveness, the balance of trade and
hence employment. Much the same conclusion has been
put forward with respect to longer holidays, with a
general increase of one week in holiday entitlement
creating some 25,000 to 100,000 jobs, but costs
increasing by approximately 2 per cent. The
situation is slightly different in the case of the
reduction of overtime. It is believed that using
this strategy jobs could be created without any
significant rise in labour costs, because the extra
costs of recruitment and training of full-timers
would be recouped through the reduction in the

number of hours paid at premium rate. However, despite this optimistic analysis, the Department does stress certain practical obstacles to overtime restriction. Overtime may be the only practical method of getting the work done and there may be problems of recruiting the necessary labour. In addition, a large number of poorly paid workers are dependent on regular overtime to supplement their low basic wage.

However, despite the purely cost-effective reasons which might militate against adopting such schemes, Blyton and Hill (1981) point out that such strategies could be very beneficial to management, in terms of reduced absenteeism and turnover and greater manpower flexibility. Additional labour costs may be more than compensated through improvements in product quality or in services to customers, or offset through product diversification or better marketing (Dey 1980). From a broader perspective there may be an even stronger case for 'sharing work' rather than the alternative of redundancy. The effects of unemployment on public expenditure are obviously important and some Cambridge economists have stressed the need to take account of balance of trade effects in any assessment of the efficiency of labour saving (Rowthorn and Ward 1979). Other objections to redundancy point to its harsh psychological and social effects, and it may also be argued that by opting for redundancy pay workers are making the labour market worse for others. Given these harsh realities it is significant that in the context of technological change, the only legislation protecting employees is that which forces employers to consult and warn workers when redundancies are pending.

The policies outlined above serve to further illustrate the fact that the impact of technology is determined by a number of factors besides those intrinsic to the technology itself. The current interest and concern about microtechnology has revitalised the debate about technological change and its impact and the special features of microtechnology make it an increasingly important area of study. However, the main argument of this chapter has been that the emergence and adoption of a new production technique, which may have substantial labour force effects, need not be associated with the widespread displacement or degradation of labour. Alternatively, there are strong arguments that such technology can and should be utilised with the objective of improving the quality of working life.

Chapter Two

THE CONSTRAINTS ON CHOICE AND THE POLITICS OF CHANGE

If it is agreed that there are 'choices' to be made in technological change, the next stage in the analysis must be the scope of such choice and the factors which may influence it towards certain outcomes. Whereas it may be possible for decision-makers to choose outcomes which contribute to the 'humanisation of work' and improve working conditions, a number of social, economic and political factors could prevent such decisions being made.

SOCIO-ECONOMIC CONSTRAINTS

A number of socio-economic factors could mediate between what management 'wants' to happen as a result of the introduction of microtechnology, and what actually does happen. In the first place, the investment situation of the industry making the changes and the nature of the market for its product will influence the course of events. For example, the maintenance of full employment with a rapid programme of automation will only be possible with a high economic growth rate. In a situation of low economic growth, maintaining labour intensive technology to reduce the level of unemployment could lead to poor sales performance and consequentially, lower living standards. However, if labour saving devices are introduced in order to increase the overall productivity of organisations, this would also create structural unemployment (Bessant, Bowen, Dickson and Marsh 1981). Within this second scenario it is usually argued that an equitable process of redeployment would redress the structural unemployment problem and improve the long term employment situation.

Another important factor will be the rate of introduction of the new technique. This will be influenced by economic viability as well as the present make-up of employment skills (Bessant et al. 1981). In a study of U.K. engineering firms, Senker (1980) found a tendency to pursue short term goals, with the implication that insufficient resources are being devoted to innovation and training. The conclusion of this study was that the U.K. engineering industry 'is grievously short of skills needed to select and implement appropriate technical change'. Such a conclusion has been supported by many others (Pavitt and Soete 1980; Rothwell 1979), and it would therefore seem that the mismatch between existing skills and future require- ments, as well as the time lag necessary to rectify this mismatch, will significantly influence 'techno- logical impact' (Large 1977). The degree of such influence will however be dependent on future government policy concerning the education and training for these new skills (Cain 1977; Edwards 1978). At the moment the British government is being criticised for its fragmented and ad hoc policies in comparison with other Western industrialised countries (Bamber 1980). A notable 15 nation study (Forslin, Sarapata and Whitehill 1979) has shown how a country's socio-economic system and its respective government policies may substantially effect the impact of advanced techno- logy upon the attitudes of workers, on work content and on working conditions.

Encouragement of government action could be seen as a movement away from the dictates of 'market forces'. However, in the 'free market' argument, it is maintained that new technologies may have 'employment creating aspects' as well as job loss aspects. The technology may create employment both directly in the industry which grows up around the new technology, and indirectly, by virtue of the multiplier effect which these new jobs have in the surrounding economy. However, such an argument is based on a number of assumptions that many believe are ill-founded (Jenkins and Sherman 1978). It is often the case that new technologies produce goods for an old market, rather than creating new goods for new markets. The digital watch is a prime example of this. Despite a fall in the price of watches overall and an increase in demand for them, the total number of people making watches worldwide fell dramatically. At present, there are few new goods for new markets, and while such goods might be developed to meet new consumer demands, at present and for the foreseeable future such a development seems unlikely (Jenkins and Sherman 1978).

Decisions concerning techological change occur within the context of international competition. In order for any country to compete internationally with other industrialised countries, her manufactured goods must appeal to prospective customers in terms of both quality and price. Because of this competition, a country without any labour saving technology could experience as high a level of unemployment as a country which has adopted the technology. Countries which fail to adopt the technology would be forced to have permanent import barriers and non-convertible currencies to shut off their economies entirely. An important assumption made in this book is that Britain will continue to trade in international market areas and will not adopt a siege economy (Bessant et al. 1981). One reason for expecting this continuation in trade is that a self-sufficient Britain would require a restraint on consumption beyond the powers of a democratic government.

Therefore, managerial decisions concerning where and how to implement a new process are decided on grounds of profitability, productivity and market share, and the exact impact of the technology will depend on the economic situation of the industry as well as on various governmental or market forces. Up to now the motives and objectives of management during technological change have not been questioned. It was clearly shown in the previous sections that management can 'choose' to use technologies in a way that will enhance the quality of working life, and can implement policies that will avoid some of the negative aspects of technological change. However, given the socio-economic constraints already mentioned, is it justified to assume that management will want to make 'such choices'? For many theorists, the introduction of 'new technologies' is viewed very much as a political process between capital and labour, the primary objective of the former being an increase in their control over working people, rather than the improvement of their working life.

THE POLITICS OF WORK DESIGN

Socio-technical systems design, utilising job enrichment and autonomous working groups, has already been suggested as a way to increasing job satisfaction while also improving the efficiency of production. While such an approach may have a sound theoretical base and highly commendable objectives there is very little evidence of such work design activity in Britain (Tipton 1982). In the isolated instances in which it has occurred, the projects frequently cover only a small number of employees, often as few as 10 in some cases (Butteris and Murdoch 1975). The time span for many of these has also often been short (Trist 1953; Melman 1958; Trist 1981).

Many reasons have been put forward to explain the limited application of these strategies. Some studies have shown that the assumptions concerning the human needs of working people do not always hold. Many people may not want 'enriched jobs' with increased responsibility, especially when, as some studies have shown, it seems to have a 'price'. This was illustrated by Paul and Robertson (1970) when studying a group of process workers whose jobs had been 'enriched'. At the time of the study there had been some uncertainty about the future of the plant, while there was a demand for labour from other employers in the district. Over the period of the study labour turnover rose from about 20% per annum to nearer 100%, with the researchers concluding that the possibilities of better pay and job security at another plant were acting as stronger motivators than job enrichment. A study by Kelly (1981) is one of the few studies that has explicitly recognised that workers' needs and interests may not be confined to psychological aspects but may also extend into economic issues. He questioned the assymetry in the treatment of employer and worker in work design projects, and concluded that in many cases workers experienced significant costs including the loss of jobs, no wage increases in return for productivity, and the tightening of managerial control over labour.

There are indeed many examples which illustrate the limited success of work design in practice. The key to the failure of the approach and its limited uptake was first evident in the pioneering studies in the mining industry. Trist (1981) argues that although the 'success' of a more autonomous organisation of work had been acknowledged, the divisional

management Board had not wished attention to be
drawn to it. It is stated that the Board feared the
power change that would be consequent on allowing
groups to become more autonomous at a time when
management wished to intensify controls in order to
accelerate the full mechanisation of the mines.
The Board's priorities were clearly shown to be
elsewhere e.g. the closing of uneconomic pits in
the older coalfields, and in securing union agreement deemed critical for full mechanisation. They
were not willing to encourage anything new that
might disturb the delicately balanced situation,
especially at a time when the industry was contract-
ing as a result of the increasing use of oil. In
the light of these reactions, it is significant that
within a year or two the conventional system of
'technocratic bureaucracy' had reinstated itself.
    Similar findings were reported in Melman's
(1958) in-depth studies of work practices in the
Standard Motor Company at Coventry. Here the
workers had formed themselves into 15 large,
internally differentiated groups varying from 50 to
500, each comprising a worker constituency which
negotiated its detailed conditions of work and operating rules within a general plant agreement. The
large groups, known as gangs, controlled up-grading
and deployment among eight broad classes of jobs,
and they negotiated the bonus for the number of
products turned out at a given time. The company
had not only increased its market share over five
years beyond that of other automobile companies in
Britain but had also introduced automated equipment
at a much earlier date, paid much higher wages with
lower unit costs), remained attractively profitable
and increased its assets by a third. However,
despite such success, the new arrangements met with
severe management opposition. Again the main
complaint was that too much power was being shared.
A further and more recent example of work design
philosophy and strategies not producing the expected
result may be found in a major change project which
was carried out by the Shell oil company in the late
1960s (Blackler and Brown 1978).
    Trist (1981) views the incidents described
above as mere 'setbacks', and as examples of what
Schon (1971) has called the 'dynamic conservatism'
of organisations. He even refers, for explanation,
to psychoanalytic theory, believing that such 'setbacks' may be seen as stemming from envious attacks
on innovations and innovators. However, the above
examples also seem to illustrate that work design

theorists have failed to take account of the political and economic aspects of the process they recommend. Carnall (1982) rightly points to the 'conditional' nature of such projects in the prevailing social structure of industry, highlighting the problems and contradictions dependent on the resource market, product market and labour market situation. In addition, the centrality of political considerations has recently been outlined by Tipton (1982). She states that changes in job content, other than of the most trivial kind, necessarily require the restructuring of traditional hierarchies of occupational prestige and control.

Therefore, a significant policy for improving the quality of working life even at the level of the work place is inevitably a complicated social and political undertaking. It may also be argued that, under normal capitalist market conditions, management initiated schemes of work design must be viewed in the context of shareholder profitability, and that they are subjected to conventional business accounting techniques which concentrate on the individual firm and the relatively short-run period. Interestingly, Braverman (1974) cites an article from the Wall Street Journal (1972), which although entitled 'The Quality of Work', focuses almost entirely on accounts of cost-cutting, productivity drives and staff reductions in banks, insurance companies and brokerage houses.

The Socio-technical theory, on which strategies of work design are based, has also been the subject of much criticism. Legge (1978) outlined one of the main problems by stressing the differences between the positive/descriptive and normative uses of this type of contingency theory. It is argued that 'contingency thinking' in its positive sense just makes the theoretical point that it is contingencies in the organisation's environment that, acting as both constraints and opportunities, influence the organisation's internal structures and processes. However, the appropriateness of any strategy in an exercise of organisational design will depend not only on the nature of the organisational and environmental characteristics and their inter-relationships, but also on the objectives sought by the exercise. The theory therefore ignores the whole question of the motivations of members of the organisations, and the problem of matching individual objectives to organisational goals (Bowey 1976). Child (1973) concludes that whereas a contingency or socio-technical approach may have some benefits as a heuristic device, what it does not consider is that managers may have preferences for outcomes other than those indicated by an application of socio-technical theory alone. Therefore, it seems that a fundamental weakness of this theory and of work design strategies is the implication that decision-making about organisations simply involves accommodating to operational contingencies, thus achieving an optimisation of various social, technical and economic elements in order to achieve maximum effectiveness. For Child and many others work design is equally a political process into which other considerations, particularly the expression of power-holders' values, also enter. Similarly, Kochan and Dyer (1976) outlined three main problems of work design studies in the United States. Firstly, the process is conceptualised as taking place in a single hierarchical organisation that has some overriding set of goals to which all parties are responsive. Secondly, the role of power in these studies is seldom considered in terms of the structural sources of power that operate in union-management relations. Finally, conflicts are approached as arising out of interpersonal sources and again fail adequately to conceptualise the structural sources of conflict that characterise union/management relations. Thus it may be concluded that the traditional framework of work design studies negates a legitimate role for the trade unions, and as such has aroused the hostility and suspicion of many trade union leaders towards such projects.

THE 'SOCIAL BIAS' OF TECHNOLOGY?

The expression of management's need for increased power and control over the workforce has been emphasised by some as the single most important factor in the invention and implementation of 'new technologies' in capitalist society. Technology is viewed here not as the autonomous force of the socio-technical school but 'as the product of a social process, a historically specified activity carried on by some, and not others, for particular purposes' (Noble 1977). Writers such as Marx (1967) and Ure (1835) insisted early in the 19th. century that technology was being used to replace labour power and to increase managerial control over the workers that remained.

Marx stated:

> Machinery not only acts as a competitor who
> gets the better of the workman and is constan-
> tly at the point of making him superfluous. It
> is also a power inimical to him, and as such
> capital proclaims it from the roof tops, and as
> such makes use of it. It is the most powerful
> weapon for repressing strikes, these periodical
> revolts of the working class against the auto-
> cracy of capital.

In fact there are both historical and contemporary
examples of how manufacturers of 'new technologies'
have attempted to sell their products by emphasising
such aspects of control. In the 'Philosophy of
Manufacturers', Ure (1835) vividly describes how
manufacturers oppressed by militant unions and
unable to control workers by reducing wages, were
led to use technological innovations for this
purpose. One example he points to is the development of the self-acting mule. Strikes in factories
in various towns in the Midlands led local factory
owners to ask a firm of machinists in Manchester 'to
direct the inventive talents of their master to the
construction of a self-acting mule, in order to
emancipate the trade from galling slavery and impen-
ding ruin'. When the self-actor was marketed in
1830, the manufacturers listed as its first
advantage:

> ...the saving of a spinner's wages to each pair
> of mules, piercers only being required, one
> overlooker being sufficient to manage 6 or 8
> pairs of mules or upwards".

E.C. Tufnell, a factory commissioner stated in 1834:

> The introduction of this invention will even-
> tually give a death blow to the Spinners'
> Union, the members of which will have to thank
> themselves alone for the creation of this
> destined agent of their extinction.

Such a view of technology is also to be found in
more recent publications. Noble (1979) believes
that there is no question that management in the
United States saw in numerically controlled machines
the potential to enhance their authority over

production and seized upon it. He cites a number of manufacturers who have promoted their machines along these lines. For example, in one trade journal article entitled, 'How can machines cut costs?', the Landis Machine Company is quoted as stressing the fact that with modern automatic controls the production pace is set by the machine rather than by the operator. Many writers view the advent of the new microelectronic systems in this historically threatening way (Cooley 1981), and similar statements to those above have been expressed by the computer manufacturers. An I.B.M. official is reported to have said:

> People will adapt nicely to office systems if their arms are broken, and we are in the twisting stage now.
>
> (Times Oct. '81).

While the Managing Director of Olivetti is quoted in the 'Office Workers' Survival Handbook' (1979) as saying:

> Information technology is basically a technology of coordination and control of the labour force.
>
> (Times Oct. '81).

Perhaps the most notable work which attempts to expose the social bias in technological change is Harry Braverman's 'Labour and Monopoly Capital' (1974). This author consistently maintains that control of the labour process, through the division of labour, scientific management and the utilisation of technology, is central to management systems in capitalist countries. Work is organised according to the principles of Frederick Taylor, who, it is stated, raised the concept of control to an entirely new level. The three main principles followed are: the gathering and development of the knowledge of the labour process; the concentration of this knowledge as the exclusive province of management; and the use of this monopoly over knowledge to control each step of the labour process. Indeed Taylor himself said of his ideas:

> The worker is told exactly what he is to do, and how he is to do it, and any improvement he makes upon the instruction given to him is fatal to success.

Labour power, according to Braverman, has become a commodity. Its uses are no longer organised according to the needs and desires of those who sell it, but rather according to the needs of its purchasers, who are, primarily, employers seeking to expand the value of their capital. He views the utilisation of new technologies as aids to capital in this 'degradation of the labour process'. It is argued that the Scientific-Technical revolution which began in the last decades of the 19th century and is still going on, has a 'conscious and purposive character' in line with the above Taylorian principles. In place of spontaneous innovation indirectly evoked by the social processes of production, came the planned progress of technology and product design. It is therefore believed that the revolution cannot be understood in terms of specific innovations but rather by the transformation of science itself into capital. In outlining the role of the scientific-technical revolution Braverman states:

> ... the unity of thought and action, conception and execution, hand and mind, which capitalism threatened from its beginnings is now attacked by a systematic dissolution employing all the resources of science and the various engineering disciplines based upon it.... In this revolution there is a displacement of labour as the subjective element of the labour process and its transformation into an object.

Braverman argues that such technological developments completed the transition to the 'real subordination' of labour, and ushered in the new phase of monopoly capitalism, as illustrated in Fig 2.1. Here it has been suggested that Braverman adopts a view of the periodisation of the labour process which is significantly different from that of Marx (Littler and Salaman 1982). For Marx, the real subordination of labour to capital occurred during 'machinofacture' or the implementation of machine based technology, whereas Braverman suggests that at the turn of the century there were still significant areas of production within which workers, especially craftsmen, maintained real control over aspects of the labour process (Stark 1978). In this Braverman is supported by the work of Bright (1958), who showed that as automatic production increased, skill level decreased. This result is summarised by a curve which Bright calls the 'hump in skill requirements' (see Fig 2.2). It describes an

Figure 2.1: The Phase of Monopoly Capitalism signifying
the 'real subordination' of Labour According
to Braverman

Technology	Automation
Division of Labour	Detailed division of labour based on Taylorism and related to automatic machinery.
Mode of Control	Formal plus real subordination only occurs now. It did not under machinofacture.
Dominant Mode of Extracting Surplus Value.	Relative surplus value (but Braverman does not seriously discuss this aspect).
Working Class	Mass of unskilled labour, including large groups of unskilled clerical and service labour, and de-collectivization of workers has occurred.

Source: Littler and Salaman (1982)

Figure 2.2:   'Hump' in Skill Requirement Curve

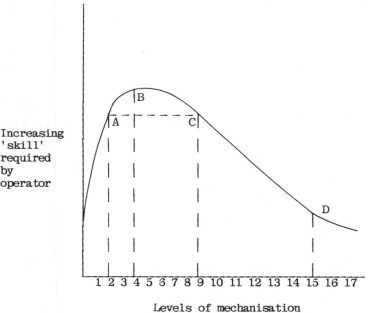

Increasing
'skill'
required
by
operator

Levels of mechanisation

Increasing degree of automatic operation

Source: Bright (1958)

average experience as mechanisation increases, and shows an increase in skill only through the first four levels of mechanisation, with a decrease thereafter and a sharp fall in skill level with the installation of those elements of mechanisation which are associated with the popular term 'automation'.

Technological progress is therefore seen as representing the progressive elimination of the control functions of the worker, with such functions transferred to a device controlled by management from outside the direct process. While Braverman does recognise the continual revolt of labour against this management process, he does not regard such a revolt as having much importance. For the habituation of the worker to the system is seen as the primary element of the functionings of the capitalist system:

> ....this manipulation is the product of powerful economic forces, major corporate employment and bargaining policies, and the inner workings and evolution of the system of capitalism itself..

Labour, its skills and knowledge, is thought to be incorporated into instruments of production, thus becoming what is termed 'dead labour'. Braverman argues that the ideal towards which capitalism strives is the domination of 'dead labour' over 'living labour' (i.e. labour which takes part directly in production). He believes that the expression Marx gave to this process at a time when it was just beginning cannot be improved upon:

> By means of its conversion into an automaton, the instrument of labour confronts the labourer, during the labour process, in the shape of capital, dead labour, that dominates and pumps dry, living labour power. The separation of the intellectual powers of production from the manual labour, and the conversion of those powers into the might of capital over labour, is, as we have already shown, finally completed by modern industry erected on the foundation of machinery. The special skill of each individual insignificant factory operative vanishes as an infinitesimal quantity before the science, the gigantic physical forces, and the mass of labour that are embodied in the factory mechanism and, together with that mech-

anism, constitute the power of the 'master'.

Capital, vol 1 p. 393-99

However, it may be argued that Braverman does not take a completely 'deterministic' view of technology, for he realises that it is not the 'productive strength of machinery that weakens the human race, but the manner in which it is employed in capitalist social relations'. He sees an all powerful capitalist force in the guise of management, intent on exerting ever more control over a refractory labour force. He concludes that the worker can regain mastery over collective and socialised production only by assuming the scientific, design and operational prerogatives of modern engineering. He believes, like Marx, that the material degradation of the workers will force them into a political revolt, which paradoxically their economic subordination has organised and prepared them for.'Short of this, there is no mastery over the labour force' (Braverman 1974).

A Critique of Braverman
While Braverman's work has been acknowledged for 'rejuvanating the sociological study of the work place' (Littler and Salaman 1982) and the labour process, it has also been harshly criticised. To summarise briefly, Braverman and his supporters (Burawoy 1979; Elbaum and Wilkinson 1979) stated that changes in type and scale of new production technology must be viewed as effects of necessary and general 'tendencies' or 'laws' of capitalist exploitation and acumulation. The object and orientation of these laws is claimed to be primarily the subordination of manual production workers and the eradication of their autonomy by simultaneously decreasing the level of skill in production and increasing managerial control (Jones 1982).

Firstly, Braverman has been criticised for his obsession with managerial control over the labour process and for viewing 'scientific management' as the method of management control. Wood and Kelly (1982) argue that it is dangerous to assume that one particular area of management concern is the overriding problem in need of solution. It is stated that the 'significance of control over labour has to be understood in the context of management having a series of objectives linked with the full cycle of capitalist production e.g. labour supply,

job performance, product sale and product market.'
     A   second criticism is that in his   search   for
universal   characteristics   Braverman   has ignored any
variability   in the labour process or in   managerial
strategies of control.   The achievement of   consent
by management (Beynon 1973), and the legitimation of
current   management   by   its claim to a   unique   and
critical competence (Offe 1976) have also been   proposed as important managerial strategies but Braverman makes no reference to them.   Also,   by assuming
an   universal   recalcitrance   of   labour,   Braverman
avoids consideration of specific instances of resistance to the process he described.   Some changes are
resisted   more   than others and some   groups   resist
more than others (Littler and Salaman 1982).
     The work of Wright (1975),   Friedman (1977) and
Edwards   (1978),   moves   beyond   such   limitations,
exploring   the   contradictions   of   each   level   of
capitalist   development and of   specific managerial
strategies.   Edwards,   for   example,   distinguishes
between   technical   and   bureaucratic   management
control   strategies.   Whereas technical control   is
embedded   in technical organisation and work   design
(direct   control),   bureaucratic   control   is
institutionalised   control,   exercised   through   the
structure   of organisations and manifest   in   rules,
procedures   and regulations.   Bureaucratic   control
represents   an   attempt   to attract   worker   loyalty
through   positive   sanctions,   and   through   the
establishment   of   a   graded hierarchy   of   benefits
available to 'responsible' and 'reliable'   employees
(Littler and Salaman 1982).
     A   final   point   about   management   control
strategies   is   that   control does   not   exclusively
occur   at   the   point   of   production.   Braverman's
concentration   on   such control   is   therefore   both
short-sighted   and   damaging.   It ignores the   fact
that the arenas of influence and control may be   the
school,   the   family,   and other non-work situations
(Baldamus 1961;   Parkin 1971; Bendix 1974; Hyman and
Brough   1975).   Recent moves by large scale   multi-
national corporations to disperse production   around
the   world,   and especially in   countries   with
congenial   labour histories and   attitudes,   permits
the   owners   of such enterprises to achieve   desired
levels of production without undue consideration   of
issues of control (Littler and Salaman 1982; Shaiken
1980).
     If   one accepts the capitalist ideology and the
existence   of a strong motivation in   management   to
control and deskill the labour process,   and even if

one also believes the claims of the machine makers
to aid this process, there still remains one criticism of Braverman's work which is central to this
book. This is the view that managerial control over
the labour process, and its utilisation of new technologies in this task, is an unilateral, uncontested
process (Cutler 1978; Friedman 1977). Braverman
ignores a number of important influential factors,
such as product and labour markets, economic
considerations and organisational structures. All
these conditions may vary between industries and
enterprises and therefore preclude any universal
order of priorities and mode of calculation in
capitalist production (Jones 1982). However, the
most criticised omission in his work in this
respect, is his view and description of 'labour
power'. As Littler and Salaman (1982) point out,
'the overall theoretical thrust of 'Labour and
Monopoly Capital' is to suggest that capitalists no
longer face the problem of labour power as a
variable and indeterminate component of the production process'. Whereas Braverman's conception of
control is in terms of the application of
'scientific management', Littler and Salaman have
also argued that control must be seen in relation to
conflict and sources of conflict, and in relation to
the potential terrain of compromise and consensus at
the work place.

Even though capital owns (and therefore has the
right to control) both the means of production and
the worker, in practice capital must surrender the
means of production to the 'control' of the workers
for their actual use in the production process
(Cressey and MacInnes 1980). Therefore while technological progress may limit the power of labour, it
never disappears altogether. It is always possible
for workers to bargain with their obedience, effort
and conscientiousness, thus making the achievement
of consent a basic aspect of all strategies of
control. Braverman has been criticised for working
implicitly with a zero-sum concept of control and
its bases, particularly knowledge (Wood and Kelly
1982). It may not necessarily be the case that if
management acquires knowledge of a production
process, the workers lose this knowledge, or are
incapable of regaining it.

Therefore, in contrast to Braverman's conception of a working class dominated by the law of
capitalism and its consequences, one may point to a
history of management/worker conflict and cooperation. It has been argued that in the mid-Twentieth

century the authority of management was challenged by workers collectively, through the development of trade unions, and that management's authority over labour utilisation is increasingly being questioned (Fox 1971). In the 'Sociology of Power', Martin (1977) argues that both managers and workers have the ability to obtain compliance from each other through the use of influence. Each group depends upon reasonable behaviour from the other for the successful achievement of individual, group and organisational goals. If such reasonable behaviour does not occur both groups have the ability to make life difficult for the other. Management has at its disposal the manipulation of overtime and bonus payments, the allocation of unpleasant work assignments and the disruption of established work-groups. Similarly, workers, collectively through various forms of industrial action and individually by 'skiving', 'pilfering' and other forms of non-cooperation, can make life difficult for management.

It could be argued that in general terms managers are more powerful than workers, individually and collectively (Taylor 1980). To adopt the idea dogmatically however, ignoring the various factors which mediate in specific circumstances, leads to an underestimation of the power of class relations and class struggle within modern capitalism (Friedman 1978). There are many examples which do not demonstrate 'the unfettered triumph of capital over labour through the division of labour and machinery' (Lazonick 1979). There are also many who argue that there is now a greater readiness to challenge managerial decisions directly in situations where they had previously been accepted. Beynon (1973), for example, showed how effective trade union organisation encroached upon practices traditionally regarded as integral to managerial prerogative, including regulation of the speed of the assembly line. Whatever the reality, it seems inevitable that the capitalist process of production, including that of technological change, is potentially one of conflict, compromise and consensus between capital and labour. The determination of the reality, and the distribution of power and influence in any particular instance of technological change, must therefore be subjects of empirical analysis, rather than of dogmatic theory.

Chapter Three

THE INDUSTRIAL RELATIONS CONTEXT OF TECHNOLOGICAL CHANGE

The course of technological change, like other
aspects of industrial life, is influenced by many
features of the general situation in which it takes
place. The previous chapter indicated how various
socio-economic factors may affect this process. We
will now consider the influence of the industrial
relations system on the problems and processes of
technological change. Key features include the
reaction of management and trade union representatives towards a particular change project, the
relationship between these two sides and the impact
of that relationship on the outcome of the change.
The importance of the industrial relations
context has been outlined by many writers. Scott et
al. (1956), in a study assessing the social factors
which promote or impede technical change in the
Steel industry, concluded that one of the most
important of these was the structure of management-
union relations. It was shown that the unions and
their members would accept technical change, and
cooperate in implementing it, provided that certain
conditions were fulfilled. Among the more important
of these was the full recognition of the union and
its role, the acceptance of agreed principles related to the reallocation of employees and the reab-
sorption of the redundant, and the maintenance and
improvement of the conditions and rewards of those
transferred. Thus, it is clear that changes in
technology may produce a bargaining situation in
which wages, conditions of employment, worker selection and organisation of work come up for reconsid-
eration. The strategies adopted by the bargaining
parties should therefore form part of the analysis
of these consequences (Reynaud 1972). For example,
it may be the case that some will assert their power
by making themselves indispensable or by capturing a

45

strategic position, while others will fall back on other means of defence. Reynaud argues that what are regarded as the consequences of a change are largely the result of the power postures of the parties, and the way they make use of the situation.

This was demonstrated by the early craft unions, which had evolved because of a need for particular skills, and then proved highly influential in dictating the course of technological change. As Reynaud states, 'craft unionism strengthened solidarity between those possessing the skills, operated against the breaking down of processes into individual jobs, increased the scarcity of the skills through limitations on occupational entry and enhanced their prestige and social standing through union power in negotiations'. Given the limited development of formal industrial democracy in Britain, policies for the management of change will have great significance in determining whether a consensual or conflict approach develops.

The aim of this chapter is to examine the position of workers and trade unions towards technological change and to outline possible managerial strategies to cope with the trade union response. It is often suggested that technical progress is retarded by the resistances to change which are apparent in our society. Is such 'resistance' an innate and inevitable occurrence, or, if it results from legitimate grievances, can it be avoided?

RESISTANCE TO CHANGE

'... of all baggage man is the most difficult to move'.

Tha above dictum by Adam Smith (1937) implies that 'people innately resist change', and this characteristic is used to explain resistant attitudes to change. It has been suggested that such a characteristic is due to 'man's strong desire for persistence of association, and the maintenance of existing routines and relations' (Roethlisberger and Dickson 1939). In support of this hypothesis, Reynolds (1960) observed the considerable emphasis that tends to be placed on 'security' in labour markets, which is evident in such phenomena as closed shops, limitations on the supply of labour through apprenticeship schemes, seniority emphasis, redundancy rules and payments and employment insurance. Others, however, have argued that resistance is due more to the adverse consequences of change, rather than to any particular human characteristic. For example, Scott et al. (1956) attributed resistance to the periodic depressions which have been characteristic of industrialism since its inception. It is argued that periods of unemployment, short-time working and other consequences of industrial fluctuation make a lasting impression on the minds of those who lived through those years; and it is possible that such memories of the past will shape people's attitudes to change even in more prosperous times. Thus, according to this latter hypothesis, people may or may not resist change, the dependent factor being the perceived consequences of that change.

Here we are specifically concerned with worker resistance to technological change, and in reviewing the literature one finds very little evidence that worker resistance to change is a major obstacle to technological progress. Indeed, there are a number of studies which have specifically indicated the low degree of resistance and conflict from employees and trade unions during the introduction of new machinery (Scott et al. 1956; Abbott 1977; Warner 1982). In one study, Francis et al. (1982) showed how the unions willingly accepted the new processes, even though there was a sharp decline in the numbers employed, and even though the company had been unable to justify the new technology in short-run financial terms. It had seemed that the unions shared management opinions that this was the technology of the future, and that the company could not afford to remain with the traditional process.

In addition, there are a number of studies which show that 'managerial resistance' to the new information technology has been a much more significant factor than any worker resistance. Shaiken (1980) showed how considerable resistance to computer technology had come from some operating managers who saw their traditional authority in the workplace shattered by a compression of the work process and by the attempt of higher management to exert increased control over every aspect of production. A comparative study of the introduction of numerically controlled (N.C.) machines in Britain and West Germany also showed the prevalence of management resistance (Swords-Isherwood and Senker 1980). In West Germany, the perceived unreliability of the new machines had caused problems and generated resistance among supervisors and managers in some firms, as did the managers' ignorance about possible consequences in terms of reorganisation.

In the British firms greater emphasis had been placed on cost factors rather than on engineering considerations. Middle managers believed that there had been some resistance from top management, and in one firm it was felt that there had been a lack of sufficient managerial and engineering expertise to get the best out of the equipment. Interestingly, in neither country did the managers consider that the workers or the unions had impeded the progress of N.C. technology significantly. Initial problems in some of the British firms had been described as 'scepticism' about the technology, rather than any resistance to it.

An historical analysis of worker resistance to technological change also shows that most instances of so called 'resistance' do not constitute an outright opposition in principle to either change or to the technology. Most conflicts have occurred over issues such as the distribution of benefits resulting from the change, or the control of the technology. As Shaiken (1980) points out:

> For those who are tempted to resist, the question is posed "do you accept new technology or do you want to return to the dark ages?" This masks the real issue, which is not support for or opposition to the new technology, but who will control it and for what purpose.

Thus it has been argued that the real problem is not technical change, but the human changes that often accompany technical innovations (Lawrence 1969). Severe costs may be imposed on workers in terms of loss of job and earnings, lower status or decreased job satisfaction, and these may be unevenly distributed amongst certain sections of the population. Although from an historical perspective technological change and modernisation may be equated with a better and healthier life for all, at a local level 'resistance to change' still occurs amongst employees, who feel themselves to be the 'casualties of an industrial revolution, the benefits of which are not immediately evident' (Jenkins and Sherman 1979).

The early 19th century example of the celebrated 'Luddites' machine breaking and rioting, is often quoted as being one of the earliest expressions of resistance to technological change. However such actions were only partly connected with any hostility to the new machinery per se, for wrecking machinery or tools, whether new or old, was

also a major method for coercing employers to grant
concessions regarding wages and conditions (Hobsbawn
1968). When employers were few and capital was
scarce the destruction of machine tools, raw
materials or even employers' houses, proved an
effective weapon in achieving such demands. A
number of worker conflicts were won, and such opposition to machinery, in Norfolk for example, was
successful in raising the wages of weavers for a
number of years. As Luddism faded in the 1820s, it
gave way to more organised activities through trade
unionism and other early forms of worker organisation in the factory. Dickson (1974) concludes:

> By imposing the discipline of the factory, the
> factory owners had unwittingly created a new
> political force, the industrial proletariat.
> The more that work tasks were fragmented, the
> greater became the desire of workers to join
> together in united industrial action.

The history of such struggles provides a great deal
of evidence for the importance of labour's role
during technological change. There have been many
examples of resistance, either taking the active
forms of organised work stoppages and slow downs, or
the passive forms of individual's holding back on
the exertion of their labour unless closely super-
vised. However, the context of such struggles is
perhaps better described as an almost continual
process of conflict, compromise and even cooperation
between capitalists and workers, over the form and
content of the components of technical change
(Lazonick 1977). Abbott (1977) found that unions in
a number of petro-chemical firms had been prepared
to agree to changes in their work methods and practices if the terms were financially attractive and
involved working fewer hours. Similarly, there are
many examples where various trade unions have been
involved in demarcation disputes, in the development
of manning standards, in the evolution of wages and
skill in the new technical situations and in achieving compensation and resettlement benefits.

However, the most notable labour struggles
during technological change, both past and present,
have resulted from the development of craft unionism
and the battles of many skilled craftsmen to maintain their status and craft control in the face of
technological progress which renders their skill
redundant. Friedman (1977) argues that much of the
early disruption was due to a change in management

strategy, afforded by the new machinery, from 'responsible autonomy' to direct control over the craftsman's work. With 'responsible autonomy', top management loosens direct control over work activity as part of a strategy for monitoring or augmenting managerial control over productivity as a whole. Such a strategy took advantage of the particular attitude of craftsmen towards their work in simple commodity production, i.e. self-respect, pride in certain standards of workmanship, and differential rewards for different grades of skill. Many examples are to be found in the early weaving, spinning and car industries of the obstruction of mechanisation on the grounds of de-skilling and the loss of craft control.

In the early 19th century the strong weavers organisation successfully resisted the introduction of steam power into Coventry workshops, and no-one even attempted to set up a steam factory until 1831. The first such factory was in fact burnt down by the weavers, its owner set on a donkey with his face to its tail and paraded through the streets. Also, in the early car industry, the Amalgamated Society of Engineers, the most important craft union in the industry, had a distinct policy towards mechanisa- tion which prevented de-skilling and loss of status. It stated that all jobs traditionally performed by craftsmen should continue to be paid at the craft rate and performed only by 'legal men', even when machinery had eliminated most of the skill required for the job (Jefferys 1946). Even when machines and semi-skilled work were introduced, craftsmen were often able to win special considerations from employers for displaced craftsmen. Therefore, as Friedman (1977) points out, 'the disruptive effects of mechanisation, and the excess of payment required to keep deskilled craftsmen employed on those machines, all slowed down the rate of mechanisation, especially in the Northern centres. Evidence of similar craft control has also been found in the early spinning industry (Lazonick 1977). Here control which had been developed over the common mule since the late 18th century was maintained well into the 20th century, despite the fact that any technical justification for such control had long been undermined.

The introduction of computerised technology has produced many more recent examples of similar craft struggles, particularly in the engineering and printing industries. Shaiken (1980) demonstrates how the change to N.C. machinery in highly skilled prototype work caused real resentment and obstruction when it was combined with strong personal feelings about the importance of craft. A notable dispute at the Times newspaper resulted in an 11 month lockout over the union demands to be given an extensive social package before they would accept the new technology. One of the central themes of this package was union control over the use of the technology. Jacobs (1980) commented:

> The union would accept the switch to photo-typesetting, even though that would cost as much as 45% of their jobs; but they would not accept that journalists could get their hands on the new keyboards, even though that would not have cost any jobs at all. To put it another way, the union was ready to go along with the part that hurt in real, material terms, but not with the bit that scarcely affected its members, except in such abstract terms as status and exclusiveness.

The strike newspaper produced by the unions underlined the devastation in store for workers who 'were to lose control of a function in the production of newspapers which had been theirs for centuries' (The Times Challenger, Jan. 1977). The objective of influencing technological change, rather than the promotion of resistant attitudes and strategies, underlies much of the present trade union policy towards microtechnology. Indeed, over the last 30 years the trade union movement has shown a great deal of interest in the debate surrounding automation and increasingly sophisticated technologies. The movement believes it has an important and influential role in shaping the direction of such developments.

THE ROLE OF THE TRADE UNION MOVEMENT

Since the late 1950s the British trade union movement has attempted to establish technological change as a major issue for collective bargaining. In 1955, the Trade Union Congress (T.U.C.) adopted a resolution which stated that Britain stood on the threshold of a technological advance, presenting the unions with new opportunities for securing higher living standards. A special report on automation was issued by the T.U.C. in 1956, which outlined both potential advantages and threats. It was argued that advantages such as improvements in wages, increased holidays and better working conditions would be made possible by greater productivity. It was also suggested that as unit costs of production were lowered greater security of employment might be gained. However, the report also recognised problems of labour displacement, of transfer, skill, training, wage rates and promotion opportunities, and it recommended that joint consultation and a greater measure of workers' participation were needed to solve them. The report stated:

> Benefits from automation will not come automatically, nor can problems be left to sort themselves out as best they may, or from the trade union point of view be left to management to deal with. There is a strong insistence by the unions therefore, that all questions pertaining to automation - as with any industrial matters - must be discussed and negotiated through the appropriate machinery in each industry.

The 1956 report emphasised the positive and constructive role the T.U.C. and its affiliated unions were adopting in relation to automation. They were firmly convinced that such automation would contribute in increasing the efficiency and productivity of industry. In 1965, the T.U.C. issued a further statement on automation and technological change, again demanding that full consideration be given to the effect of these proposed changes on working conditions and conditions of employment. It insisted that threats to job and income security should be minimised, that there should be adequate facilities for retraining, and that union representatives should be consulted at all stages.

The advent of microtechnology has revived this historical concern of the trade union movement with technological change, and the most recent T.U.C. report, 'Employment and Technology' (1979), dealing with the introduction of microelectronics, is very similar to the earlier documents. The recent publication, like its predecessors, adopts a positive attitude to the 'new technology', confident in its contribution to the productive capacity of the U.K. industry. It lends support to evidence which suggests that high productivity growth leads to high economic growth and improved employment prospects (Cornwall 1977). The belief is again expressed that

new technologies will offer great opportunities –
not just for increasing the competitiveness of
British industry - but for increasing the quality of
working life, and for providing new benefits to
working people. It is admitted, however, that
'change has not always been easy, and its benefits
not always clear'. The report also suggests that it
is the responsibility of the government and the
trade union movement to face the challenges of technological change and to ensure that the benefits of
this change are distributed equitably. It states:

> Scientists will be absorbed in the exploration
> of new processes and techniques; managers will
> be searching for greater financial returns and
> profitability. Only trade unions and govern-
> ment can insist that the use of new technology
> must take account of the widest human and
> social - as well as economic - implications.

The report refers to a number of policies which may
be used to smooth the process of adaptation and to
distribute the benefits. Examples of such policies
include provisions for job and income security,
worksharing and reduction in working hours, improvements in working conditions, monitoring of health
and safety implications, and provisions of increased
opportunities for training and retraining.
However, there is one important difference
between the earlier statements on automation and the
more recent document. Microtechnology has provided
a focus for trade unionists' attempts to extend
their ability to influence and control key areas of
decision-making. The 1979 report argues that the
trade union response should widen the debate about
new technology into the area of industrial democracy, and that trade union involvement should begin
at an early stage in decision-making, through
collective bargaining. The report includes a
'checklist for negotiators', covering such
procedural issues as the level at which the bargaining should take place, the nature of the
discussions, the stage at which negotiations should
begin, the use of a trial period, the information
that should be available and the development of
monitoring machinery. As the report points out:

> It is at the design stage for a technological
> system that decisions will be taken that affect
> the technology's influence and control over
> those who work with it. Negotiators should

therefore seek full involvement at this stage.

The approach advised by the T.U.C. for combining the development of collective bargaining machinery with a response to technological change, is the pursuit of 'new technology agreements'. These, it is envisaged, might initially incorporate various aspects of existing agreements such as 'status quo' and 'mutuality clauses', but seek to turn them into more positive provisions. However, the specific response of different union organisations will vary according to a combination of factors (Mainwaring 1981). These are likely to include the effects of the new technology on particular jobs, the threat to members' skills, and the bargaining power which unions have established prior to the change. While no union has declared outright opposition to the new microtechnology per se, the degree of willingness to change does vary considerably.

Figure 3.1 shows a range of possible union responses to 'new technology'. The Electrical, Electronic, Technical and Plumbing Union (EETPU), in particular, seeks to take advantage of the increased demand for the skills of their members or skills which their members can learn. This is reflected in their anticipation of being able to earn product-ivity payments, their demand for revision of job evaluation along with technological change and their ommission of any demand for a reduction in hours or a shorter working week. The EETPU believes that with the new skills and increased responsibility its members should be able to demand higher wages than other craft grades. Such a response contrasts sharply with those unions taking a hard line approach to change. Two examples are the National Graphical Association (NGA) and the Association of Cinematograph, Television and Allied Technicians (ACTT), who fear that the new microtechnology threatens to bypass the demand for their skills. Thus, the NGA, for example, is seeking the retention of traditional demarcation lines on typographical input so that journalists and advertising clerks do not 'key in' copy.

For the vast majority of other unions the res-ponse consists of establishing minimum guarantees through negotiation. These typically refer to such procedural issues as the importance of a joint agreement between management and union before the introduction of the new machinery, the disclosure of information to the unions, and the use of trial

Figure 3.1:   Scale of Union Agreement to Change

Agreement   Disagreement

◀--▶

See advantages to   Realisation that new   Feel threatened
members provided   technology will lead   by new technology
that certain   to fewer jobs, but   and are only
minimum safeguards   that resistance to   prepared to
are met.   productivity   accept change
                        improvements would not   subject to
(POEU & EETPU)   not help members.   rigorous
                        Extent to which the   conditions.
                        benefits outweigh the
                        disadvantages depend   (NGA & ACTT)
                        on extent to which
                        they can control the
                        implementation and
                        price of change.

                        (APEX;   BIFU;   NALGO;
                          TASS)

periods to test the new machines before full implementation. Important substantive issues refer to job security and no redundancies, increases in pay, reduction in hours and a shorter working week, demands for retraining and the monitoring of health and safety implications. This latter issue has received a great deal of attention from many of the white collar unions, especially in connection with the introduction of the word processor. Most of this attention has been paid to the ergonomics of the hardware and the physical environment, with great emphasis on attaining detailed standards (Williams and Pearce 1982). It has been suggested that trade union pressure for high design standards has been a major stimulus to companies marketing their products on the basis of user acceptability (McKechnie 1981).

However, one fundamental criticism of this trade union concern with the numerical aspect of ergonomic design, is that it seems to have drawn attention away from important issues that are difficult to quantify, such as job satisfaction and stress at work. The potential of using work design strategies during technological change to improve the quality of working life has already been referred to, but trade union policies concerning the utilisation of such strategies are not well developed. Interestingly, a recent international comparison of union attitudes to work organisation and design found that British unions adopted a neutral position on the subject (Asplund 1981). Fig 3.2 suggests a number of factors which may be in operation to shift the focus of trade union concern away from issues of job design and towards the physical hazards of using the equipment e.g. radiation and eye damage from VDUs. These include the availability of more precise knowledge, easier access to information and legal rights concerning the physical aspects of work.

However, even outside the 'technology debate' the trade unions have played little part in the design of work or the initiation of work design experiments. There are very few strikes over the routine nature of work, and few trade unions are making work interest and challenge one of their bargaining issues. This seems to be a national as well as international norm, with only a few exceptional cases, for example Lucas Aerospace (1976). Part of the reason for this lack of involvement has already been suggested. It has been shown how some such experiments may have high 'costs' in terms of

Figure 3.2:   Summary of Factors Affecting Union Uptake of Job
Design as Opposed to Health and Safety Issues.

	VDU Hazards/Physiological	Job Design/Stress etc.
Scientific Knowledge	Greater precision, universality, and therefore authority.	Knowledge less precise/universal. Need for detailed local determination requires greater resources.
Access to information	Established provisions for educating and informing workplace safety representatives. Union structures for research, policy formation, information coordination and dissemination.	Structure not yet well established.
Legal rights	Legal duty on employers to consult and provide information, means of redress in case of employers failure to comply.	Legal duty not clear. No redress

Source: Williams and Pearce (1982)

security and equity (Kelly 1980); and the paternalistic approach of management, traditional in such
projects, arouses union suspicions that there is a
goal of undermining the union position.
Another important factor could be the lack of
union education and training in this area. Hull
(1978) puts much of the blame for this on the 'anti-
intellectualism of the organised labour movement',
whereas others have questioned the 'anti-unionism'
of the intellectual or expert (Becker 1973; Giddens
1979; Tipton 1982). The general opinion seems to be
that substantial resources need to be made available
to worker representatives, particularly at a local
level, and that these representatives need to have
sufficient training to use this knowledge
effectively (Tipton 1982; Williams and Pearce 1982).
In Germany, for example, work councils have long had
access to resources to investigate the design of
work systems under the umbrella of 'the quality of
working life' (Asplund 1981).
Alternatively, job design projects have been
criticised for adopting too narrow a definition of
the quality of working life. Encompassing a broader
definition, trade union influence may be perceived
as more significant, and it may be recognised that
there is a long tradition of trade union/worker
resistance to the scientific management of production through the implementation of new systems
(Williams and Pearce 1982).
The above review of national level trade union
policy illustrates clearly that while there are
significant differences between the responses of
individual unions, their overall approach is moder-
ate and generally favourable to micro-technological
change. For instance, the trade union report in
1979 did not deal directly with the arguments that
either massive unemployemnt might result from the
adoption of the new technology or that deskilling
might be widespread. Therefore, a most significant
point about the trade union response, and one which
is central to this book, is the underlying assumption that technology itself is neutral and can
provide benefits for all. If the environmental
conditions in which the technology is applied are
favourable, greater benefits may well be achieved by
increasing trade union involvement in the process.
Unions do not adhere to the labour process model of
change outlined in the previous chapter, and while
fully aware of 'potential costs' unions assume that
with full participation these costs will be reduced.

The approach advised by the T.U.C. to ensure union involvement and an equitable distribution of the benefits of micro-technology, is the pursuit of 'new technology agreements'(NTAs). Over the last five years a number of unions have attempted to secure NTAs as a means of influencing technological change. A review of these agreements will enable us to identify the potential problem areas.

THE NEW TECHNOLOGY AGREEMENT

Over the past 5 years various unions have attempted to secure new technology agreements (NTAs) as a means of influencing technological change, and much of the recent work in this area has therefore concentrated on such agreements. In the TUC 1979 report, management and unions were encouraged to sign NTAs, 'so as to combine the development of collective bargaining machinery with a participative and flexible response to technological change'. It was advised that these agreements should include:

- status quo and mutuality clauses, so that major change will not be introduced unilaterally

- a guarantee of full job security for the existing workforce

- guarantees to workers, whose pay and status is lowered through job reorganisation, that their individual earnings and status will be maintained.

- adequate redundancy provisions, with continuing earnings related payments to redundant workers rather than lump sum payments

- a reduction in working time with priority given to the 35 hour week; to reducing overtime; to longer holidays; and to providing opportunities for time off for public and union duties.

- earlier retirement for older workers on improved pensions.

Williams and Moseley (1982) view the objectives of the trade unions in signing NTAs as three fold

Firstly, NTAs represent an attempt to ameliorate the negative effects of new technology on, for example, employment, skills and health and safety. Secondly, NTAs should secure trade union involvement in the decision-making process, not only in the implement-ation of any given technical change but also by giving access to information and consultation over change. Thirdly, NTAs should ensure the distribu-tion of the benefits arising from the new techno-logy. At the national level almost every union has produced 'model agreements' which are based on the above objectives and which serve to provide guide-lines for negotiators at the local level. However, the question remains as to what extent these objec-tives have been achieved in the agreements already signed. Over the last three years, a number of research projects have analysed the content of NTAs.

Such agreements are still in many ways an exceptional response for dealing with microtechno-logical change. Most technological change is there-fore being handled without these agreements, especially in the manual and blue collar sectors. The most recent analysis by the Labour Research Department (1982) uncovered 225 such agreements, of which 217 covered the office and related areas. While all these cannot be described as NTAs, most did nevertheless refer to new technology. A more thorough study, using a stricter methodology, was conducted by Williams and Moseley (1982). They collected and analysed one hundred NTAs, precisely defined as 'agreements which directly and explicitly attempt to exert trade union control and influence over the process of technological change, and its effects on work and conditions of employment'. Excluded from their analysis were agreements which simply represented the application of well established collective bargaining approaches to technological change. These included revisions to the general terms and conditions of employment in the annual round of wage negotiations, redundancy agreements, a productivity agreement, and a few which were limited to the safety aspects of the new technology.

Williams and Mosely found that almost all of the agreements covered white collar workers, with only 7 out of the 100 dealing with manual workers. There were inter-industry differences in the readi-ness to conclude such agreements, with the vast majority occurring in engineering, high technology and insurance companies. Another significant feature was that 3/4 of the agreements had only one union signatory, despite the fact that new production and administration systems frequently crossed traditional demarcation lines. Conclusions from the various studies of NTAs will be presented using the classification system proposed by Williams and Moseley. The three main classes are (1) provisions for trade union involvement; (2) defensive measures used to ameliorate any negative effects; (3) the distribution of benefits.

Trade Union Involvement
While it could be argued that the very act of signing a document or agreeing a code of practice indicates some acceptance by management of the fact that the introduction of new technology should be negotiated, it is possible for the provisions of such an agreement to be so vague and limited as to render it almost meaningless. Such vagueness is characteristic of many of the NTAs signed, and there is some difficulty in assessing what the practical implications would be. Some agreements provide for 'joint discussion', others use the term 'consultation', or alternatively 'consultation and negotiation'. Only by the study of such agreements in action could one make an assessment of the types of union involvement these different terms reflect. Williams and Moseley (1981) investigated the extent to which agreements indicated that technological change was to occur by mutual agreement between the two sides, an important objective of the TUC. They concluded that while 'some period of discussion' was provided for in nearly all the agreements, prior to changes being implemented, mutuality was certainly an exceptional achievement – occurring in only 8 of the cases studied.

In addition to the type of union involvement, the stage at which such involvement occurs is also important. Williams and Moseley categorised their agreements according to the provisions made for involvement at a number of different stages. Three stages of involvement were outlined – the planning stage, where involvement is concerned with formulating proposals for future change; the decision stage, where unions are concerned with selecting options for change and discussing the results of feasibility studies; and the implementation stage, where involvement concerns how to put into practice a decided technical change. The authors found only limited provision for union involvement at the earliest stages of decision-making, with only 7 of the agreements outlining involvement in the planning stage. This contrasted with 27 agreements which provided for involvement at the implementation stage.

The effectiveness of union involvement is also related to the access they have to certain information. The NTAs analysed typically provide for access to information in one of two ways - by specifically listing the information to be provided, or by a more general agreement for provision of information. With the former there is much variation in the detail of information provision agreed. Some agreements have been successful in establishing a long list of information which management has agreed to disclose to union representatives before final decisions are taken. Such information may include:

- management proposals, together with the results of research or feasibility studies

- the areas involved together with a statement of proposed changes

- the present structure by job grade of the department where grades are expected to be affected, or where jobs are expected to no longer be required

- proposed revised organisational structure by job grade in the same department

- a summary of the changes indicating the likely effect on present numbers of staff e.g.

- no change

- change in job grade

- redundancy

- rates of staff turnover, if relevant

- expected number and location of visual display units in the revised organisation

- information on the new equipment which could have an effect on the health and safety of staff

- the expected effective date of the new system
  and the plan of expected progress during the
  time leading up to that date

- training and retraining requirements

(taken from the Norwich Union and ASTMS agreement)

In terms of a more general requirement for the
provision of information, Williams and Moseley have
distinguished between three categories of NTAs -
those where no such general requirement exists;
those where there is a restricted requirement for
information; and those where there is an open
requirement for information. The latter type of
agreement may include such phrases as 'equality of
information between management and the union'.

Thus, while examples of 'good practice' in
terms of provision of information may be found (as
in the Norwich union - ASTMS agreement), a substantial number of agreements contain no such provision.
One third of the agreements analysed by Williams and
Moseley contained no clause relating to the provision of information, while the Labour Research
Department (1982) showed that only in 53% of their
agreements (119 out of 225) had management undertaken to provide information on some or all of the
overall effects of new technology.

Provisions for Ameliorating Negative Effects
The threat of job loss and labour displacement are
obvious areas of trade union concern during technological change, and this is illustrated by the fact
that in the majority of agreements manning levels
are discussed. However, as a general conclusion, it
could be argued that present agreements have been
relatively successful in protecting the job and
income security of existing employees, but not of
working people as a whole. Clauses relating to this
issue have frequently been found to be ambiguous,
combining 'no redundancy commitments' with
provisions for natural wastage or voluntary redundancy. The Labour Research Department found that in
only 8% of their agreements was there an assurance
that there would be no job loss, the more usual
provision being for 'no compulsory redundancy' of
existing employees. This finding is also supported
by Williams and Moseley, with a fairly high percentage of the agreements they studied allowing for
manpower reductions either by natural wastage (36%)

63

or voluntary redundancy (14%).

These provisions for manpower reduction have been strongly criticised for confusing the job position with the person holding the job (Mainwaring 1981). While the avoidance of compulsory redundancy clauses may be successful in protecting the job security of the job holder, it does not help to preserve the job position, and Mainwaring argues from this that management are ensured of introducing the changes they want in the long term with minimal resistance. A similar situation occurs with 'protection of earnings clauses'. Although Williams and Moseley found that 39% of agreements stipulate that an individual's wages/grading would be maintained even though the job might be downgraded, replacement labour might well be recruited at a lower grade.

The most notable union achievements in these agreements have concerned the protection of the health and safety of employees from potential hazards of the new technology, especially those associated with visual display units (VDUs). While there is still considerable controversy and no conclusive evidence about the health and safety risks of VDUs, many agreements nevertheless successfully guard against any problems which may emerge. The Labour Research Department found that 39% of the agreements they examined contained sub-stantial detail of the health and safety aspects of VDUs, covering such areas as rest periods, eye testing and the setting of certain ergonomic standards. In contrast, there are very few provisions in these agreements dealing with issues of job design and work organisation. The limited nature of trade union involvement in this area has already been outlined, and this is certainly reflected in the agreements which have been signed. In the unions' defence, McKechnie (1981) argues that the union representatives have often sought concrete standards on equipment design and operational standards, because employers are often unwilling to discuss seriously the implications of operators' complaints of fatigue and strain.

The Distribution of Benefits

All the commentators on NTAs (Williams and Moseley; Labour Research Department; Mainwaring) are agreed that the unions to date have been largely unsuccess-ful in securing an equitable share of the benefits from new technology in these agreements. Two of the

main union demands, in light of the potential
increases in productivity and profits from the new
technology, are a reduction of working hours and
increases in pay. Williams and Moseley (1981) found
that only 13 of the agreements explicitly linked the
introduction of the new technology to shorter hours
and higher pay. A much larger number included a
loosely worded commitment that unions and management
would discuss questions of shorter hours and
increases in pay following any productivity or
profit increases. The Labour Research team also
commented on the small number of cases in which they
were able to obtain specific information of pay
improvements. Only 15 agreements contained a
general reference to the need to reduce working
hours, and improvements in arrangements for holidays
was also found to be unsatisfactory. Therefore,
although the TUC has argued that the case for
accepting technological change rests largely on a
fair distribution of the benefits, it appears that
relatively little progress may have been made in
achieving this, particularly in certain areas of
concern.

The above conclusions highlight several
possible trade union weaknesses in achieving satisfactory agreements with respect to new technology.
The most significant factor of the trade union
approach is the demand for full involvement in order
to influence the direction of change. To date,
however, there has been a lack of rigorous analysis
and examination of the elements of such a participative relationship in the area of technological
change. There is a need to examine the feasibility
of union participation during the introduction of
new technology and to consider, if such participation does occur, the effect that it has on the
outcome of the change. And even if the trade union
movement, at national level, does demand full
participation, the demand at a local level, may be a
poor reflection of the movement's ideal.

THE MANAGEMENT-UNION RELATIONSHIP AND CHANGE

A participative consensual approach between management and employees seems to be a major factor facilitating change in organisations. One of the earliest studies demonstrating the benefits of participation was carried out by Coch and French (1948). A minor change in work procedure was introduced, with varying degrees of participation, to four groups of factory workers, and the results were carefully recorded to examine any problems which occurred. The two extreme groups used in this study were a 'no participation group' and a 'full participation group'. In the 'no participation group', the operators were told that there was a need for a change in their work procedures. Staff explained the change to the operators in detail, and provided them with reasons for the change. The operators were then sent back to the job with instructions to work in accordance with the new method. In contrast, the 'full participation group', having been convinced of the need for change, discussed with the staff representatives how existing methods could be improved and unnecessary operations eliminated. When the new work methods were agreed and all the operators were trained in the new methods, all were observed by time-study specialists in order to establish a new piece rate for the job.

The results of the study showed a remarkable difference between the two extreme groups. In the 'no participation group', resistance developed almost immediately after the change had occurred. This was evident in marked expressions against management, including conflict with the methods engineer, hostility towards the supervisor, deliberate restrictions of production and lack of cooperation. The output of the group dropped to about 1/3 of the previous rate, and stayed at this level throughout the experimental period. In addition, 17 of the subjects left the experimental group during the trial. In contrast, the group which fully participated showed a smaller initial drop in output and a rapid recovery leading eventually to an increased output. There were no signs of hostility towards the staff or supervisors and no worker left during the experimental period.

A more recent study by Gallie (1978) showed how the degree of participation in decision-making influenced worker reaction towards organisational change in British and French oil refineries. The companies were both faced with the problem of reducing and restructuring their workforce, a result of the growing competitiveness of the oil industry in the 1960s. The static nature of the industry meant that such problems could not be solved by redeployment. The respective managerial strategies used to cope with these problems, however, differed quite remarkably between the refineries. In the French case, management had regarded its prerogative in decisions concerning organisational change as absolute. The preparation of proposals for change had been placed entirely in the hands of managerial study groups, to which the union representatives had no access. The French workers felt that they had no power to veto decisions they disliked, and they were confronted by piecemeal changes, the long term implications of these not being made clear to them. Serious feelings of frustration and disenchantment ultimately led to industrial conflict and a strike. The trade union representatives resented the fact that they did not have the right to examine the results of the original studies, and argued that only if they knew all the technically feasible options could they meaningfully discuss and influence the reorganisation proposed. An additional problem was that the main decision-making centre was in Paris, and management was reluctant to engage in meaningful plant discussions.

In contrast, the British refinery had well established industrial relations machinery at plant level. Industrial relations officers had the full time job of familiarizing themselves with shop-floor problems, and had direct access to the refinery manager. These institutional arrangements guaranteed a high level of security, and as the process of negotiation continued such security grew steadily higher. By the final stages of negotiation the work force was confident that any proposals which elicited strong feelings would either be modified or abandoned. A productivity agreement was eventually adopted, the basic principle being that any savings made through the reorganisation would be split 50:50 between management and the workforce. As this process of participation increased, the change in worker reaction was evident. As Gallie stated, 'there was a constant diminution in the level of anxiety of the workforce from an initial state of panic, to one of ambivalence and restrained dissatisfaction, to finally one of overt legitimation of the processes and procedure of organisational change'. Thus, whereas French management had regarded organisational structure as part of managerial prerogative and imposed changes by 'managerial fiat', British management had sought to carry through organisational change by consent with much more positive results. Gallie also concludes that these differential strategies may also provide an effective explanation for the greater hostility in the attitudes of the French workers towards their firm.

In some European countries, legislation has been adopted which has established and built up enterprise level participative structures, and these, it has been argued, greatly facilitated the introduction of change. Jacobs et al. (1978) outlined how differences in such institutional arrangements radically influenced approaches to change in Britain and Germany. In Britain virtually all consultation and negotiation over change took place between management and trade unions. Such involvement developed to the point at which it formed the single channel for employee representation on all matters from national economic policy to the day to day shop-floor problems. Institutions for consultation tended to be poorly established, making consultation haphazard and irregular and not a familiar part of the industrial environment. There was a reluctance on the part of the British management to reveal information for fear of arousing opposition before plans were complete. As a result, management approached change hesitantly, secretively and fearfully, while the workforce responded suspiciously and aggressively. Change, as was concluded, thus became inseparable from a mood of crisis. In contrast, in Germany it was felt that workers exhibited greater confidence with regard to change, due mainly to government support in fostering mechanisms for resolving conflict peacefully within the enterprise. These mechanisms largely consist of a dual system of representation, with powerful trade unions operating largely outside the place of work, and legally established work councils providing an enterprise based negotiating partner for management on most matters affecting the enterprise. Jacobs et al. found a much greater willingness on the part of the German management to reveal information about change to their employees far in advance of its implementation. These authors even go as far as to conclude that the style of conflict resolution in Germany (cooperative as opposed to adversary in Britain) may not only smooth the process of change, but may also account for the greater economic performance of that country.

In relation to technological change, similar advantages have been found from the occurrence of greater management-union participation. Abbott (1977) concluded from his study in the engineering industry that all of the companies which had indicated a highly consensual or harmonious relationship during technological change had placed special emphasis on union-management consultation, and on the fact that the introduction of new machinery had been discussed well in advance. In one of these firms the stated philosophy was that industrial relations should be founded on the principle of 'management by workforce consent'. Communications were considered to be extremely important and once a week there was a period when the factory was stopped for sessions in which grievances could be aired and information passed on. Similarly, Scott et al. (1956) concluded from his work in the steel industry that the formal structure of management-employee relations, supported by the traditional values favourable to the maintenance of cooperation, has effectively limited the conflicts and problems arising from technical change. For many years both parties shared a belief in the importance of avoiding conflict, and of limiting such conflict when it did emerge, and to this end had consolidated a formal structure for the purposes of negotiation, conciliation and arbitration. Certain functions had come to be recognised as legitimate and appropriate to each party. Management's right to make technical changes, and to select the labour force for a new process had been conceded by the unions, while the unions' claim to determine seniority and to participate in promotion procedures had been recognised by management. It was argued that the firms' full recognition of the unions' function in these respects had reduced the conflict of interest between management and the unions.

In some countries legislation has been introduced to aid the process of technological change by seeking to increase the degree of management-union participation. The new Norwegian law on Worker Protection and Work Environment has given unions important legal rights for participating in the design and implementation of new technology. The legislation ensures that employees and their elected representatives will be kept informed about systems employed for planning and effecting work, and about any changes in such systems. Although in Britain there is no such legislation, the Department of Employment study (1979) concluded that participation during the introduction of microtechnology will be declined by management 'only at their own peril'.

In view of the above evidence supporting the importance of management-union participation during change, it is perhaps surprising to find that most of the change models described in the literature do not capture the dynamics of management-union interaction (Katz and Kahn 1966, Lewicki and Alderfer 1973). The models advanced largely accept management's prerogative to initiate and implement change, and participation is viewed only as an appropriate managerial strategy for overcoming resistance. The most prevalent model in the literature is that which advocates a contingency approach to the management of change. In such a model it is demonstrated that managers, in choosing a strategy for change, will make a number of choices. Decisions need to be made regarding the speed of the effort, the amount of pre-planning, the involvement of others, and the relative emphasis given to the different approaches. Available options are conceived as ranging along a continuum from 'coercive' to 'participative' management (Greiner 1967). With coercive strategies, management will attempt to overcome any resistance, resulting at the extreme in a 'fait accompli'. More participative management will be utilised to reduce resistance to a minimum, resulting in a much slower change process, a less clear plan, and the involvement of many people other than the change initiators. According to Lorsch (1976), the strategic position for such a change effort depends on a number of situational variables. These include the amount and type of resistance anticipated, the position of the initiators in relation to the resistors, the locus of the relevant data for designing change and of the needed energy for implementing it, and the stakes involved e.g. the presence or absence of a crisis. If organisational performance and survival is at risk, then the management strategy for change will need to be more coercive. If, alternatively, anticipated resistance is likely to be strong, the management strategy will need to be more participative.

A significant feature of the above model is that the choice of a change strategy is viewed as a unilateral management decision. None of the models include a role for the trade unions, or discuss any unique features of organisational change involving unionised employees. In view of past trade union influence, and present union interest in microtechnology, such paradigms are obviously inappropriate, and there is a need for improved models of the change process (Thomas and Bennis 1972; Kahn 1974). Some progress is being made in this direction, and improved models of organisational change in the context of management/union relationships are now being outlined (Kochan and Dyer 1976). There are a number of assumptions which should underlie any new model. Firstly, it should be assumed that employers and employees interact in an independent relationship that resembles a mixed motive game situation, i.e. some of the goals held by the parties will be compatible and others will not (Kornhauser, Dubin and Ross 1954; Fox 1971). Secondly, the presence of a union implies that employees have formed a permanent structure, protected and legitimated by law, for pursuing their interests. It is assumed that, unlike non-unionised situations, the relationship is a structurally based power-sharing arrangement (Leavitt 1965). Finally, because power is shared between organisations with partially conflicting goals, it should be assumed that structurally based conflict is a natural and inevitable phenomenon in the relationship (March and Simon 1958; Strauss 1963; Fox 1971). These assumptions require an interest group or sub-system approach to the study of change. Only with this type of an approach can we understand the dynamics of union-management change efforts and determine their effectiveness (Kochan and Dyer 1976). There is therefore a need to examine the potential for management-union participation during change, in settings where clear structural sources of power and conflict are inherent features.

Labour, through the trade union movement, is a 'force' which needs and deserves consideration during technological change. While there are some instances of resistance to what are seen as the negative effects of such change, the most significant factor of the trade union approach to micro-technology is the demand for full involvement, in order to influence the direction of change. However, to date the literature lacks a rigorous analysis and examination of the elements of such a relationship in this potentially problematic and frequently occurring situation. There is a pressing need to examine the feasibility of union participation during the introduction of new technology and the effects that this might have on the outcome of change. While it has been clearly stated at national levels that the trade union movement demands full participation in the formulation of proposals for technological change, the situation at local level may be very different. Indeed, there may be a great deal of tension and problems within such a trade union position, e.g. over the issue of 'responsibility'. One of the aims of the research to be reported is to provide an assessment of the strength of this demand at local level, and to examine whether or not such a demand is being met.

Chapter Four

PARTICIPATING IN CHANGE

The trade union movement, in its demand for
increased involvement in the introduction of new
technology, has advocated the extension of
collective bargaining as an appropriate means of
achieving this end. For example, the white collar
union, the Association of Professional and Executive
Staff (APEX) has called for an extension into areas
such as 'the level of output, investment, range of
products and diversification'. Similarly, the
General and Municipal Workers Union (GMWU) has
stressed the importance of a new technology
committee concerned with such issues as investment,
research, and equipment and process design. The
various policy statements suggest that most unions
are in favour of some sort of joint problem-solving
forum which would co-exist with a more distributive
type of bargaining over the outcome of change. It
is suggested that in this way an agreement which
will be of 'mutual benefit' is more likely to be
achieved. Therefore, one of the main concerns of
the unions is the potential for increasing
management-union participation through the
collective bargaining structure.
    Many authors argue that in negotiations
concerning technological change there is the
possibility for the development of 'integrative' as
well as 'distributive' bargaining relationships.
Such a proposition was put forward by Reynaud (1972)
who identified four conditions in which integration
or cooperation between management and unions would
be likely to develop. Firstly, he argues that the
parties must have already tested their strength and
acquired the practice of discussion, particularly on
the traditional subjects of bargaining. It is also
stated that zero-sum games must precede non zero-sum
games because (a) the unions need to assert their

powers of opposition before accepting semi-collaboration; (b) it is better for the relations of the parties to be worked out on verifiable results, rather than on issues with more remote and uncertain consequences; (c) management will not tackle problems affecting entrepreneurial initiative before the other party has been tested. Secondly, Reynaud believes that management must encounter sufficient union power to conclude that prior negotiation is preferable to leaving matters for settlement after the event. Thirdly, there should be a delimination of the zone of shared power i.e. a demarcation of the matters which are to be settled by negotiation. Finally, Reynaud states that no negotiation of a specific change can take place in the absence of wider institutions dealing with more general problems of unemployment, placement or vocational training.

The above outline clearly highlights the importance of a powerful trade union movement for any type of cooperation between the two sides. However, the ease with which cooperative and conflictual subprocesses may be separated, and the conditions and behaviours underlying the occurrence of each, are issues not addressed by Reynaud. Indeed, in reviewing the vast literature which has accumulated around the subject of management-union participation in Britain, there is a distinct 'gap' in empirical work assessing the feasibility of co-operative bargaining relationships. Indeed, the majority of the research studies involving participation have a number of serious shortcomings.

Before examining the research already conducted on integrative bargaining, more general work on participation will be reviewed. Participation is defined as the potential for allowing workers an influential role in the management of the enterprise, involving equalisation of influence and power sharing (Tannenbaum et al., 1974).

THE IDEOLOGY OF PARTICIPATION

> Into this social atmosphere, with momentous and almost incalculable effects on the behaviour of men in their various groupings, we see entering successive waves of thoughts and feelings, which spread over entire communities, and with increasing inter-communication, increasingly over the whole world.

The above quotation, taken from 'Methods of Social

Study' by Webb and Webb (1932), is instructive in highlighting the influential effects that ideology may have on human behaviour. Poole (1975) has effectively illustrated how this influence has operated in relation to the concept of 'participation', having both positive and negative consequences. On the negative side, it is argued that whenever the predominant ethos of society has been authoritarian, and whenever the main assumptions of leaders have been based on their belief in man's essential evil rather than good, the prospects of enhancing human freedom by way of participation have been limited and circumscribed. However, on the positive side, Poole argues that 'participation' has been a mainspring for many broadly humanitarian philosophies, whether socialist, democratic, libertarian or religious.

In this section, we are broadly concerned with movements and ideologies which have as their objective the promotion of worker participation in industry as well as society. We will later concentrate on the practical problems and difficulties of translating those ideologies into reality. The Webbs (1932), with respect to the effects of ideologies on social institutions, distinguished between those arising from (1) religious emotion; (2) humanistic ideals; (3) deliberate planning for efficiency in carrying out social purposes. In relation to the concept of worker participation, three categories of ideological assumptions have, corresponding roughly also been identified, to the above classification. These ideals are political, humanistic and efficiency, and although there are similarities between the categories, it is that the differences outlined in the proceding discussion legitimise the divisions, especially between political and humanistic ideals.

The concept of participation has its origins in many political debates, being mainly promoted by the labour movement as part of its struggle for the emancipation of workers. The value of increased participation is viewed as a means of optimising individual freedom and self determination within a collective context. It therefore derives its legitimacy from the need to equalise the internal distribution of power and involvement in industry, redressing what is seen as the existing inequality in the possibility for individuals to be involved and make decisions in their own jobs (Qvale 1979). Indeed, it has been argued that the democratic character of society as a whole is profoundly influenced by the nature of social relationships in the industrial sphere. Almond and Verba (1965) proposed that 'political efficacy and political consciousness are largely developed in the work context'. A vision of socialism has also provided the ideological commitment to industrial democracy. An example of this may be found in the constitution of the British Labour party, which includes a call not only for the common ownership of the means of production, distribution and exchange, but also 'for the best obtainable system of popular administration and control of industry or service'. As argued by Cole (1972):

> Socialism cannot be soundly built except on a foundation of trust in the capacity of ordinary people to manage their own affairs - which requires methods of management on a scale not so large as to deprive them of all possibility of exercising any real control over what is to be done.

Within the radical political framework, the type of participation aimed for is complete workers' control over the means of production. Such participation has been attempted in recent years in the formation of worker cooperatives. However, such endeavours are still few and small in scale and they are a virtually insignificant aspect of the British industrial scene. It is widely believed by political activists that a more widespread adoption will only be achievable by an overthrow of the capitalist system of production.

A second set of ideological assumptions underlying increased worker participation is related to the quality of the worker's life on the job. It is argued that by giving workers more autonomy, their sense of powerlessness and dehumanised regimentation will be reduced, and their work may be given more meaning (Walker 1970). Numerous industrial psychologists in the Human Relations tradition have demonstrated how satisfaction at work may be just as dependent on the fulfilment of ego-needs such as self-actualization, as upon the satisfaction of physical needs (Mayo 1933; Maslow 1943; Herzberg 1959). Many studies have also provided evidence that participation, power and responsibility on the job tend to satisfy these basic ego-needs (Morse and Reimer 1956; Vroom 1960). Lewin, Lippitt and White (1939) even conclude that 'of all the generalisations growing out of the experimental study of groups, one of the most broadly and firmly established is that the members of a group tend to be more satisfied if they have at least some feeling of participation in its decisions'. It has also been argued that traditional forms of authority in economic enterprises, in which employees are allowed little or no right of participation, directly contravenes the psychological needs of mature adults (Blumberg 1968). Whereas mature individuals strive to take an active part in their world, the chain of command at work renders them passive. Similarly other psychological needs of maturity such as independence and control of one's own behaviour, and the desire to have an equal or superordinate role in society, are all stifled by the autocratic organisation (Argyris 1964).

A third set of ideological assumptions is related more to the management perspective of organisations. Basically what is argued here is that greater worker participation will improve the overall efficiency of the organisation. Such assumptions form part of a 'Human-Resources' model of organisations, in which the worker is viewed as a 'factor of production' which must be taken into account if it is to be used with maximum effectiveness (Miles 1965). It is argued that through greater participation a more effective utilisation of the human resources in the organisation will be achieved. Walker (1970) presents the following reasons for this effect:

- workers may have ideas which can be useful
- effective communications upwards are essential to sound decision-making at the top
- workers will accept decisions better if they participate in them
- workers will work harder if they share in decisions which affect them
- workers will work more intelligently if, through participation in decision-making, they are better informed about the reasons and the intention of decisions
- workers' participation will foster more cooperative attitudes among workers and management, thus raising efficiency by improving teamwork and reducing the loss of efficiency arising from industrial disputes
- workers' participation will act as a spur to

managerial efficiency.

According to the Human Resource model, such strategies of labour utilisation are necessary if the organisation's environment becomes too dynamic to be handled by traditional business strategies or tactics. The development of internal flexibility and commitment to the company in order to cope with the variability of the environment, would be contingent upon employee involvement in the job and the perceived legitimacy of the leadership (Qvale 1979). Finally, the frustration of the psychological needs of the workers may be dysfunctional for the organisation as well as for the workers. Such frustration may be expressed in aggression, ambivalence, apathy, restriction of output, and other activities which reduce the overall effectiveness of the organisation (Argyris 1957).

The three sets of ideologies outlined above imply that an increase in worker participation would benefit both management and labour. Workers, it may be argued, have a democratic right to participate and also have psychological needs which can only be satisfied through increased participation. It is also possible that such concessions will lead to greater organisational efficiency. There is, however a need to provide empirical evidence to justify such assumptions and it is to such empirical work that we now turn.

EMPIRICAL RESEARCH

The vast amount of empirical work which has been carried out in the area of employee or worker participation prevents the inclusion of a complete review here. However, much of the research to date has been criticised for methodological weaknesses and for its adoption of a narrow and unrealistic approach to the problem of participation. The intention here is to present a brief review of the different types of research which have been conducted, and to outline some of the conclusions concerning the feasibility and success of different participative schemes. The participation literature may be conveniently divided as focusing on four main areas of interest

- the extent workers' desire to participate
- their ability to participate

- the effectiveness of different types of participative structures
- the impact that greater participation will have on the organisation.

A brief review of the empirical findings in these areas will be presented.

Workers' Desire for Participation

One of the necessary prerequisites for participation in the decision-making of a group or organisation is that members must be motivated to participate (Walker 1970; Mulder 1971). Empirical data in this area may be divided into those studies which have investigated 'immediate participation' and those that have examined 'distant participation'. In the former, issues concerning the worker's own job such as work methods, job design, speed of work and other working conditions would be the appropriate subjects for participation, whereas in the latter, topics would include various aspects of routine personnel decisions and company policy making, such as capital investments. Information has typically been collected by attitude surveys of blue-collar workers, examining their opinions and interests in these various areas. The evidence to date, although prolific, is still inconclusive.

Many studies show a desire amongst workers to participate on issues which immediately concern them and their own job (Pateman 1970; Hespe and Little 1971). Warner, M., Heller, F., Wilders, M. and Abell, P. (1979), while presenting evidence in agreement with this proposal, also conclude that there is no evidence from the shop-floor of a radically different degree of influence or control to that which already existed, despite the fact that the present level is very low indeed. It was stated that workers who were now merely 'informed beforehand of decisions affecting them personally, wanted instead to be able to give their opinions'. However, they stopped short of insisting that their opinions should be taken into account when the decisions were made. It is argued that the same modest aspirations for greater involvement were also expressed for other kinds and levels of decision. However, as Warner and his colleagues point out, generalisations in this area may be grossly misleading, and each individual's desire to participate may be contingent on a number of other factors, such as the type of industry and the level of job that an employee holds. Wall and Lischeron (1977) also demonstrated that different opinions were in turn related to configurations of attitudes on a range of wider social issues, which in turn could also be related to factors such as age, skill and experience. Evidence concerning worker interest in participation at a higher level is rare and general or indirect in nature (Holter 1965; Tabb and Goldfarb 1970). It is concluded that the worker on the shop-floor is not interested in issues which concern top level management, even when worker representatives are closely involved. There is a great deal of empirical evidence which shows that the motivation to participate is limited even in the Netherlands, Yugoslavia and a few other European countries. Such participation, it is argued, is mainly promoted by members of the intellectual, often academic, levels of society (Broekmeyer 1968). Mulder (1971) suggests that:

> The intellectuals decide that more participation is needed, that certain structures such as work councils with certain rules of decision-making are the most appropriate means, and that such participation is best. In other words, the intellectuals are making up the game, and the rules of the game.

Such findings, highlighting a lack of motivation, may provide one explanation for the low level of worker participation actually found in these councils, and in other similar bodies. For example, studies of Dutch (Van der Velden 1965) and Yugoslav work councils (Kolaja 1965; Broekmeyer 1968) found that managers and specialists contributed most of the communication in the councils, and were usually responsible for the greatest number of proposals accepted by the councils. Analyses of the substantive content of discussion have also shown that even after many years of operation their focus was still on personnel matters, health and hygiene and various task related issues, with an insignificant amount of decision-making taking place in higher level policy areas (Gevers 1977, studying Belgian work councils). Similarly, Brannen, P., Batstone, E., Fatchett, D. and White, P. (1976), in their study of the worker director scheme at the British Steel Corporation, showed that the contributions of those directors to the Divisional Board were heavily balanced towards personnel matters. However, the extent to which this low level of participation is due to a lack in workers' desire to participate, is an empirical question which cannot be satisfactorily answered by the past research.

Workers' Ability to Participate

Walker's description of the 'propensity to participate' includes not only the willingness of workers to do so, but also their ability, in terms of the knowledge and skills required for them to participate fully in managerial decision-making. A number of organisational studies have shown how knowledge and information are important power sources which can be used to manipulate the outcomes of decision-making. King (1975), in his study of capital investment decisions in large firms, has demonstrated the influence specialists have through their ability to define and structure information. Once they have built up commitment to a project, it becomes difficult for others to change or reject it. Pettigrew (1972) also demonstrated how one strategically placed manager can act as a 'gatekeeper', filtering information so as to influence the outcome of a board decision. Finally, Pahl and Winkler (1974) observed how senior managers are able to manipulate and ultimately control their boards through a skilful structuring of the information available to the board. Unless trade union decision-makers are aware of these strategies they are highly likely to receive biased information which would serve only to limit the options open to the unions, thus tying them down to managerially described objectives.

It is a common complaint in experiments in 'participative management' that employees or employee representatives have insufficient information with which to participate in the decision-making process in a meaningful way (Ahlin and Svensson 1980; Carnall 1979). Brannen (1976), commenting on the worker director scheme at the British Steel Corporation, pointed out that 'management had a monopoly of language of authority; the worker directors were individuals with no sanctions and no power'. The statutory provisions concerning the disclosure of information by management to employees are of little benefit. The Employment Protection Act 1975, refers only to the provision of information in traditional areas of collective bargaining and does not examine issues of 'strategic planning'. The employer does not have to allow inspection of any document other than the one specifically prepared for the purpose of providing information. He is under no obligation to provide any documents, accounts or other materials to verify the facts or to show that the information disclosed does not contain misleading statements. This contrasts with the right of the shareholders' auditor to go into the firm and examine any original document (Companies Act 1948).

Managers also see a number of problems surrounding the disclosure of information. The main argument against it is usually based on the need for commercial secrecy and confidentiality. There is also an argument that the information which would be required is not routinely available and would be too costly to compile. Many employers feel that existing consultative and briefing machinery ensures the provision of sufficient information, and that no further provision is therefore needed. However, if information was freely disclosed, this would not guarantee union involvement in management decisions, and where such information is controlled by management it is also more likely to maintain or even strengthen management's position (Mulder and Wilke 1970).

Another significant factor concerning the 'ability to participate' is the strength of the trade union organisation. Qvale (1979) demonstrated that participative bodies were more democratic if unions were present in the plant and were represented within these bodies. Qvale also found that high worker influence was related to influential 'external bodies'. For example, the workers as a group were found to become stronger within the enterprise if the local union was linked to a strong national union system. In their study, Daniel and Stilgoe (1978) also discovered that the presence of a trade union organisation had the single biggest influence on the strategies used by management to reduce their manpower. Surveys undertaken in America and Britain seemed to confirm that consultation is likely to be perceived by employers as most effective when unions are weak or non-existent (Clark, Fatchett and Roberts 1972).

For the unions to be able to achieve greater participation, it would obviously be necessary to have union organisation at a number of levels and in particular at the levels of the plant and company. However, it is precisely company level organisation, especially in large multi-plant companies, which is still under-developed (Cressey, P., Eldridge, J., MacInnes, J., and Norris, G. 1981). The most important reasons for this are the heterogeneity of many multi-plant companies, the complexity of union structure and government, and in many cases straightforward management and official union opposition to 'combine committees'. However, it is being increasingly realised that strategic decisions made at this level affect investment and reorganisation and that even in the context of so called decentralised collective bargaining, there is often quite tight central management control.

Different Types of Participative Structures
Interactive structures of some kind are obvious prerequisites for any kind of participation. A comprehensive classification of different forms of participation was produced by Walker (1970), who distinguished four principal dimensions - structural/informal, integrative/disjunctive, individual/collective and task level/enterprise level. Figure 4.1 shows how various forms of participation may be classified in terms of these dimensions. For example, it may be seen that 'disjunctive participation' is exemplified by collective bargaining, in which workers form their own counter organisations which then interact with the formal organisation of the enterprise. Integrative formal participation involves a formal organisational structure intended to provide for participation such as works councils at the collective and enterprise level, or job enlargement or enrichment at the individual or task level. Individual forms of participation may also be regarded as 'direct methods', for in such schemes subordinates take direct responsibility for controlling part of the enterprise. In collective participative schemes indirect methods are generally more appropriate with managers interacting with subordinates through representatives.

Which type of participative scheme is considered most effective depends largely on the theoretical approach taken by the particular author. Job enrichment and other direct participative schemes are usually criticised for their 'apolitical' approach to organisations. As pointed out by Loveridge (1980), critics following this line of argument adhere to the notion that the separate bases of market dependency make it imperative for employees to maintain strong independent means of

Figure 4.1: Classification of Forms of Workers' Participation in Management

Formal (modification of formal organisation)			Informal	
Integrative		Disjunctive		
Individual	Collective		Individual	Collective
e.g. suggestion schemes	works councils	collective bargaining	participative supervision of individual workers	
delegation and 'flat' organisations	employee directors	tripartite grievance procedure; tripartite promotion tribunals		participative supervision by group methods
job enlargement and enrichment	autonomous working groups	unilateral work rule making by union	informal individual restrictive practices	informal group restrictive practices

84

involvement with management through a trade union. Political economists tend to regard such participative schemes as anti-union devices. They have been accused of focusing on task level relationships as a means of diverting employee attention from the strategic decisions which have greater implications for their long term futures (Kerr 1964).

Similar objections have been made against collective schemes such as Joint Consultative Committees and Workers' Councils. Perhaps the most significant objection is that such committees are not the place or level where the decisions are made. Simon (1965) outlined the fact that management decision-making was not equivalent to a system of taking decisions at boards or in committees where people sit down and say 'yes' or 'no'. According to Simon, management decision-making comprises three principal phases. The first phase consists of finding occasions for making decisions; the second phase consists of finding possible courses of action. This means working out alternatives, and then analysing and evaluating them. The third phase, often regarded as the least significant involves selecting from among well prepared, analysed and evaluated courses of action. It is therefore most important that employees or their representatives understand the process of company decision-making and become involved as early as possible. Brannen et al. (1976) highlighted the problem in the worker director scheme they studied, concluding that the worker representatives had been involved not in decision-making but purely in a 'rubber stamping process'. A number of studies have shown that in many participative schemes workers are admitted to the process far too late, and when designs are well on the way to completion (Ahlin and Svensson 1980). However, it has been argued that the effectiveness of such committees was improved in the 1970s both by the introduction of productivity bargaining as a type of participative mechanism, and by a recognition of the 'pecuniary interests of the workforce' (Loveridge 1980).

Critics of the above schemes of formal participation (Clegg 1960; Dahrendorf 1959) usually refer to collective bargaining as the only appropriate and effective means of management-union participative relationships. These theorists view the nature of control in modern organisations to be essentially conflictual, and any system which does not recognise conflicts of interests is viewed as inherently unstable (Dahrendorf 1968). Such arguments will be discussed in the following section.

One final point concerning the choice and effectiveness of participative schemes is that limitations may arise as a result of a number of socio-technical factors. Walker (1970) isolated four such factors, although he admitted that the ways in which they operate are far from clear. These were (1) the autonomy of the organisation; (2) size; (3) type of technology; and (4) organisational structure. A number of studies indicate that the relationships between organisational structure and internal democracy are indeed complex. Under certain conditions employees may be more secure and feel more involved and influential in a highly structured, formalised and centralised organisation than in a more decentralised less structured system which may be more open also to management manipulation (Crozier 1964; Gustavsen 1973). Also Qvale (1979) found that, even within a single country, enterprises with the most highly developed system of participation were also the ones with the most democratic distribution of power. In addition, companies that scored highly on functional differentiation, and were relatively dependent on customers, were also more democratic. Guest and Fatchett (1974) postulated the importance of product market on the degree of shop-floor participation, although again the precise nature of the effect was far from clear. On the one hand, firms operating in an uncertain environment may require greater decentralisation in order to be effective, and this would increase the chances of shop-floor involvement; but on the other hand it was also noted that some of the better known experiments had taken place in relatively stable markets. In relation to organisational size, there is still more confusion. For whereas smaller organisations have been shown to give better opportunities to their workers, in the larger organisations representative bodies are more powerful, and thus provide better opportunities for indirect participation.

Loveridge (1980) has also indicated several characteristics of organisational structure which are in some degree shaped by technology, and which particularly affect participation. Firstly, the distribution of influence between the parties is greatly affected by the division of labour, whether derived from the vertical (authority) structure or the horizontal (task) structure (Burns and Stalker

1960). Secondly, Loveridge argued that technology enables participation on a group basis, for bringing people together in one place enables them to identify with one another socially or in task related terms, to build up common interests, and to express these at a particular level of command within the organisation (Sayles 1958). Thirdly, the mode of decision-making may be affected by the existence and predictability of deadlines, the length of deadlines on product delivery and stoppages in production schedules. While such factors cannot be ignored, it would be wrong however to present here a fatalistic interpretation of participation in organisations. It has already been stated that decision-makers have a 'choice' regarding organisational structure, working methods and technology. It can be argued therefore that there is a similar degree of choice with regard to the type of participative structure adopted.

The present volume adopts the current Aston model 'in which the cognitive frames of reference used by actors may have more permanence than the objective structure of the market place and technology'. As Loveridge (1980) states:

> The introduction of participative procedures must be seen as a process of negotiation in which the prevailing normative structures that shape management and labour relations have both ideological and emotional significance in shaping their respective views on the way they ultimately want to participate in the future.

The attitudes of managers and trade unionists towards various participative schemes will be discussed fully later.

The Impact of Participation

Numerous studies have been carried out to measure the effectiveness of participation, although the evaluative criteria used fall broadly into only three categories - satisfaction or morale, productive efficiency and lowered resistance to change. Little comment and even less systematic evidence is offered in relation to any other consequences of participation such as an increase in trust, less fear of victimisation and the quality and quantity of the pattern of communications (Wall and Lischeron 1977). However, despite the preponderence of research within this very narrow area, few unequivocal conclusions can be presented. It is not the intention here to review these studies, as excellent and thorough reviews have already been compiled by a number of authors including Guest and Fatchett 1974, and Wall and Lischeron 1977.

In general, two conclusions may be drawn from these reviews. In relation to the productivity criterion there does not seem to be any trend in favour of participative leadership as compared to more directive styles. Secondly, with respect to satisfaction, while the results generally favour participative over directive methods, 40% of the studies failed to show that participation had provided any advantage. Wall and Lischeron (1977) also cast further doubt on the participation-satisfaction hypothesis by outlining four major drawbacks with the studies that confirm the thesis. Firstly, they point out that one cannot infer causality from the correlational studies which link increased participation with increased job satisfaction. It could be that because workers are satisfied they tend to see supervisors in a more favourable way i.e. as more participative.

Secondly, these authors question the relevance of leadership styles as indices of participation. It is argued that participation is only one facet of these leadership styles, others being respect, trust, warmth, and concern for the needs of subordinates. Thus what might be seen as a participative leadership style, based upon the above factors, does not necessarily enhance the subordinates' opportunities for influence. Thirdly, Wall and Lisheran refer to a certain tautology in the findings, with investigators often correlating two measures which, although ostensibly different, include essentially the same components. Finally, they question both the validity of behavioural measures as indices of job satisfaction, and the reliability of findings which are based mainly on small samples from outside Britain. Guest and Fatchett have also criticised these studies, arguing that 'the inability to control the variety of intervening variables - and the lack of control groups of any sort - has been a serious limitation to much of the evaluative work in this as in many other types of behavioural research in industry'.

Having briefly surveyed the bulk of research surrounding the concept of participation, what conclusions may be drawn? Many studies have shown a low degree of participation in operation, a lack of interest among shop-floor employees and misgivings about its benefits. Should we then conclude that the subject is not worthy of further study, and participative management not a viable prospect in industry? One important reason why such a conclusion cannot be substantiated is that the inadequacies and methodological problems of the past research cast a dubious light over the findings so far produced.

It has already been argued that despite the volume of work published on the subject of participation, very few conclusive findings can be presented. This has been mainly blamed on the quality of the research conducted. One of the main criticisms concerns the fact that a substantial part of this research has consisted of attitudinal questionnaire surveys amongst shop-floor employees relating their desire to participate at both immediate and distant levels. It is argued that such techniques, used in relation to the desire for 'distant participation' in particular, present an unrealistic and meaningless approach to the subject. Fatchett (1978) puts it effectively:

> to ask questions about the desired level of participation in those areas of decision-making which have traditionally been beyond the scope of the worker, may be as relevant as asking about the colour of the Rolls-Royce car which he is going to buy with his next wage packet. There is an unreal ring about the whole approach.

It is unlikely that a desire for collective involvement will take precedence over more immediately attainable shop-floor goals, and objectives such as higher wages may be felt to be more within the range of realistic expectation for the average shop or office worker than is the sharing of authority and responsibility for managing their place of work (Loveridge 1980). Also, in relation to attitude surveys, Marchington and Armstrong (1981) point out that it is hardly surprising that the distant decisions seem to have attracted such little interest, for these surveys have failed to take account of the essentially collective nature of union and shop-floor representation. It is argued that it is inappropriate to ask individuals how much involvement they themselves would like on a series of issues which are normally taken at higher levels of decision-making. Whereas a number of studies do indicate that shop-floor workers seem to want greater involvement at this level, many of these workers feel that such involvement would be best exercised through their representatives (Marchington and Armstrong 1981; Blauner 1964).

Another important criticism of these surveys is that questions about desire for participation are asked without reference to any particular context. General attitudes towards industrial democracy may bear no resemblance to the participative behaviour demanded and achieved when the vested interests of different groups in the organisation are threatened. Motivation to participate, therefore, may not be stable but may increase when promoting conditions are created (Mulder 1958). In support of this, a study by Goldthorpe (1968), showed that questionnaire schedules provided little guide to the subsequent choice of action by shop-floor workers or their response over time to management initiatives.

Apart from the criticisms of the questionnaire data collected, which apply to most participation research, there is a second major failing in this area. Much of the work has ignored the roles of the shop-steward and the manager as key figures in making participation work. Recent studies have begun to focus on the frames of reference of these actors in the participation debate, and these will be discussed in the next section. There has also been a failure to discuss the contribution which collective bargaining might make towards participation. In analysing the desired role of the trade unions in technological change, it would seem that collective bargaining provides the only appropriate means through which participative relations may develop.

MANAGERIAL AND TRADE UNION ATTITUDES

Comparatively little empirical work has been carried out in relation to trade union and managerial attitudes towards industrial participation. This may be rather surprising as the success of such schemes in unionised settings would seem to very much depend on the commitment of the two groups. As a recent study on employment participation concluded - 'in order to gauge the likely success of any specific proposal for democracy, participation or involvement in industry, and in order to understand the controversies that surround the different proposals, it is necessary to identify the beliefs and values which enter into management's and trade unionists' calculation of interests, and their perception of losses and gains in respect of relative power positions' (Dowling et al. 1981).

A few studies do present findings which show both groups expressing a general commitment to industrial democracy. In a study by Ursell et al. (1978), 89% of a sample of trade unionists were 'basically' or 'strongly' in favour of the idea, with the remainder being neutral (8%) or against (3%). Similarly, 70% regarded industrial democracy as an issue of central importance; 85% were optimistic that it could be made to work in practice, and 78% felt much more industrial democracy should exist than at present. A survey of managerial attitudes by the same authors also indicated that the majority were broadly in favour of industrial democracy. However, an examination of the attitudes of these groups to specific 'participative' schemes is instructive in highlighting the various meanings given to 'participation'.

The debate surrounding participation reached a climax in August 1975, when the then Labour government established a Committee of Inquiry on Industrial Democracy under the chairmanship of Lord Bullock. The report, which was published in 1977, recommended that participation be achieved through a reform of the structure of large British companies (those with more than 2,000 employees), to allow equal numbers of employee and shareholder representatives to sit on company boards, balanced by a third group of independent board members. The Employers Federation completely rejected these proposals, many accusing the report of being biased towards the trade union. A number of recent surveys have also indicated strong opposition by managers to worker director schemes. In one study the following reasons were highlighted – managers could not see worker directors making decisions that would have adverse consequences for workers; continual conflict and negotiation overflowing into the boardroom would create delays and difficulties in decision-making; there would be difficulties in reconciling collective bargaining with the presence of worker directors; and there would be problems of training worker directors and in coping with multi-unionism (Dowling et al. 1981).

The responses of the trade union movement, both

officially and from the reactions at a local level, were more divided, however. Whereas the TUC General Council is reported to have supported the proposals, a number of affiliated unions voiced disagreements. The Amalgamated Union of Engineering Workers (AUEW) drew a fundamental distinction between trade union participation in management in public and private sector companies, supporting board level representation only in the former. The GMWU wished for a widening of the options of types of legally backed participation, while the EETPU expressed open hostility to trade union participation on policy making boards. The leaders of these three unions therefore rejected the proposals of the Bullock Committee, despite the fact that participation was to be conducted through the trade union channel. While a number of studies have indicated some support amongst trade unionists for worker director schemes (Warner et al. 1979; Marchington and Armstrong 1979), there is nevertheless a suspicion amongst many trade unionists concerning the advantages of their representation on company boards. Their general fears are reflected in the writings of Clegg (1960), who made a powerful case for a strong and independent oppositional body to management. This, in his view, provided the only means for developing and sustaining the power of resistance among working people, and hence was the mainspring of industrial democracy. He argued:

> If the unions were to become an organ of industrial management, there would be no-one to oppose the management, and no hope for democracy. Nor can the trade union enter into an unholy alliance for the joint management of industry, for its opposition functions would then become subordinate to, and stifled by management.

The importance of a strong opposition force in the form of trade unionism is also supported by a number of other authors including Dahrendorf (1959) and Strauss and Rosenstein (1970). It is feared that the shop-steward will have many problems in participative schemes, including role conflict, loss of touch with the membership, and a lack of expertise in comparison to management. These problems have in fact been outlined by stewards who were questioned about the difficulties that they felt would confront them if they became worker directors (Marchington and Armstrong 1981).

However, perhaps the most serious danger as seen by
the above theorists, is that unionists, through
increased participation, might acquire managerial
definitions of the proper functions of the
enterprise (Clegg 1960) and, seen in this way, such
participation is perceived not to be in the long
term interests of workers.

Ironically, some of the objections of
management to certain participative schemes also
related to a fear of losing power and authority,
being based on the premise that management is
responsible to the owners of the enterprise and
cannot legitimately share its authority without
abdicating its responsibility. In addition, there
are a number of managerial arguments which are
sceptical of the advantages that participation may
bring to the organisation. There are anxieties
concerning the increased time which would be taken
over decision-making, as well as the capacity of
workers to contribute usefully to managerial
decisions (Marchington and Loveridge 1979). Brannen
et al. (1976) noted that the acceptance of
participation is often perceived as a threat to a
manager's sense of professionalism, and the idea of
non-useful and generally destructive contributions
from shop-stewards would appear to exert a
particularly pervasive influence over British
management thought. According to Poole (1975)
'modern management have internalised an ideology
which defends their decision-making authority on the
basis of expertise, and will be unwilling to
threaten this by encouraging democratic and
participative practices'.

Therefore in general, managers would seem to
prefer 'direct forms of participation' (Ursell, G.,
Nicholson, N., Blyton, P., Wall, T.D., and Clegg,
C., 1978), and as concluded by Cressey et al.
(1981), participation is mainly viewed as
'complementary' to their right to manage and make
decisions, and not a challenge to that power, or a
diminution of it. In Cressey's study, it was found
that managers wished to retain the initiative in the
decision-making process, as well as complete
discretion over the subject matter, timing and
handling of any participation. The managers
outlined what they saw as the two main roles of
participation. Firstly, a broadly educational role,
which was a question of getting the correct message
over about where the company stood, the market
problems it faced, its performance over the current
period and the role of each plant and section of the

workforce in that performance. Secondly, they viewed it as facilitating the input of shop-floor expertise and knowledge to the managerial decision-making process. There were areas where direct experience counted, e.g. job evaluation committees or decisions on the purchase of new machinery, and also areas where the reaction of the shop-floor was seen as having a potential bearing on how a course of action might be implemented. Not surprisingly, the trade unionists interviewed in the same study envisaged a much more influential role in a participative process. Their differing perspectives were summed up as follows:

> Managers feared the prospect of discussions promoting challenges and opposition to their plans, rather than an understanding of them; conversely representatives feared that unless they could influence and challenge managers' plans, rather than simply being able to understand and explain them better, they would be seen by the workforce as just another set of managers, rather than as representatives. (Cressey et al. 1981).

It is the opinion of a number of theorists (e.g. Clegg 1960) and trade unionists surveyed (Dowling et al. 1981), that the development and extension of collective bargaining is the only appropriate means of improving trade union influence in a capitalist system where there exists a fundamental conflict of interests between the two sides of industry. An extension to the range of issues subject to collective bargaining necessarily limits managerial autonomy in decision-making, and it is therefore not surprising to find managers generally against this form of participation (Dowling 1981). However, it is this type of participative structure which was outlined in Chapter three as being the most effective means of securing trade union involvement in the introduction of new microtechnology. It is recognised that such a process could involve them at different times in both conflict and cooperation with management, and there seems to be some interest, at least from the union side, in an 'integrative' or 'problem-solving' relationship between the sides during a technological change project. The feasibility and possible mode of operation of integrative bargaining, as a means of improving management-union participation in technological change will be the main focus of the final section of this chapter.

BARGAINING RELATIONSHIPS BETWEEN MANAGEMENT AND UNIONS

The idea of extending collective bargaining in order to improve management-union participation is firmly rooted in the conflict tradition of labour relations. The most significant characteristic of this type of participation is the strict maintenance of the distinct responsibilities and loyalties of the parties. This is believed to be of the utmost importance because of the basic conflict of interests, and the difference in preferred outcomes between the management and union groups. It is only through some sort of 'bargaining process' that a reasonable agreement will be reached between the parties. These ideas have perhaps been most clearly set out by McCarthy and Ellis (1973) in 'Management by Agreement'. Here a situation is visualised in which future management problems are analysed and their solutions negotiated between management and unions:

> One way of symbolising this concept would be to say that within a system of management by agreement there would no longer exist any area of management decision-making where management itself could claim an absolute and unilateral right to resist union influence in any form.

Collective bargaining is most frequently used to mean any form of agreed-upon association between union and management (Chamberlain and Kuhn 1965). It has typically been treated by economists and game theorists as a rational process in which the important variables are economic factors, such as the utility functions of the bargaining parties, and political factors, such as the power to strike (Zeuthen 1930; Hicks 1942; Nash 1950). However, the above theorists often admit the existence of psychological or emotional factors in bargaining which are not included in their models (Cross 1969), and in fact in recent years the stream in bargaining theory tends to be heading in this 'behavioural direction'. These models have generally focused on such factors as the level of aspiration of the parties (Siegel and Fouraker 1963); attempts to influence perceptions (Pen 1952); and the learning process which may affect estimates of the opponents' rate of concession (Cross 1969). An excellent review of each of the above bargaining models has been produced by Peterson and Tracy (1976). The majority of the models describe a competitive orientation between the two sides involving power strategies, coercion tactics, threat and deception. Such bargaining arises out of sheer functional necessity to reach an agreement so that operations, on which both sides are dependent, may continue (Chamberlain and Kuhn 1965). However, many have argued that a more cooperative type of bargaining process is available to negotiators, and it is on this type of participative management-union relationship that emphasis will be placed here.

The notion of 'integration' during management/union bargaining derives historically from Follet (1940), who viewed it as a creative process by which bargainers discover new options that are better for both parties than those currently under consideration. Integrative agreements may therefore be considered essential if the process is to be viewed as beneficial by the conflicting interest groups. Pruitt and Lewis (1975) indicated that where both parties have high aspirations or limits, it is conceivable that agreements may only be reached if highly integrative options are found. It is also argued that such agreements are tantamount to achieving the greatest good for the greatest number, and also, as Follet pointed out, non-integrative agreements may often fail to resolve long run conflict. However, the achievement of 'integrative agreements' is not without difficulty in a conflict based industrial relations system, and a number of problems may arise.

Firstly, there is always the fear of cooperation itself, which has already been outlined more generally in relation to participation. It will suffice to say that the fear may be prevalent amongst management, union, and employees, so that any potential benefits of integration are outweighed by potential dangers. As stated by Chamberlain and Kuhn (1965):

> For managers, it is a loss of their prerogatives; for union leaders, it is a loss of function, rendering their role and office unnecessary; for employees, it is the fear of the possibility of increased insecurity caused by improved efficiency and reduction of jobs.

Secondly, there is a difficulty relating to the

style and content of integrative bargaining which
results mainly from the very tentative and
exploratory nature of the process. It involves
cooperation on many levels including the pooling of
information and ideas, consulting one's own
colleagues for suggestion and trying out possible
solutions together. However, perhaps more
significant is the need for a willingness on the
part of the bargainers to talk about what they are
really aiming for, avoiding hard, dogmatic
conclusions until many different loose ends have
been tied up (Warr 1973). Several studies indicate
that such behaviour is not typically exhibited in
inter-group bargaining. There are usually strong
psychological pressures on negotiators to win and
this typically rules out any integrative behaviour
(Rapaport 1970). It also means that most
negotiators try to find out as much as possible
about opponents' payoffs, while keeping opponents
ignorant of their own (Bartos 1970). The problem
may be further complicated by the fact that much
bargaining will probably involve both cooperative
and conflictual elements, and the usual tactics of
competitive bargaining, such as secrecy and inflated
demands, may militate against the occurrence of
greater integration. Negotiators might also find it
difficult to change their style of behaviour from
deception and distrust at one point in time to a
later style which emphasises openness and common
purpose.

Over recent years a number of research studies
have sought to outline the necessary conditions for
overcoming the above difficulties during
'integrative bargaining'. The most notable work to
date has been conducted by Walton and McKersie
(1965) and because most other studies have taken a
lead from the writings of these authors, their
propositions will be reviewed first. Walton and
McKersie conceived 'integrative bargaining' as one
of four bargaining subprocesses, each having 'its
own function for the interacting parties, its own
internal logic, and its own identifiable set of
instrumental acts or tactics'. Their main
distinction is between what they term 'integrative'
and 'distributive' bargaining processes. The latter
describes the process of resolving pure conflicts of
interest between the parties. This is analogous to
the most competititve type of bargaining, with one
person's gain resulting in a loss to the other. The
subjects of such bargaining are described as
'issues' which refer to an area of common concern in

which the objectives of the two parties are assumed to be in conflict.

In contrast 'integrative bargaining' is used to refer to a system of activities instrumental to the attainment of objectives not in fundamental conflict with those of the other party. Such objectives are said to define areas of common concern, which Walton and McKersie call 'problems'. A third process, 'attitudinal structuring', functions to influence the attitudes of the participants towards each other, particularly such attitudes as friendliness-hostility, trust, respect, and the motivational orientation of competitiveness-cooperativeness. The final process is 'intraorganisational bargaining', which has the function of achieving consensus within each of the interacting groups. While these four processes are conceived as being entirely separate, they do facilitate and interfere with one another.

Walton and McKersie's model of integrative bargaining consists mainly of three important elements. The first is the integrative potential of various situations. Here they distinguish between the 'problems' of common concern which have a high integrative potential, and 'issues' which are purely sources of conflict between the sides. They argue:

Agenda items involving strictly economic values are much less likely to contain integrative possibilities than are items referring to the rights and obligations of the parties. Secondly, they outline the process of integration, essentially a problem-solving process involving the following three steps:

1. Identifying the problem
2. Searching for alternate solutions and their consequences
3. Preference ordering of solutions and selecting a course of action.

The first step involves the maximum exchange of information about the problems perceived by each party, the problems being formulated in a clear and accurate manner. In the second step there is a thorough and accurate gathering of information about alternative solutions, with the suggestion that parties should attempt to be imaginative in perceiving alternatives, and persistent in exploring the fullest range of alternative solutions. In the final step there is a free exchange of accurate and believable information about utility structures. It is envisaged that bargainers will firmly uphold their own viewpoints unless and until they are convinced that these are not viable. In Follet's words (1947) 'mushy people are no more good at this than stubborn people'. In this way premature compromises will be avoided and trouble taken to seek an agreement that provides high joint profit.

The development of the above integrative process is dependent on the presence of several psychological and informational states, providing the third aspect of the integrative model. Firstly, it is argued that the parties must have a motivation to solve the problem, and also to regard the problem as significant enough to take time and discuss. Secondly, those participating in the process must have access to the information relevant to each step and be authorised to use it. It is also important that they have the language and other means and skills of communication adequate to exchange this relevant information. A third important condition outlined by Walton and McKersie is the existence of a supporting and trusting climate. This, it is argued, will lead to more accurate perceptions of communications (Blake and Mouton 1961) as well as providing confidence for more experimentation with attitudes and ideas.

With regard to the relationship between integrative bargaining and other bargaining sub-processes, the authors point out that the above conditions are generally antithetical to the requirements of distributive bargaining, which, for success, requires a certain amount of suspicion and withholding of information. However, the processes of 'attitudinal structuring' and 'integrative bargaining' may be generally regarded as mutually enhancing. It has already been stated that before any integrative process can take place the two parties need to develop a good measure of trust and friendliness, while the problem-solving process serves to improve the relationship even further. In relation to intra-organisational factors, it is argued that integrative bargaining may be impeded by pressures from constituents to act in a specified way. They may not tolerate off-the-record discussions, subcommittees, and the other tactics necessary for integrative bargaining, and may not be satisfied with an agreement that has been reached via problem solving.

A recent review of the experimental literature on bargaining (Peterson and Tracy 1976), revealed a number of studies which lend support to some of

Walton and McKersie's propositions concerning problem-solving or integrative bargaining. Frey and Adams (1972) agreed on the importance of trust within the bargaining teams as well as between them for problem-solving to occur. Healy (1965), using interview procedures, suggested three ways in which labour and management could facilitate problem-solving. These were (1) continual attempts to improve day to day relations (2) formal study committees on particularly difficult problems and (3) fact finding and study during the life of the contract.

Some further support for Walton and McKersie's thesis has also been established in the laboratory using simulated negotiation exercises in the context of purely 'economic exchanges'. In one of these, subjects were made to role play in accordance with either a problem-solving or individualistic orientation, being told that their company had developed a bargaining technique which all of its negotiators had been instructed to use (Pruitt and Lewis 1975). For the problem-solving orientation, the instructions were - this approach views the bargaining situation as a solvable problem, and one must attempt to play down the conflict nature of the task and view it as a problem. Naturally, you want to make as much profit as you can, but you are also interested in the needs of the other company. Alternatively, for the individualistic orientation, the instructions were - 'your job is to make as much profit for your company as possible, and the needs and the profits of the other negotiators are unimportant to you'. Profit limits for various subjects were manipulated, as was the type of communication. In what was termed a 'truthful communication' condition, subjects were told that any information they chose to divulge about their profit schedule had to be truthful. In the 'free communication' condition, subjects were told that they could say anything they desired, and could if they wished bluff with respect to the profit sheet. Both members of the dyad were given the same orientation, aspiration and communication levels, and Pruitt and Lewis were able to distinguish between three approaches to bargaining which seemed to influence the level of joint profit in the final agreement. Firstly, there was a distributive approach, which entailed the use of threats, positional commitments and arguments about why the party should concede. Secondly, there was a heuristic trial and error approach, in which the other party's reactions were sought to a large variety of tentatively advanced options and general proposals. Thirdly, an information exchange approach, in which bargainers requested and provided valid information about their profit structures. The important conclusion in relation to Walton and McKersie's thesis is that the distributive approach was shown to reduce the likelihood that integrative agreements would be adopted, while heuristic and trial and error approaches increased this likelihood.

In real life, integrative bargaining between management and the union has often been attempted within joint or cooperative committees. There has been a proliferation of these in the United States, mainly concerned with quality of working life, and organisational effectiveness issues. However, due to the limited success rate of many of these projects, an important area of research has been the identification of factors that are critical for their success or failure (Kochan and Dyer 1976; and Drexler and Lawler 1977). In the limited empirical work carried out in this area to date, some support may be found for the hypothesis of Walton and McKersie.

Kochan, Lipsky and Dyer (1973) found that approximately 60% of a union sample favoured joint programmes outside of collective (distributive) bargaining for quality of work issues. However, only about 20% of the sample were found to favour dealing with the traditional bargaining issues (such as wages, fringes and job security) outside of the formal process. They conclude therefore, that one of the conditions necessary for joint programmes to succeed is the willingness of parties to separate integrative from distributive issues. This will require that management and union officials maintain enough differentiation in the overall relationship to allow them to effectively cooperate in integrative issues, while still aggressively pursuing their constituents' interests on distributive issues through normal bargaining channels. Nadler, Hanlon and Lawler (1980) found that some of the variables which most strongly correlated with project success related to aspects of organisational context or climate, and the functioning of the labour-management committee. The variables highlighted the importance of an open and trusting environment. A major test of Walton and McKersie's model was conducted by Peterson and Tracy (1976) in a study concerned with identifying the conditions, behaviours and procedures that enhance problem-solving in labour negotiations. Respondents were drawn from a nationwide sample of American private sector negotiations of contracts involving 500 or more employees, and usable responses were gained from 37 management and 27 union representatives. They found that a large number of the variables which were tested were significantly associated with successful problem-solving behaviour. This was especially true for those which had been derived from the work of Walton and McKersie, namely, the subvariables relating to a cooperative working relationship and the frequency of contact and openness of communications between the two sides. Bargaining power also showed a strong relationship with perceived success in problem-solving. This result is consistent with the idea that meaningful cooperative bargaining cannot succeed until employees have become convinced that their special interests have been fully considered (Chamberlain and Kuhn 1965) or until the union side is sufficiently strong to participate (Poole 1975).

Interesting differences were observed between the management and union responses. For the management negotiators, the variables associated with success in problem-solving related to a condition underlying the negotiations and an aspect of intra-team freedom. For the labour negotiators on the other hand, the important variables were aspects of interteam climate, bargaining procedures and perception of results. However, perhaps more significant than these differences is the fact that a number of the variables in the categories of interteam climate and bargaining procedures were significantly related to perceived success in problem-solving for both sides e.g credit and praise for the other team, constructiveness and supportiveness of the other side, trust and respect of other team, other side's rate of concession and availability of information.

Peterson and Tracy's study is different in a number of respects from the work of Walton and McKersie. They showed that respondents found it very difficult to distinguish between 'issues' and 'problems', with many unionists even maintaining that there was nothing that was 'non-distributive'. This finding is also consistent with an interim evaluation carried out in 1980 of 16 quality of work projects (Lewin). It was found that unionists and managers in these joint projects displayed adversarial distributive bargaining behaviours as

well as cooperative integrative ones. Such
behaviours included management's reluctance to give
up its authority, the union's unwillingness to give
up its control, a lack of interest displayed by some
managers and rank and file union members, and the
parties' slowness in developing an appropriate
organisational structure for the projects. Thus it
may be argued that the suggestion that problem-
solving or a more participative approach cannot deal
with 'conflict issues' fails to appreciate the true
nature of management-union relationships.
Management and union respondents were also shown to
differ in the meaning they gave to problem-solving.
Management interviewees tended to speak about
problem-solving in terms of major issues affecting
both sides, e.g. they mentioned problems such as
meeting the requirements of the Equal Employment
Opportunities Commission, whereas union negotiators
seemed to have a much broader definition, referring
to all negotiations over non-economic matters in
terms of problem-solving. Peterson and Tracy also
suggested that much problem-solving occurs in
relation to separate or overlapping problems of the
sides, rather than in relation to mutual problems.

However, the most significant differences
between the two pieces of work relate to the
distinction between the processes of distributive
and integrative bargaining. Walton and McKersie
(1965) indicated that many of the strategies and
tactics required for success in problem-solving are
counter productive for distributive bargaining and
vice versa. Peterson and Tracy, however, found a
positive correlation between the two processes,
highlighting only one instance in which there was a
clear conflict. The latter even found that several
variables showed significant relationships in the
same direction for both success in problem-solving
and distributive bargaining. As a result, they
suggest that it is perhaps more helpful to consider
distributive bargaining and problem-solving as polar
extremes on a continuum, rather than following
Walton and McKersie's proposition that these were
two distinct processes. They argue that parties
tend to identify whether the adversary or
cooperative approach was most appropriate for a
given issue, and to act accordingly.

A replication of the Peterson and Tracy study
has recently been carried out by Smith and
Turkington (1981) in New Zealand, and similar
results regarding the conditions and behaviours were
found to be necessary for problem-solving to take

place. However, no support was found for Peterson
and Tracy's hypothesis in relation to distributive
bargaining, the discrepancy being explained by
differences between the two countries in the way in
which such bargaining is approached. As a result,
findings from the New Zealand study showed less of
an overlap between the independent variables related
to success in integrative bargaining, although the
friendliness of the other side, and far sightedness
of both sides about future bargaining issues,
contributed to the success in the two bargaining
subprocesses. As in the American study more
significance was given to the similarities in the
management/union responses than to any differences,
and Turkington and Smith concluded that it did not
seem that the parties approach integrative
bargaining from diametrically opposed standpoints.
The importance of the above studies is that they
illustrate the feasability of a cooperative type
bargaining relationship in the context of a conflict
based industrial relations system. They are
interesting because they highlight a number of
conditions that are necessary for such cooperation
to occur, even though they were not direct studies
of microtechnological change or of British
industrial relations.

PART II

A CASE STUDY – THE BREWING INDUSTRY

Chapter Five

A MODEL AND A METHODOLOGY

The model and methodology of the study to be described emerged as a result of initial case study
work of the experiences of change in two large
brewing companies. These were useful in illustrating a number of the problems and implications of
applying microtechnology. Information was collected
from both management and union representatives, and
of particular interest in this initial research were
the different working relationships which had been
formed between these two parties during the change.
In addition to this, it was shown that the company
which had adopted a more participative, consensual
approach to the introduction of the new technology
had made a far greater attempt at improving general
personnel policies as a result of the change, and
all parties involved felt that these two factors
were causally linked. As a consequence of these
findings, and by drawing inferences from the literature concerning technological change and
management-union participation, the following
conceptual model was formulated.

CONCEPTUAL MODEL

It is suggested that the behavioural relationship
between management and unions is an important deter-
minant of technological change. Such change is
viewed as a political and problematic process with
the different interest groups in the organisation
attempting to achieve their 'preferred' outcomes.
The consequences of the change will therefore tend
to be those desired by the main interest groups. As
shown in Fig 5.1 the model is arranged in four
sections. Section one outlines factors outside of
the management-union relationship which may have an

Figure 5.1: An Analysis of the Impact of Integrative Bargaining on the Outcome of Micro-Technological Change

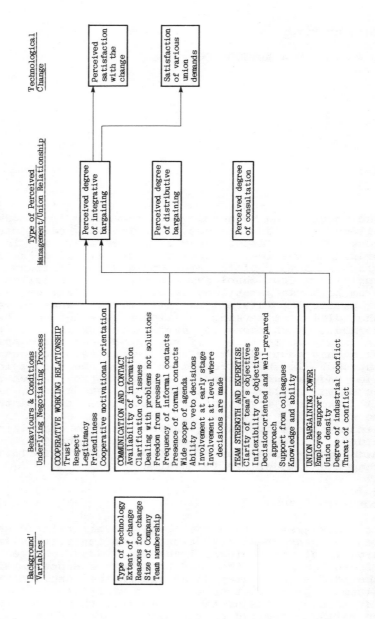

effect on the outcome of technological change. The second includes the procedures and behaviours of the negotiating teams. The third deals with the respondents' perception of the type of management-union relationship which arise, and the fourth concerns certain 'outcomes' of the change. The components of each of these sections will be examined in the following discussion.

It is assumed that within the context of micro-technological change three different types of man-agement-union relationships may co-exist - integra-tive bargaining, distributive bargaining and consul-tation. Such a situation occurs because of the multiplicity of issues which may be covered, from the type and extent of the technology, health and safety matters to wage negotiations. These three types of relationship are defined as follows. A 'consultative' relationship is one in which manage-ment conducts most of the decision-making unilater-ally, with the trade unions merely being kept infor-med. This relationship, for the trade unions at least, may be regarded as a 'non-relationship', with the unions being unable to exert any influence at all, and such a relationship results typically in 'win-lose' outcomes in management's favour.

Secondly, a 'distributive bargaining' relation-ship is defined as one in which management and unions adopt adversary positions with agreement usually reached by means of a compromise of the opposing demands of the two parties. The resulting outcome may be defined as a 'lose-lose' situation, with neither party obtaining the best deal for it-self. However, in contrast to the first type of relationship, the trade union will have some power, and the degree of such power will be largely dependent on the bargaining strength of the union. The third type of management-union relationship, labelled 'integrative bargaining', is defined as a cooperative rather than a conflictual relationship. It is assumed that during the negotiating process typical of such relationships, management and unions, in dealing with issues or problems, will search for alternative solutions until they arrive at a mutually satisfactory agreement. Integrative bargaining may therefore be seen as a 'win-win' method, because there is an attempt to meet the needs of both parties. There is a conflict in the literature concerning whether integrative and dis-tributive bargaining are two distinct processes which are counterproductive to each other (Walton and McKersie 1965); or whether they are simply polar extremes on the same continuum with much in common (Peterson and Tracy 1976). Most of the elements found by Peterson and Tracy, showing significant relationships in the same direction for success in both integrative and distributive bargaining, relate to conditions within one's own team rather than between the teams. Both types of relationships were therefore included in the present model in order to test more thoroughly whether the two processes can be easily differentiated or whether there is much overlap between the factors important to each.

The units of measurement used were the perceived extent of integrative and distributive bargaining, rather than the perceived success of these processes. This strategy was designed to prevent confusion between feelings of satisfaction with the outcome and the means by which the outcome was achieved, a confusion which critics have levelled against Peterson and Tracy's work. To study the degree of mutual benefit achieved by management and unions as a consequence of technological change, a social justice approach to the evaluation of change is utilised in the model (Keeley 1978; Carnall 1980). Such an approach takes into account the different frames of reference in the organisation, and prevents evaluation being biased towards the interests of any particular group. As it is assumed that management, who are generally the initiators of such change, will ensure that the new technology serves the interests of the group it represents, most of the variables tested in this part of the model are designed to illustrate the degree of union success in achieving improvements in terms and conditions of employment.

The model identifies four major independent variables assumed to be associated with the perceived extent of integrative bargaining during technological change. These independent variables are derived mainly from previous work by Walton and McKersie (1965) and Peterson and Tracy (1976). The majority are behavioural variables, and it will be beneficial to describe briefly each of them here, and to consider the support for their relevance in the literature.

A Cooperative Working Relationship

Peterson and Tracy (1976) suggested that integrative bargaining or problem-solving requires a modicum of cooperation between the parties. The specific elements of this type of relationship include trust, respect, acknowledged legitimacy, friendliness and a cooperative motivational orientation. Walton and McKersie identify four of these five elements (omitting respect) in their discussion of attitudinal structuring. In relation to non-distributive bargaining they state: 'we are convinced that some minimum level of trust and support is a precondition to the process'. Further support for the importance of these five elements may be found in the literature.

Gergen (1969) concluded from his research that major gains for both parties were possible only when there was mutual trust, and another negotiation experiment indicated the importance of trust within as well as between parties (Frey and Adams 1972). In relation to respect, Julian, Hollander and Regula (1969) found that competent spokesmen were significantly more likely to be endorsed by their respective parties than those persons identified as low in competency.

Failure to accept the legitimacy of the other side and its negotiators would seem to preclude any attempt at problem-solving, and while Peterson and Tracy (1976) did not find a significant relationship between mutual acceptance of the negotiating parties and perceived success in problem-solving, the correlations were in the predicted direction. Peterson and Tracy also argued that although friendliness does not ensure success in problem-solving, its absence is likely to retard problem-solving activity. A number of research experiments in non-labour management situations demonstrate that friendliness is related to effectiveness in attitudinal structuring of one's opponent, a condition necessary for problem-solving. Swingle and Gillis (1968) found that subjects were initially more cooperative when playing against a liked partner, while Johnson (1971) has observed that expressed warmth was causally related to the degree of favourable interpersonal relations.

Walton and McKersie considered a cooperative motivational orientation to be crucial to nondistributive bargaining, with both parties willing to solve the problem, and this hypothesis was confirmed by Peterson and Tracy (1976). Blake and Mouton (1961) concluded from their studies of labour/management relations that both sides have to share an internal motivation to solve common and distinctive problems while retaining group boundaries. Furthermore, Healy (1965), in his studies on creative collective bargaining, concluded that the most critical element is a mutual attitude of determination and commitment.

Contact and Communication

Walton and McKersie outlined the importance of frequent contact and openness of communications for successful problem-solving, and the specific attributes expected to enhance the process include (1) the greater availability of information (2) ability of both sides to clarify the issues (3) exploration of subjects without commitment (4) freedom from pressure (5) discussion of feelings and alternatives surrounding the issues prior to offering of solutions and (6) greater frequency of informal contacts between the parties.

Whereas much of the literature on distributive bargaining demonstrates that this process entails the withholding of information from the opponent, integrative bargaining on the other hand normally requires the availability and communication of information between the bargaining teams. The dilemma for the negotiator is that bargaining power usually increases as more information is gained about opponents' reward structures. Thus, if information is to be communicated it must be done in such a way as to ensure that the other side does not use it for manipulative purposes. In an experiment in which individuals bargained anonymously with each other, it was found that when both parties had complete information negotiations were concluded more rapidly, and that they tended towards a solution which maximised the joint payoff more than under conditions of incomplete information (Siegel and Fouraker 1960). Clarity in defining issues is also outlined as a facilitating condition, and where the parties attempt to solve difficult problems, clarity of communication and understanding are important. Johnson (1971) found that there was a causal relationship between the expressed accuracy of understanding and cooperation. Peterson and Tracy (1976), although finding no difference between the extent one's own side clarifies issues in problem-solving and distributive bargaining, found that there was a difference between how negotiators perceived the activity of the other side in the two processes. A significant relationship was found only between problem-solving and the clarification of issues by the other side.

Walton and McKersie suggest that brainstorming and other methods of exploring subjects without

112

commitment enhance the likelihood of successful problem-solving. It is possible that the very process of moving directly into the solution stage preempts the possibility for both parties to convey their concerns and feelings for each other's problems. Walton and McKersie considered it important that the negotiators have opportunities to convey their true feelings and to raise alternatives prior to proposing solutions, and empirical support for this variable was obtained by Peterson and Tracy (1976). A number of other studies have examined the way the positions adopted by the bargaining teams may affect negotiations. Druckman (1968) for example, concluded that problem resolution was facilitated by negotiation experience that either involved unstructured discussion, from a unilateral perspective, among team mates; or a bilateral study with an opposing representative, irrespective of whether he was to be a bargaining opponent. Klimoski (1972) pointed out that the independent adoption of a group position was generally associated with intense feelings of competition. Rapaport (1960) also emphasised the importance of bilateral discussion prior to commitment if problem-solving was to occur.

Healy (1965) argues that successful problem-solving or creative bargaining is more likely to occur when the parties are removed from pressures. Pressure, it is argued, will result in narrowing down both the number of issues in discussion and the time given to each issue by the negotiators, such conditions being inconducive to problem-solving. Peterson and Tracy found that perceived success in problem-solving was related both to personal freedom from team pressure, and to team freedom from constituent pressure. In the present model, the impact of freedom from pressure exerted by the opposing side was a focus of investigation.

Greater frequency of informal contacts were found by Healy (1965) to be associated with creative bargaining. Peterson and Tracy also showed a significant relationship between the number of grievance meetings held over the past year and perceived success in problem-solving. However, in respect of formal communication, there seems to be some contradiction between the literature based on psychological studies and those arising from the industrial relations context. Empirical work on negotiating behaviour by Morley and Stephenson (1970) led these authors to conclude that where the communication system favours formality the representative aspect was encouraged, and problem-solving behaviour would be constrained by commitment to the negotiators' own groups. The authors maintain that formality essentially depersonalises the relationship between the negotiators and encourages negotiatiors to concentrate on representing their individual cases. However, there is alternative evidence that if rules for participation are more formalised then the means for increasing employee involvement and for equalising the distribution of power will be more efficient. Whether participation is legitimised through legislation, collective agreements or company policy, however, does not seem important, as long as the rules are enforceable (Qvale 1979).

Healy (1965) recommended the setting up of formal study groups to enhance creative collective bargaining. Given the well documented evidence of the persistence of the managerial prerogative in many areas of decision-making, it is suggested by the present model that some degree of formal arrangements will be beneficial to problem-solving, provided that there is a mutual determination not to let inter-party conflict create inter-party hostility. In addition to the formality and frequency of contact, the model also suggests the importance of other prerequisites in this category for meaningful participation and problem-solving. These include a wide scope of agenda for discussion, the ability to veto the other side's decision, the opportunity for union involvement at an early stage in decision-making, and the importance of involvement at the level at which decisions are made.

Team Strength and Expertise

In the category of 'team strength and expertise', five elements are suggested in the model as being important for the occurrence of integrative bargaining. These are - the clarity of the team's objectives; the flexibility of objectives; a 'decision-oriented approach' by the team; support for the team; and the knowledge and ability of team members. There is evidence that problem-solving will be more successful in situations where team policy and administration are well understood by the team's negotiators, and provide a high degree of intragroup acceptance (Balke, Hammond and Meyers 1973). Gospel (1978) also pointed out the importance of clearly formulated objectives if the trade unions are to achieve increased involvement in decision-making. The inflexibility of objectives has also been regarded as important. In one laboratory study, integrative solutions were most likely to be developed in a situation which combined high relatively inflexible limits or aspirations with a problem-solving orientation (Pruitt and Lewis 1975). Similarly, Follet (1940) argued that integrative solutions are adopted when bargainers firmly uphold their own viewpoints unless and until they are convinced that these are not viable. On the other hand, it has been shown that the higher the opponent's rate of concession, the more likely the respondent will be to perceive success in problem-solving (Peterson and Tracy 1976). Gospel (1978) has also stressed the importance of a 'decision-oriented' approach as the most efficient strategy for trade union use of information in a participative or problem-solving situation. Such an approach emphasises that the information sought must be relevant to the decisions unions need to make to meet their objectives. Consistent with this proposition is the finding from Peterson and Tracy's study that the effectiveness of own's own team policy and administration is related to the success of problem-solving.

Recognition and support of objectives is included in the present model as a source of strength to a team's position. Peterson and Tracy found that expectation of constituent satisfaction was significantly related to perceived success in problem-solving. Also, in relation to union strength, Qvale (1979) found that high worker influence coincided with the relative influence of 'external bodies' in relation to the enterprise.

Knowledge and ability have been shown to be important sources of power in a problem-solving or participative situations (King 1975; Pahl and Winkler 1974), and it would therefore seem impossible for such processes to occur without some equality in this area. In the context of technological change, unless they have adequate knowledge of the technical system, it may be impossible for trade unions and non-technical managers to play a meaningful role in negotiations.

Union Bargaining Power
There is some agreement within the literature that problem-solving is enhanced by a reasonable balance of power between the parties (Mulder and Wilke 1970). The predominance of power by one of the parties would seem to provide that party with little

motivation for integrative bargaining. It may be
also argued that a sense of security is a prereq-
uisite for the union side to be willing to take the
risks involved in non-distributive bargaining, and
that bargaining power may provide such a sense of
security. Peterson and Tracy found a fairly stong
relationship between perceived bargaining power and
perceived success in problem-solving. In the
present study a more thorough test of of the value
of bargaining power is undertaken. The conceptual
model outlines four specific elements - the degree
of union density; the amount of employee support for
the unions; the occurrence of industrial conflict
during negotiations; and the threat of such
conflict.

Conflict has been highlighted by a number of
authors as beneficial to the achievement of aims
during problem-solving. Pruitt and Lewis (1975)
concluded that a period of conflict is often
necessary before people look beyond the easy,
obvious options in search of those that provide
greater joint profit. Qvale (1979) also concluded
that 'disagreement would seem to be more widespread
when power is relatively equally distributed across
levels'. Conflict may therefore be seen as a
constructive result of employee involvement, with
new arguments, new criteria for decision-making and
new solutions to problems becoming available.
However, Peterson and Tracy (1976) found in their
study that a strike or even a threat of one was
counter productive for perceived problem-solving.
But when the data was analysed separately for
management and union respondents, the occurrence of
a strike, while significantly negatively related to
problem-solving for management negotiators, showed
only a weak negative relationship for unionists.
The effect of a strike threat therefore needs to be
tested further. Wilkinson and Burkitt (1973)
pointed out that it is strike potential as shown by
the level of unionisation, rather than by the
occurrence of a strike, that is significant to union
power. Whereas a union's strength may derive
ultimately from the threat of a strike, such a
threat need not be put into practice. Indeed it may
be argued that the most powerful unions rarely need
to resort to strike action, since a threat to do so
will modify the employer's attitude.

In the present model, it is suggested that the
outcome of technological change will reflect the
behaviours and conditions which occur within the
management/union relationship, and which give it

form. Previous chapters have outlined the 'choices' which are available to organisations at times of change, but given the essentially political nature of organisational activity, it can be argued that what results will depend on the 'dominant coalitions in the enterprise' (Child 1972). However, the potential influence of other organisational and environmental variables cannot be completely ignored and the importance of two such variables, size and technology, has been stressed in much of the literature (Woodward 1965; Perrow 1970; and Hickson et al 1969). The present model therefore takes into account the type and extent of the new technological system and the size of the operations.

Another factor beyond the management/union relationship, and included in the model, relates to the reasons why the change in technology occurred. This variable highlights the 'motives' behind the changes, a factor which might indeed have the most influence on the type of management/union relationship which occurs, and which might provide the 'blue-print' for the results of that change. A final 'background' variable considered by the present model relates to team membership. Examination of which will allow an analysis of the different management and union perceptions of the bargaining process. It has already been stated that in the literature on collective bargaining there is limited systematic treatment of differences between union and management negotiators in attitudes or behaviours (Peterson and Tracy 1978), most of the research treating these parties as if they were interchangeable. Although a recent study concluded that there was very little difference between the perceptions of management and union negotiators towards the integrative bargaining process (Turkington and Smith 1978), the paucity of evidence, especially in a British context, justifies its further investigation. Also, known differences in the background, status, philosophy and internal political situation of these two groups, would lead one to predict differences in the way they perceive and react to the bargaining process (Gottschalk 1973).

In conclusion, whereas many of the above variables have already been tested, and their importance for integrative bargaining and participation confirmed, their occurrence in the specific context of technological change has not as yet been examined. It is argued that in such a context, which clearly has a high potential for conflict, the

117

elements of management/union cooperation need closer
examination. The conceptual model provides a framework in which the occurrence and content of cooperation may be studied, and it therefore constitutes a
first step towards a predictive model of integrative
bargaining between management/union negotiators in a
British context.

RESEARCH METHODOLOGY

The information to be presented is based on data
collected in 1981/82 from a sample of managers and
trade unionists recently involved in discussions or
negotiations concerning the introduction of microtechnology. The research consisted of one main
study conducted within the brewing industry. This
industry was chosen because of a number of distinctive features, relevant to both microtechnological
change and to management/union participation.
Firstly, there are a number of factors related to
the economics and structure of the industry which
make it well suited to the introduction of sophisticated technologies. The United Kingdom is the third
largest producer of beer in the world, following the
United States and West Germany. Beer production in
1980 reached 39.6 million bulk barrels (roughly 11.4
billion pints). In 1975, the gross output of the
industry was valued at almost £2 billion, the
industry contributing some £575 million to the
Exchequer in excise payments and giving employment
to approximately 69,000 people. In relation to the
manufacturing industry as a whole, the industry
accounts for slightly less than 2% of net output, 1%
of employment and almost 5% of capital investment.
Prior to the development of a national beer market
in the post war period, local breweries dominated
the industry. However, the number of breweries in
Britain decreased from 247 in 1960 to 80 in 1979.
During this period the British Brewing industry was
taken over by six large brewing groups, - Bass;
Allied; Whitbread; Grand Metropolitan; Scottish and
Newcastle and Courage - which supply three quarters
of Britain's beer. This restructuring of the
industry was achieved almost entirely by merger.
The emphasis on merger as a means of corporate
growth is due to the vertical organization of the
industry. Breweries own the majority of retail
outlets through which their beer is sold, and since
these outlets are restricted by licensing policies,
the acquisition of competing firms with their tied

retail estate has been the only feasible growth path.

The industry is also one which has been able to maintain its profitabiltiy in line with that of manufacturing as a whole (Price Commission 1977), and despite the more recent downward trend in sales, demand for the product is still fairly stable. Its structure has been shown to benefit from 'economies of scale', which flow chiefly from capital and labour as the scale of the brewing plant is increased (Cockerill 1979). Under such conditions technical efficiency becomes an important variable. However, despite this trend in the structure of the industry, there are still many small single plant firms in existence. This may be explained by the differentiated market for beer, where consumers may express a preference for local beers with particular taste characteristics. Small firms can gain additional protection through the possession of their own distribution networks. A Price Commission Report in 1977 even showed that the rates of return on capital employed in production and wholesaling for regional breweries (46%) and local breweries (53%) were significantly higher than for the larger ones (32%).

In terms of labour relations, despite the fact that the industry is historically paternalistic, union membership in the production and distribution areas is very strong, with a large number of closed post-entry agreements. The Transport and General Workers Union (TGWU) has a membership of approximately 45% of the total workforce, the General and Municipal Workers Union (GMWU) 30%, the Association of Scientific, Technical and Managerial Staff (ASTMS) 15%, and the Union of Shop, Distributive and Allied Workers (USDAW) most of the rest. Another significant feature is that plant negotiations have a far greater impact than any national suggestions or industry guidelines, reflecting the way in which the industry has developed on a local pattern.

The study was conducted in two parts. The first consisted of an analysis of the microelectronic potential of the industry, together with a national survey of current and planned applications. A list of the major breweries in the country was obtained from the Brewers Society, and questionnaires were sent to different operating companies, enquiring about micro-applications in 12 different areas of the brewing process. From the companies which responded, 50 breweries were selected for the second part of the study, selection being based on the likelihood that the technological changes which these breweries had carried out would have had manpower implications. In addition, interviews were conducted with key decision-makers in 25 of these breweries. The breweries visited covered the whole of the country from Scotland to South Wales, and they were choosen because they had carried out the greatest degree of microtechnological change over the last few years. Twenty of these breweries were operating companies of one of the six large brewing groups, and only five were independently owned. Therefore, most of the breweries in the second stage of this study, and especially those visited, were medium to large in size, i.e. brewing in excess of 100,000 barrels a year.

Although the study gains a number of advantages by being industry specific, this fact also imposes limitations, especially in the degree to which one can generalise from the results. In an attempt to overcome this problem, information was also collected from a more general sample of managers and trade unionists. A questionnaire survey was sent to a selected sample of managers from the Food, Drink and Tobacco industrial sector, and to full time trade union officials of 10 different unions. The managers were selected from companies where it was assumed that microtechnological changes were likely to have occurred. Therefore, mainly large companies were chosen, with some information concerning various technological change projects gained from newspaper articles and case study reports in journals. In total approximately 150 questionnaires were sent out over a three week period. The trade unionists represented a broad cross section of working people, including electricians, office workers, and print workers as well as the skilled and unskilled manual trades. Due to a lack of available information, selection of the sample was of necessity fairly random, and therefore of the 160 questionnaires which were sent out, a number were returned from officials who reported no involvement in negotiations about technological change. Fifteen of the trade unionists, chosen from those who had completed and returned the questionnaire, were also interviewed. As the following chapters will clearly show, the findings from the general sample were very similar to those in the brewing industry.

Chapter Six

THE APPLICATION OF MICROTECHNOLOGY IN THE BREWING INDUSTRY

THE POTENTIAL FOR MICRO-APPLICATIONS

Extensive reorganisation in the industry since the mid-fifties has provided the basis for technical innovation, and the whole brewing process, from the malting stage to the packaging of the product, is highly suited to the introduction of microelectronics. Despite seasonal peaks, the industry enjoys high and stable levels of demand which permit continuuous year round production. The large size of many breweries in the U.K also enable them to make wide use of the new technology. Microelectronic controls offer flexibility, large data handling capabilities, relative cheapness and improvements in performance (Brewing Sector Working Group Report 1980). While hard wired logic systems have long been in operation in many companies, the application of microtechnology has in recent years made a significant contribution in improving the efficiency of the process. There is a potential for such applications in the control of the physical elements of production, as well as in the area of information technology.

Control of the Physical Elements of Production
Microtechnology has played a major part in improving the technical efficiency of the process. Sensor devices may be programmed for weighing ingredients, mixing, controlling temperature, monitoring and recording and also for automatic in-place cleaning. The utilisation of 'micro-chips' as control devices in the fermentation process has been made possible by the replacement of open stainless steel or aluminium fermenters with enclosed vessels of roughly the same capacity. In recent years there

has been a marked trend towards very large vertical conical-cylindrical fermenters. Because of the height of the column of wort in these vessels, agitation during fermentation is intense, and as a consequence the time required for the process is reduced to about 60 hours. The large capacity of the fermenters also produces substantial economies of scale both in capital and operating costs. In addition, it is possible to place these vessels in an outside setting, thus avoiding expensive housing costs.

The development of post-fermentation treatment since the 1950s has opened up another area for the implementation of microtechnology. Microprocessors can facilitate automatic line product changes for lines handling different container sizes. Palletiser programmes may be microelectronic instead of electro-mechanic, and 'chips' may be used to recognise tare weights of kegs, as well as to check, to weigh, and to calculate weight averages and standard deviations. This information may then be rapidly assessed and fed back for correction of filling head performance. In addition, on line machine monitoring by microprocessors is able to provide information on machine efficiencies and to indicate where improvements can be made.

Information Technology

The use of microprocessors in the provision of information to management represents a qualitative improvement in operations rather than a structural change. Such applications also present vastly different problems in terms of capital resource and effects on manpower. A number of areas connected with the brewing process may be subject to microtechnological change in assisting with the provision of information.

- Maintenance

A programme may be developed to plan schedules for maintenance work and to produce management figures on labour, material and contractor costs.

- Warehousing and Stock Control

Process control systems may be used to measure accurately the volume of beer in the tanks. The assessment of batch size, lead time, cost of batch ordering and service level can help to achieve a rapid determination of the ordering programme.

- Distribution

Microtechnology may be used for the identification
of the whereabouts of containers, and for monitoring
the utilisation of vehicles, their maintenance and
costings. Information can also be provided on
vehicle routeing, thus enabling better cost effectiveness and higher levels of efficiency.

- Energy Audit

The statistical presentation of data will be
enhanced. This will improve the general auditing of
utilities, allowing an effective apportioning of
costs and allowing management to act efficiently to
counter any negative trends observed.

- Retail Control

Electronic cash registers are able to produce more
information and can be linked to stock control.
Microtechnology may be used to facilitate stock-
taking by recording stocks, calculating cash
expected and indicating variances in managed houses.
Benefits include a reduction in the amount of time
needed to stock-take in each outlet and an increased
ability to check errors in stock-taking on site.
Information may be passed back to the head office
via 'viewdata', enabling the managers of houses to
send their returns direct to the main frame
computer, thus meeting the need for faster information at relevant control points.

- Administration

Word processing will increase the productivity of
the typist. Computerised maintenance of personnel
records will result in easier information retrieval,
more accurate option assessments, and the saving of
clerical time.

- Accounts

Computer technology may be used to calculate interest and tax for deposit and loan ledgers and
subsequently to print statements. It may also be
used to calculate budgets and to calculate product
profitability.

THE EXTENT OF CURRENT AND PLANNED MICRO-APPLICATIONS IN THE INDUSTRY

Of the 140 or so brewing establishments in England, Wales and Scotland, 11 cannot be included in the calculation either because they refused to participate in the survey, or because they had ceased or were about to cease production. As the few breweries which did not respond were mainly small concerns, the calculation is based on the assumption that they have no microelectronic applications. Of the sample of 129 establishments, responses to the questionnaire from head brewers showed that 76 (58%) had adopted microtechnology in one or more of the 12 possible areas of application, and that almost all were planning further applications.

In terms of current applications it is not surprising that the highest proportion of establishments have implemented microtechnology in the areas of accounts (56%) and stock control (31%), although over 20% of the companies surveyed had applications in 7 or more of the 12 areas examined. Responses about future plans indicated that the degree of application is expected to increase, and while accounts and stock control will still have the highest percentage of applications (74% and 59% respectively) over 40% of establishments estimate applications in four other areas, namely brewing, packaging of large containers, distribution and administration.

A general dimension of microelectronic application was constructed to give a more overall indication of the degree of this application in the industry. Five categories of classification were used, and a percentage degree of application was calculated for each respondent by dividing the number of current and planned applications by the number of possible applications. Table 6.1 illustrates that there is currently quite a substantial decline in the number of cases with micro-applications in 50% of the categories. However, in the context of planned applications this is much less dramatic. Whereas only 1% of companies surveyed had at that time implemented new technology in over 75% of their brewing operations, if the existing plans are implemented this 1% will rise to 21%.

Table 6.1:   Current And Planned Micro-Applications
In The Industry.

Degree of Application	Current		Planned	
0	16	(20%)	10	(12%)
1 - 25%	38	(47%)	23	(28%)
26 - 50%	19	(23%)	21	(26%)
51 - 75%	7	(9%)	10	(12%)
76 - 100%	1	(1%)	17	(21%)

n = 129

As indicated earlier, the areas of application
examined may be usefully divided into two types –
information technology and the control of physical
elements. The average use of microtechnology in
both was calculated. Currently 20% of companies are
using microtechnology in the control of physical
elements (i.e. in either the maltings, brewing or
packaging processes) and 23% in the area of 'information technology'(i.e. in areas such as distribution, stock control, accounts, maintenance, warehousing, retail control procedures, administration
and energy auditing). The number of companies
planning such applications increases to 33% for the
control of physical elements and 44% for information
technology.

Impact of Size on Microelectronic Applications
Not surprisingly, a significant difference was found
between brewery size and the level of microelectronic applications in most areas. This was
true of current and planned applications (see tables
6.2 and 6.3). In terms of current applications,
over 50% of the large companies surveyed had
implemented microtechnology in at least four
operational areas of the brewing process. However,
in estimating future applications, over 50% of the
large companies believe that they will make microtechnological changes in 10 of the 12 possible
areas. It is interesting to note that all of the
large companies surveyed either already had or were
planning for the future, micro-applications in the
actual brewing process and in the packaging of large
containers.

Table 6.2:   Current Applications of Microelectronics
by Size of Company.

Area of Application	Number and % of establishments					
	Small	%	Medium	%	Large	%
Maltings	1	3	1	4	3	25
Brewing	2	6	12	43	10	83
Packaging - Large	4	11	9	32	7	58
Packaging - Small	3	8	7	25	8	67
Distribution	4	11	11	39	4	33
Stock Control	11	30	11	39	2	17
Accounts	18	50	19	68	7	58
Maintenance	0	0	11	39	3	25
Warehousing	0	0	5	18	2	17
Retail Control	4	11	7	25	2	17
Administration	7	19	10	36	5	42
Energy Audit	0	0	3	11	1	8

Large:(n=12) in excess of 1 million barrels p.a.;
medium:(n=28) between 100,000 and 1 million barrels
p.a.; small:(n=36) less than 100,000 barrels p.a.

Table 6.3:   Planned Applications of Microelectronics
by Size of Company.

Area of Application	Number and % of establishments					
	Small	%	Medium	%	Large	%
Maltings	2	6	2	7	5	42
Brewing	7	19	20	71	12	100
Packaging - Large	6	17	15	54	12	100
Packaging - Small	5	14	10	36	9	75
Distribution	6	17	19	68	7	58
Stock Control	17	47	19	68	8	67
Accounts	22	61	25	89	9	75
Maintenance	3	8	17	61	8	67
Retail Control	5	14	14	50	4	33
Administration	7	19	19	68	7	58
Energy Audit	1	3	13	46	7	58

Large:(n=12) in excess of 1 million barrels p.a.;
medium:(n=28) between 100,000 and 1 million barrels
p.a.; small:(n=36) less than 100,000 barrels p.a.

Differences in current and planned applications were also found amongst medium sized breweries. Whereas there is only one area where currently over 50% of medium sized companies have adopted microtechnology (accounts), the same percentage indicated plans to implement microtechnology in 9 out of the 12 areas in the near future. In the smaller companies the level of current application is lower, but there are still estimates of substantial increases in the future.

One of the most interesting differences between the very small and large companies is in the areas where microtechnology has already been applied. Both in terms of current and planned applications smaller companies indicate more micro-applications in the area of information technology than in the control of physical elements. For large companies the situation is reversed, with a greater percentage of companies adopting micro-electronics for the control of physical elements rather than in the provision of information. One explanation for this is that micro-applications in the former entails much greater expense and therefore is more cost-effective for large scale production. The apparent lack of application in the area of information technology may be misleading due to the non inclusion by these companies of the use of main frame computer technology. With medium sized companies, there is a greater adoption of microelectronics in information technology, although 25% or more of such companies reported current and planned applications in the control of the physical elements of production (See tables 6.4 and 6.5).

Table 6.4: The Average Current Use of Microelectronics in Two Application Areas by Size of Companies.

Area of Application	Small	%	Medium	%	Large	%
Control of Physical Elements	3	8	7	25	7	58
Information Technology	6	17	10	36	3	25

Large n=12; medium n=28; small n=36

Table 6.5:   The Average Planned Use of   Microelectronics   in   Two   Application   Areas   by   Size   of
Companies.

Area of Application	Small %		Medium %		Large %	
Control of Physical Elements	5	14	12	43	10	83
Information Technology	8	22	18	64	7	58

Large n=12; medium n=28; small n=36

The 50 breweries selected for more detailed analysis
in part 2 of the brewing study were those where most
microtechnological   change seemed to have   occurred.
From   the questionnaires collected in the first part
it was calculated that 57% of the sample included in
part 2 had more than a 25% degree of   micro-applications   (i.e.   applications in more than 3 of the 12
areas   investigated),   and that 85% of the sample had
plans   to   introduce   a similar level   of   microtechnology.   However, when managers were asked, both in
a second questionnaire and in interviews,   about the
extent   of microtechnological change experienced   by
their companies,   their responses showed more variation   than was expected.   Seventy per cent   of   the
management   sample felt that only a minor degree   of
such   technological change had taken place.   The 25
companies   visited were chosen on the basis that   a
great   many   innovations   had   occurred,   but   even
experiences   of   microtechnological applications   in
these   companies turned out to be extremely   varied.
However,   one can broadly categorise these companies
into two types,   which gives some indication of   the
reasons for this confusion.
      Firstly,   there   are   those companies (14 out of
the 25) in which micro-applications are being implemented   in   a   gradual and piecemeal   fashion   in   a
number   of different areas.   This usually   involves
the use of microelectronics for the modernisation of
existing   equipment,   and   the   technology   is   used
primarily for the control of various aspects of   the
brewing process,   such as the regulation of cleaning
and   washing functions,   temperature control in   the
fermentation   process,   and the replacement of solid
state   equipment in the control of keg   lines.   One
reason   for such limited application of   microtech-

nology in these companies is the fact that there had been a great deal of development prior to micro-electronics, through the use of main frame computerisation. A substantial number of the companies visited had been the subject of major investments of this first generation of computer technology.

It was felt by the management of several of these breweries that their companies would not be able to justify any large scale investment of microtechnology. One company had invested 6 years ago in solid state electronics used for the control of the kegging lines. This technological change had involved a great deal of training of instrument technicians, and now that this equipment had become very familiar, it was felt that there would have to be very good reasons for making further microtechnological changes. In situations where there had been recent major investments, only one company had decided not to adopt microtechnology, choosing instead a hard wired logic system. To summarise then, a group of companies in the sample have been gradually updating their technology over the last two decades. Their breweries, even without microelectronics, were already fairly modern, and further technological advances were therefore being carried out only in a 'limited piecemeal way'.

The second category of companies consists of those where a more dramatic change of the technological system may be observed. In six cases completely new breweries were built to incorporate microtechnology, four of these being greenfield sites. In the other companies there had been a major application of micro-technology in at least one area. In one example, a packaging hall had been commissioned with built-in micros. This was one of the most modern of its kind in the country. In fact many of the applications in these companies were in the area of packaging, of either kegs or cans, with few direct applications in the control of beer production. In only three of the breweries in which there had not been a move to a new site, did it seem that microtechnology was a major advance. These breweries tended to be independently owned and had not carried out gradual improvements in their technology. As the head brewer in one of these companies stated:

The plans for microtechnological changes in 1976 was the brewery's first move into the 20th century.

Thus, in conclusion, about half of the breweries visited were adopting limited microtechnology as just another step in technological progress. Whereas such companies may have indicated a number of areas of application in answer to the first questionnaire, the extent of application in these areas could be regarded as fairly minor. In contrast, other companies have invested heavily in microtechnology, either by setting up large new sites or by converting a major part of their process to microtechnological control.

Chapter Seven

THE IMPLICATIONS FOR THE WORKFORCE

The impact of new technology on working people will partly depend on the assumptions which lie behind the technological designs. It is possible that a particular technological design could be so inflexible and rigid that it would be seen as the most important factor influencing 'impact'. Information about the designs of new brewing equipment may therefore indicate some of the likely implications for the workforce. The APV company, one of the largest manufacturers of brewing equipment, outlined what they see as the essential 'elements of automation' as follows:

> ...to replace the intelligent functions of man by instrumentation and engineering. The brain is replaced by the control unit, the eye by the sensing device and the hand by the operating device. An automated installation thus embodies control equipment that receives instructions on the process and ensures that they are carried out correctly.

New equipment manufactured by this company is based on such principles, and their aims concerning technological progress in brewing focus on principles of control, cost-efficiency and labour reduction. A number of key advantages are anticipated as a consequence of these designs. These include an increase in productivity, consistency of operations, efficient manning levels, product security against accidental loss or contamination, self diagnosis of plant faults and increased flexibility. This raises questions about the extent to which the manufacturer's design and purpose have been implemented, and the extent to which the above 'advantages' have been achieved? An important ele-

ment here is the extent to which decision-makers
have been convinced of the advantages of the new
technology and the subsequent reasons they give for
making the investment.

WHY IMPLEMENT MICROTECHNOLOGY?

> Breweries today can no longer make a profit
> despite themselves, like it was 10 years ago.
> They must become more efficient.

This quote from a personnel manager exemplifies the
philosophy behind technological change in a brewery
where a major investment in a new micro-controlled
greenfield site had been made. There was almost
unanimous agreement amongst those interviewed in
this company that microtechnology aided efficiency.
In fact, only one brewery in the study had made a
conscious decision not to adopt microtechnology in a
new investment. Two reasons were given for this
decision. Firstly, that jobs would be more boring
for the workers in a microtechnological system as
they became more detached from the actual process.
Secondly, there was a fear of trade union reaction
to the new technology, and particularly that the
unions would demand better terms and conditions as a
result of the change.
     Reasons for the adoption of microtechnology in
the breweries sampled were categorised under three
main headings - people, production and finance.
Table 7.1 illustrates the findings of the questionnaire responses from the management sample.

Table 7.1:   Reasons for the Introduction of Microtechnology in the Brewing Industry.

People		
To reduce the workload	23	52%
To improve conditions	10	23%
To make work places safer	7	16%
Production		
To replace worn-out machines	23	52%
To expand production	15	34%
To improve the quality of the product	33	75%
Finance		
To reduce labour costs	26	59%
To reduce capital costs	8	18%
To meet competition	22	50%

n = 44

(1) People Reasons

The three reasons investigated in this category were the reduction in workload, the improvement of working conditions and safety at work. The latter two were little stressed in responses to the questionnaire, and it is also significant that only one manager interviewed indicated this type of reason as being important in the decision to introduce new technology. In contrast to the apparent neglect of this category, the managers interviewed seemed to place a great deal of emphasis on the increase in managerial control which was afforded by the new technology. In one company the manager commented – 'there is no longer a reliance on individual expertise, and discipline is easier when the computer dictates orders to the operator'. Similar sentiments were expressed by many others and it was felt that the new technology gave a greater certainty 'of getting things right'. One manager pointed out that the process 'could no longer be interfered with by the operator', while another stated that 'it removed the possibility of operator error or shortcuts from the system'.

(2) Production Reasons

Fairly high percentages for all three production reasons were obtained as shown in table 7.1, and almost all the companies visited pointed to one or more such reasons for the adoption of the new technology. In most plants production capacity increased within a range of 25% to 70%. The new systems were also thought to improve the consistency and accuracy of the process, thereby improving the quality of the product. Cleaning functions were more intensive and carefully controlled, and other potential advantages and reasons for adoption included close monitoring of the process, easier detection of errors, simpler maintenance and less supervision. The thoroughness of some of these operations was felt to be beyond the capabilities of the human operator, with more information being generated about the process, and new operations being introduced. Thus, while it was seen that the new technology may be used to replace the human operator, it was also believed to be able to perform beyond human capacity. Finally, reference was frequently made to the role of suppliers in dictating technological decisions, with a number of managers pointing to the difficulty of getting replacement parts for the old equipment, this being an important reason for change.

(3) <u>Finance Reasons</u>
It may be seen from the table that 59% of the
questionnaire sample mentioned the reduction of
labour costs as an important reason for the
introduction of microtechnology. The most important
reason given in the interviews also was the reduction of labour costs which could be achieved per
unit of output. An interesting distinction was
found in the sample between companies adopting
either 'cost-reduction' or 'cost-avoidance' strategies. In 14 out of the 25 companies, it was openly
admitted that a reduction in labour costs had been
one of the main reasons for adopting micro-technology.

One manager stated:

> It is obviously the most important reason for
> investment; other reasons such as improved
> quality are not good enough, because the fact
> that it is better quality does not mean that it
> will sell.

In the other 11 companies, although it was stated
that no labour savings were made, and that the
technology was introduced for other reasons,
examples of 'labour cost avoidance' were evident.
For example, it was usually the case that production
had increased two to three fold as a result of
technological change, and while it was true that
there had been no reduction in labour, neither had
new jobs been created. In one brewery, the change
from a bulk loading operation into tankers to keg
packaging had not increased the numbers employed and
if anything had resulted in some job loss. The
packaging of beer into kegs has traditionally been
more labour intensive, but the full utilisation of
new technology in this area has avoided any need to
increase labour costs. With 'information technology' applications, cost avoidance may be even more
pronounced. As one manager said, 'there is often
the choice between buying one computer or employing
three people'. Therefore, the importance of financial reasons was stressed above all others. One
company pointed to the importance for economic
survival of updating one's technology when other
companies in the market are doing so. There were
also a few illustrations of how microelectronics

could cut capital costs in certain areas. In one example, a saving of approximately £12,000 to £15,000 a year was made on detergents and other materials when microelectronics were utilised in the cleaning of tanks. Many of the trade unionists interviewed accepted these 'cost-efficiency' reasons for technological change, and took the principle of labour reduction as given. However, those who felt that microtechnology shouldn't be judged or implemented according to a set of strict financial rules, were powerless in their opposition to managerial objectives. On a few occasions it was stated that breweries had been threatened with closure if proposals were not accepted, and as one unionist said, 'if we hadn't gone along with the principle of labour reduction, the new brewery would still have been built, but with less union involvement'. Thus, it may be concluded that a number of production and financial advantages have been gained by companies who have adopted the new technology. The two main reasons for change were the reduction in labour costs and the improvement in the quality of the product. People considerations in decisions to change technology, such as improving working conditions and providing better health and safety, did not seem to focus strongly.

The reasons given by the managers in the more general sample were very similar to these from the brewing industry. For these managers, too, 'people reasons' and the reduction of capital costs were the categories to which there was least frequency of response. In contrast, reduction of labour costs was indicated as being an important reason for technological change by 78% of the sample. In only two categories were significant differences found between the two groups of managers. The improvement of the quality of the product seemed to be a more important reason for introducing micro-applications for brewing managers than for the general sample (chi-squared = 5.35, significant at .05), while the ability to meet competition and survive economically was a more important reason for introduction for the general management sample (chi-squared = 6.1, significant at .05). This latter difference may be explained by the relative financial stability of breweries in comparison with much of British industry.

CHANGES IN EMPLOYMENT POLICIES

Various trade unions, in their policy statements concerning the introduction of microtechnology, demand the 'equitable distribution of the benefits from technological change together with an avoidance of any negative effects such as redundancy and de-skilling'. The extent to which these demands have been achieved were investigated in the brewing study.

(a) The Avoidance of the Negative Effects – Redundancy and Deskilling

The questionnaire data revealed that a large propor-tion of the breweries studied (76%) had experienced no redundancies as a result of technological change. In companies in which redundancy had occurred there were only two examples in which compulsory redund-ancy had been needed. In one there had been a severe reduction in manning with 120 out of 300 being made redundant. However, even here 90% accep-ted voluntary redundancy. In the other case, major technological changes had been carried out 15 years before and it was felt that the plant was grossly overmanned. There were threats of closure unless there were immediate redundancies and jobs were lost from the highest to the lowest grade.

The voluntary redundancy package offered by many of the breweries was extremely attractive. For example, in one company, compensation was based on 150% of the relevant state payments. Early retire-ment was also available to staff over 50 and pensions were not offset against redundancy pay-ments. As is traditional in the industry many of the employees had long service with the company and decided to take the options which were being offered. Eventually, 40% of the people employed at the new brewery had to be recruited. A survey carried out by the company of employee reasons for accepting the voluntary package, indicated that the principle reason was a fear of insecurity. This was expressed with respect to both changes in the type of work with the new technology, and the introduc-tion of a new three shift system. It was usual for technological change to be 'phased in' over a number of years, and thus both redeployment and natural wastage were commonly used. In one company natural wastage had achieved a 20% reduction amongst produc-tion workers over the last two years.

From such data, it may be concluded that the management of these breweries had introduced 'new technology' in a fairly humane way. There had been very few compulsory redundancies and generous voluntary packages and redeployment for all who did not wish to give up their jobs. Out of the 25 companies visited, only 14 stated that the new technology had led to a reduction in the number of people employed. However, some doubt may be cast on the accuracy of this figure. One manager admitted that there was obviously an attempt not to associate manpower savings with micro-applications. There were also a number of indications that changes such as reduction in numbers may occur sometime after the technological change. In the present economic climate redundancies may easily be blamed on the recession and the drop in beer sales, after or before a technological change has occurred. Department of Employment figures show that most breweries have reduced their labour force over the past few years, with a substantial loss of 8,000 between 1980-1981. This has also been a time of rapid microtechnological change, and there is enough evidence in the present research to link these two factors.

One manager stated that his plan in introducing new technologies was 'to eventually automate everyone out of the production system, even myself'. But, while the technology exists to design a fully automatic brewery requiring no manual involvement, the more general attitude expressed was that the brewing industry was still a long way off from taking the human element from the process. As one head brewer stated, 'such a system would be very expensive and difficult to maintain, for when things go wrong the workforce would not have a day to day working relationship with the system except at a very high level'. Interestingly, the two manpower objectives of this company with regard to technological change were:

Firstly, that the system adopted must not replace the operator, but rather should increase his involvement in the brewing process. It was felt that this could be achieved by allowing the system to take over repetitive mundane tasks so that the operator would be able to concentrate on the more important decision-making aspects.

Secondly, the system must ensure minimum manning levels consistent with the overall aim of labour reduction.

The degree of labour reduction obviously depended on the type and extent of change which had

occurred. It usually ranged from a saving of about
2 or 3 men in an area such as brewhouse operations,
to much more significant savings in the area of
packaging. For example, one company was able to
reduce numbers employed from 100 to 6 with a new
micro-controlled canning line. The most dramatic
changes in the sample studied occurred when the
complete process was moved to a new modern site.
Savings then ranged from between half and two-thirds
of the workforce. There was wide agreement amongst
all the managers interviewed that there was no likelihood of any expansion of their labour force with
the increasing sophistication of the technology in
the industry. For example, in one company at the
time of the study, 15 men were employed in a
fermenting operation involving 7 vessels. There
were plans to increase the capacity to 14 vessels,
without the use of any additional labour.

Thus, in almost every situation studied, the
fact of redundancy, and the loss of jobs (as opposed
to people) were taken as given. The rationality in
doing this was almost unanimously upheld. Only one
manager out of the 26 interviewed had felt guilty
about making people redundant or reducing job opportunities in areas of already high unemployment and
in almost all cases the trade union had been powerless to prevent this. As one representative stated:

> The breweries are very generous when they want
> change. People will rush to give up their jobs
> because of the attractiveness of the redundancy
> package. There is nothing the unions can do,
> no way they can react as long as members take
> the money.

In a number of cases there were more volunteers to
accept redundancy than the number required by the
company, and there was no instance of industrial
action over the occurrence of redundancy. With
regards to 'deskilling', it did not seem to be a
particular problem of technological change in this
industry, as many involved in production are unskilled or semi-skilled workers.

Similar findings to these were found in the
general sample of managers and trade unionists.
Very few managers in this sample indicated that any
compulsory redundancy had occurred as a result of
technological change, although a significantly
larger percentage (41% as compared to 20% of brewery
managers) indicated that some form of voluntary
redundancy had taken place. Job loss was also shown

to be a major problem for the sample of full-time trade union officials. None of those interviewed had succeeded in securing agreements to prevent a reduction in jobs, and many felt helpless when companies offered large financial handouts to employees for giving up their jobs. A number of these unionists highlghted the problem of trying to convince management that the technological change had amounted to a 'new system'. Many situations were described where management had believed that it was merely an extension of the old, and therefore needed 'no special consideration'.

b) <u>Positive Effects - Improvements in Pay and Conditions.</u>
Fourteen positive 'employee effects' were investigated and table 7.2 outlines the frequency of their occurrence. As the table shows, the most frequent outcome recorded was retraining and improvements in skills. This occurred in 67% of the cases. Job enrichment and increased job satisfaction were also frequently recorded by management, occuring in 61% and 50% of cases respectively. Only three other benefits occurred in around 50% of the cases, namely job evaluation changes (50%), less overtime (50%) and better health and safety (45%). Therefore six of the outcomes studied regularly occurred, but only one of these related in any way to the possibility of increased payments. The evidence available therefore indicates that the employees are not obtaining increased payment for retraining and any new skills they are learning. An increase in pay was recorded as a result of technological change in only 34% of cases, improved bonus payments and productivity bargaining in 9% and 7% respectively. Working hours were only reduced in 20% of the cases, less shiftwork and worksharing in only 11%, and longer holidays in only one company. Earlier retirement was not recorded at all. In five of the companies visited, technological changes had resulted in an increase in shiftwork.

Table 7.2: The Frequency of Positive Employee Effects as a Result of New Technology in the Brewing Industry.

Increases in pay   15 34%
Job evaluation changes   22 50%
Bonus payments   4   9%
Productivity bargaining   3   7%
Reduced hours   9 20%
Reduced overtime   22 50%
Reduced shiftwork   4   9%
Earlier retirement   0
Increase in holidays   1   2%
Work-sharing   5 11%
Job enrichment   27 61%
Improved skills/retraining   31 67%
Health and safety   21 45%
Job satisfaction   27 58%

n = 44

Technological Change and Payment.
A reluctance was voiced by many of the managers interviewed to pay for technological change, and only 38% of that sample stated that there had been an increase in pay with the introduction of new equipment. Only one manager referred to the rights of both employees and employers to benefit from technological change. It was more usual to want to try and dissociate changes in terms and conditions of employment and the introduction of new equipment. One strategy carried out by two companies was to conduct a job evaluation exercise and completely change the terms and conditions of everyone employed on the sites, rather than singling out as a special case those directly affected by the new technology.

Increases in pay were also found to result mainly from a collapse of the grading system due to the reduction of the numbers employed and a decrease in supervision. In one company technological change had resulted in there being only three grade levels from the lowest labourer to management. The reduction of overtime in some technological change projects had led to a slight reduction in wages, although this had been counter-balanced to some degree by an increase in shiftwork and the relevant increases in payment. The questionnaire data revealed that job evaluation changes were much more frequent than were increases of pay. This could be interpreted in one of two ways. Either the new jobs performed are valued less, or that the value of the work is not significantly greater to warrant extra payment. Many managers felt that increased job satisfaction resulted from the changes, and that this provided an adequate reward.

Training and Technological Change.

Retraining and skill changes were benefits most frequently recorded both on the questionnaire and during the interviews. The employees most affected were the maintenance workers, but in only three of the companies visited were there any stated plans to teach such workers 'programming skills'. There was also a tendency in some breweries to make such positions staff or managerial. Although different skills would be needed in the future, it was felt that everyone could be retrained.

Job Content, Working Conditions and Technological Change.

'New technology' has transformed brewery work from that of a dirty labouring process to one of button pressing and machine supervision. While there were obviously problems with the former, there is also much evidence that the latter is not ideal. Changes in job content such as increased worker flexibility, job rotation and the consequent reduction in numbers have created many employee problems. Firstly, there is evidence from a number of cases that the new technology has greatly reduced the social element of the job. An individual's work has become very isolated and in many companies there were complaints of loneliness. One manager stated that in his company increased pressure amongst 'programme controllers' has resulted in two heart attacks and one nervous breakdown amongst those employed in such work. It was felt that the isolation of jobs had greatly reduced any feeling of team spirit among employees, and that this had been compounded in some companies by the operation of continuuous shift-working.

Secondly, it would seem that in the new techno-logical environments the workers are far more tightly controlled, despite there being less super-vision than at the old plants. In one company, workers who had been transferred from an old brewery resented the increased formalisation of the new, and there were many signs of resistance and frustration with the system. These materialised in about half a dozen cases a week of verbal and written warnings. At the old brewery it was felt that there were more informal, friendly relations with management. At that time, supervisors and managers were mainly 'man-managers', whereas they were now seen to possess far greater technical knowledge and expertise. In two of the most sophisticated breweries visited the philosophy of single-status employment was adapted both in theory and practice, with the eventual aim of being able to run a 100% staff brewery.

However, some managers stated that while more automation could have been achieved, manual tasks had been intentionally built in to give the operators a specific degree of responsibility for the smooth operation of the plant and to enhance job satisfaction. In addition, the questionnaire data indicated that job enrichment was a frequent outcome of technological change (61%), and a number of the managers interviewed felt that the new technology demanded greater initiative and sense of responsibility from the operators. This was seen to result from the fact that with reduced numbers one operator supervises far more process operations and that therefore the knowledge required is widened. One manager envisaged that such changes in technology could lead to a brewery team made up of a few highly skilled operators. These would be termed 'operator technicians' and would have the flexibility to carry out maintenance and other supervisory functions. However, with the potential prospect of a great reduction of numbers employed in these new environments, it would seem reasonable to conclude that increased job enrichment and job satisfaction for some, will exert its 'price' on others.

The data collected on manpower implications shows an interesting difference between those companies where gradual piecemeal changes have been made and those where major one-off projects have been undertaken, the former category representing the largest proportion of the sample. Table 7.3 shows significant differences with regard to a number of benefits, illustrating the likelihood that the benefits of technological change will be greatly reduced if these changes are introduced in a gradual fashion. In such cases only four benefits occurred in 50% or more of the breweries, again the most frequent being retraining. However, where there were one-off major projects, seven benefits occurred in well over 50%, with increases in pay in 73% and

less overtime and job enrichment in 90% of the
companies.

Table 7.3: Differences Between Manpower Implications of Piecemeal Micro-applications and Major
Projects.

	Piecemeal Applications		Major Projects	
Pay Increases	3	17%	8	73%
Job Evaluation	9	50%	7	64%
Bonus Payments	4	22%	0	
Productivity Bargaining	1	5%	2	18%
Reduced Hours	1	5%	4	36%
Less Overtime	6	33%	10	90%
Less Shiftwork	1	5%	2	18%
Earlier Retirement	0		0	
Longer Holidays	0		0	
Work-Sharing	1	5%	2	18%
Job Enrichment	9	50%	10	90%
Improved Skills/ Retraining	15	83%	8	72%
Deskilling	0		1	1%
Better Health & Safety	7	39%	9	82%
Increased Job Satisfaction	9	50%	9	82%

Piecemeal applications   n = 18
Major projects   n = 11

The pattern of results from the general sample of
managers and trade unionists were again very similar
to those of the brewing industry. The most
frequently recorded outcome from the general sample
of managers was also retraining and an improvement
in skills (71%) followed by changes in job evaluation, job enrichment, health and safety policy and
job satisfaction. In contrast, payment issues,
reductions in hours and changes in conditions of
work were very infrequently recorded in this sample.
In fact in 21% of these companies the technological
change had led to an increase in shiftwork, as
compared to 11% of the brewing sample. It may
therefore be concluded that in the general sample
also there seems to be a reluctance on the part of
management to 'pay' for technological change and to

prevent job loss by shortening the working week. Although many more full time officials than brewery trade unionists (64% compared to 44%) indicated that pay increases had been secured, such data alone may give a misleading picture of the situation in general. A number of the full-time officials interviewed stated that increases of pay were achieved only at the expense of most other things. In a few of the agreements, in return for slight pay increases, companies had been given a 'carte blanche'. The problem, as seen by one official, was that 'members seem to want to work these new machines, and start operations before details have been finalised, seemingly satisfied with the smallest of improvements'. As in the brewing industry, the results indicate a general failure in achieving a reduction in working hours, increases in holidays, earlier retirement, or the introduction of work-sharing. However, some trade union officials did not support these changes because they felt they were not cost-effective.

Chapter Eight

THE MANAGEMENT/UNION RELATIONSHIP

The study also examined the process of introducing
new technology, especially the type of relationship
between management and unions which occurred during
the period of planning and introduction. This
chapter reports the nature of this relationship, as
seen by unions and management. The importance of a
participative relationship in 'change' situations
has by now been well established. Three types of
management/union relationships, with varying degrees
of participation, were investigated within the
brewing industry. One of these relationships,
integrative bargaining, is distinguished by a high
level of participation in searching for alternative
solutions and arriving at a mutually satisfactory
agreement. The second type of relationship, distributive bargaining, is a process where the two sides
find it easier to adopt adversary positions. Agreement is reached less by participation and the
discussion of alternatives, than by compromise
between the opposing demands of the two parties.
The third type of relationship is consultation, in
which most of the decision-making is carried out by
management and with the unions merely being kept
informed.
    Respondents to the questionnaire were asked to
analyse their management/union relationship in the
introduction of new technology along three separate
dimensions, which were defined and labelled A, B,
and C. These corresponded to integrative bargaining, distributive bargaining and consultation
respectively. The format of the question was based
on the assumption that the management/union
relationship during technological change may contain
elements of each of these relationships.
Respondents were therefore asked to place a percentage beside each, the three totalling 100%, so that

the percentage mark reflected the part it played in
the overall relationship. Information was also
collected on the behaviours and conditions underlying these three relationships and their perceived
influence on the outcome of technological change.
Interesting differences were found between management and union perceptions of the relationships that
occurred, and the information collected from these
groups will therefore be treated separately. The
significance and implications of these differences
will be discussed towards the end of the chapter.

THE MANAGEMENT PERSPECTIVE

According to the brewery managers the relationship
which occurred most frequently in the implementation
of new technologies was one of consultation. As
shown in Table 8.1, 50% of this sample scored 50% or
over on consultation, compared with 19% indicating a
similar score for problem-solving and 3% for bargaining. When specific areas of decision-making were
examined, over 50% of the managers indicated that
the unions were not involved at all in four of the
areas - the initial investment decision; the cost-
benefit analysis; discussions regarding the type and
extent of the technology to be introduced; and
regarding redundancy decisions (see Table 8.2). The
percentage reported as participating in the redundancy decision may be misleading in that it may only
reflect the fact that this issue was not applicable
in a majority of the cases. Table 8.3 presents data
concerning the occurrence of the various types of
relationships in the eight decision-making areas.
The prevalence of the consultative type of relationship in many of the individual areas is again very
evident. Most joint decision-making seems to take
place in the areas of pay and grading and health and
safety, and most distributive bargaining with pay
and grading and redundancy.

Table 8.1: Analysis of Types of Relationship Between Management and Unions During Technological Change (Brewery Management Data).

Degree	Problem-Solving %		Bargaining %		Consultation %	
0	6	17	14	39	2	6
1 - 25	17	47	15	42	4	11
26 - 50	6	34	6	16	12	33
51 - 75	5	13	0		5	14
76 - 99	2	6	0		8	22
100	0		1	3	5	14

n = 36

Table 8.2: The Frequency of No Union Involvement in the Eight Decision-Making Areas During Technological Change (Brewery Management Data).

Area	No Union Involvement	
Type and Extent of Technology	21	58%
Redundancy	21	58%
Pay & Grading	8	22%
Investment Decision	25	69%
Cost/Benefit analysis	23	64%
Selection/ Training	11	31%
Job Redesign	9	25%
Health & Safety	7	19%

n = 36

147

Table 8.3: Type of Management/Union Relationship in Different Decision-making Areas During Technological Change (Brewery Management Data).

	Joint Decision-making		Bargaining		Consultation	
Type & Extent of Technology	1	6%	0		15	94%
Redundancy	3	19%	6	37%	7	44%
Pay & Grading	11	42%	6	23%	9	35%
Investment Decision	0		0		12	100%
Cost/Benefit Analysis	0		0		13	100%
Selection/ Training	4	17%	2	8%	18	75%
Job Redesign	4	15%	2	7%	21	78%
Health & Safety	6	21%	1	3%	22	76%

Many of the managers interviewed felt that it was impossible for both sides to fully participate in the introduction of new technologies. As one manager stated:

> Even if the unions did recognise the need for the new technology, they will not be a party to a reduction in manpower and will fight hard to get the best terms.

Another manager outlined the problem of working with the unions in this situation. He stated that in his company a joint working party had been set up to try to decide the jobs which were going to be lost through technological changes. The management had found a possible 8 - 10 jobs under threat, and since there were a number of options which could achieve such a reduction, the management told the unions that they could choose their preferred option. However, the unions did not agree with the initial decision to reduce the labour force (which had not been discussed with them), and would therefore play no part in its implementation. The manager stated that he saw this as a rejection of the managerial offer to unions to participate. Many managers felt that, no matter what they did, a union reaction of 'conflict' and 'obstruction' was inevitable. One manager suggested that the difference between the

two sides was that the union was concerned about the preservation of the number of jobs, whereas management was concerned only for the existing workforce.
In an attempt to make an objective assessment of the degree of participation, information was obtained concerning the levels and the stages at which there had been union involvement. It was found that in none of the companies visited had there been any consultation concerning the initial investment decision taken at board level. In all cases decisions were finalised by management committees before they were put to employees and the unions. One manager suggested that the union only wanted to be confronted by the final decision, because they had too much vested interest to be involved, or to be seen to be involved, any earlier. Further, it was thought that the union was unable to give much feedback in the conceptual stage of the introduction of new technologies because of a lack of technical expertise.
However, in those few cases in which some integrative bargaining had occurred, the managers involved had felt it to be very useful. In one company, it was stated that the joint management/union job evaluation exercise had been one of the most interesting features of the whole programme. Management believed that this exercise had helped the integrity of the individual trade union representatives and managers to overcome the pressures from their respective interest groups, to give a result generally felt to fairly show the relative weights of the different jobs. It was only after completing the evaluation by a joint approach that management and unions took up their separate roles for negotiations to 'price' the system. A problem-solving approach was also used to determine and implement various personnel policies and management felt that this had been particularly useful in achieving a reduction in the overall numbers employed, without any loss of production or standards during the transition period! Thus, ironically, according to management, integrative bargaining had helped to obtain an agreement from the workers regarding the negative implications of the change.
Using Kendall's tau to measure correlations, an analysis of the questionnaire data revealed that 7 subvariables were significantly correlated with integrative bargaining at the 0.05 level. Most of the significant correlations involved variables relating to contact and communication, namely the

uncommitted exploration of problems between the two sides (tau = 0.38), the degree of informal (tau = 0.25) and formal (tau = 0.30) contact, and an extension of collective bargaining (tau = 0.27). The degree of employee support for the unions was also positively correlated with integrative bargaining (tau = 0.21). It is of special interest that two of the subvariables relating to team expertise were found to be negatively correlated with the degree of problem-solving for management. These were 'a well prepared decision approach by one's team' (tau = -0.22), and 'the adequacy of the team's knowledge concerning the new equipment' (tau = -0.20). Thus, it would seem that when management was less prepared, and when their knowledge concerning the new equipment was inadequate, they perceived more integrative bargaining in their relationship with the trade unions.

Two important reasons for the limited occurrence of integrative bargaining were consistently stressed by managers during the interviews. Firstly, it was felt that the unions lacked the necessary knowledge and expertise in this area, and only one manager interviewed believed that the union district officials had sufficient expertise to be usefully involved. One head brewer stated that a 'fait accompli' should be presented to the workforce, but suggested that there should be a willingness to change the plan if there was good reason. In four cases it was explicitly stated that the original plan had not been changed at all after discussions/consultations with the employees or unions.

Secondly, management realised that the position of the trade unions in a time of economic recession was very weak. In a number of cases employees had been told that any industrial action resulting from the change of technology might close the brewery as there was sufficient capacity elsewhere in the company. The union had found difficulty in getting support, as people became increasingly concerned about keeping their jobs at a time of high unemployment. An example of this weakness in the union's position was demonstrated in one company where ACAS had become involved because of a dispute between management and the unions. When the workforce were balloted, employees accepted management's proposals.

Most managers interviewed resented the bargaining stance which they felt was prevalent in the union approach to technological change. One manager stated, 'the unions will try to squeeze money out of the company and will not operate the new machinery unless there are guarantees'. In another company, even though it was felt that the cause of a dispute which had occurred was lack of union involvement in the process, the manager still believed that conflict was inevitable because 'the unions use technological change to get more money'. Many of the managers insisted that new technology was not a negotiable issue, although in the larger projects there was more likely to have been negotiations and bargaining over terms and conditions.

From the questionnaire data, ten variables were found to be significantly correlated with distributive bargaining although only two in a positive direction. The two positively correlated variables were 'pressure placed on the team by the other side' (tau = 0.44), and an 'extension of collective bargaining' (0.300). The negative correlations, which are presented in Table 8.4, relate broadly to the team's expertise, and to a cooperative working relationship with the other side.

Table. 8.4: Variables Showing a Negative Correlation with Distributive Bargaining (Brewery Management Data).

Subvariables	*Kendall Tau Correlations
Well prepared decision approach	-0.479
Knowledge Concerning the new equipment	-0.430
Employee support for unions	-0.265
Friendliness	-0.414
Trust	-0.323
Legitimacy	-0.286
Respect	-0.422
Constructiveness	-0.381

* Correlations are significant at the 0.05 level.

As stated earlier, the most common scenario perceived by the managers was one in which they had achieved most of the decision-making unilaterally and in which the unions and employees were simply kept informed. In the majority of cases change was dealt with through the normal communication channels which ranged from 'briefing systems' to monthly consultative meetings. In six companies visited emphasis was placed on communicating directly with employees in this situation rather than on cultivating a special relationship with the trade unions. In this way it was felt that grape vine distortion would be avoided, and it was also admitted that such a process took away an element of the shop-stewards' power. The aim, according to one company, was to get people into 'the right frame of mind' so that information presented to them could be 'manipulated' by management, and statements phrased in such a way that the right questions would be asked by employees. This plan broke down in only three cases, the union in each case complaining and instigating industrial action because there had not been enough prior information and agreement.

The questionnaire data revealed a number of subvariables which were significantly correlated with consultation. These correlations are presented in Table 8.5. Five of these subvariables, relating to the type of communication and contact between the sides, were found to be negatively correlated, and only one, the degree of decentralisation in the decision-making, was positively correlated. Two variables relating to the management team's expertise and strength and three relating to the cooperativeness of the management/union relationship were also positively correlated with the occurrence of consultation. Thus the degree of consultation was related directly to feelings regarding the legitimacy and constructiveness of the union side. This would seem to indicate a rather patronising attitude on the part of management, praising the unions while allowing them no involvement in decision-making.

In conclusion, it would seem that the brewery managers who indicated more problem-solving and bargaining in their relationship were also those who were less confident about their knowledge and expertise in this area of decision-making. These two kinds of relationship were associated with similar procedural issues. In contrast, when the relationship was predominantly consultative, the management team was much more confident and the union side was seen to have few procedural advantages.

Table 8.5:   Variables Showing Significant   Correlations with Consultation (Brewery Management Data).

Sub-variables	*Kendall Tau Correlations
Uncommitted exploration of problems	-0.314
Pressure from the other side	-0.303
Degree of informal contact	-0.237
Degree of formal contact	-0.287
Extension of Collective Bargaining	-0.331
Decentralisation	0.206
Well prepared decision approach	0.330
Knowledge concerning new equipment	0.266
Friendliness	0.196
Legitimacy	0.238
Constructiveness	0.276

* Correlations are significant at the 0.05 level.

The General Management Sample
Information collected from the general sample of managers working within the Food, Drink and Tobacco industrial sector indicated a similar pattern of management/union relationships in technological change. Here, too, the most prominent type of relationship was that of consultation.

As shown in Table 8.6, 50% of this general sample scored 50% or over for consultation, while only 20% indicated a similar score for integrative bargaining and a mere 3% for distributive bargaining. In this sample too, a high percentage of managers indicated that the unions had not been involved at all in initial areas of decision-making such as the investment decision, cost-benefit analysis and the type and extent of technology (see Table 8.7); and where there was any involvement in these areas it was predominantly consultative in nature. Table 8.8 outlines the frequency of occurrence of different management/union relationships in the eight decision-making areas.

Table 8.6: Analysis of the Type of Relationship Between Management and Unions During Technological change (General Management Sample).

Degree	Problem-Solving %		Bargaining %		Consultation %	
0	8	20	15	38	1	3
1 - 25	15	37	18	45	4	10
26 - 50	9	23	6	15	12	30
51 - 75	5	13	0		5	13
76 - 99	2	5	1	3	8	20
100	1	3	0		5	13

n = 40

Most joint decision-making took place in the area of health and safety, and most bargaining, not surprisingly, in the areas of pay and grading and redundancy. It is interesting that whereas only 13% of the present sample indicated joint decision-making as being the main process for settling pay and grading issues, 42% of the brewing sample believed such a relationship occurred in this area. This would seem to indicate that a greater degree of harmony was perceived by the brewing managers in what has been shown to be a very conflictual issue during technological change. This fits in well with data which shows a significant difference between the perceived threat or occurrence of industrial action during technological change in the two samples (chi-squared = 6.35, significant at 0.05). Whereas 47% of the general sample of managers indicated that industrial action was either threatened or occurred, only 21% of brewery managers reported this to be the case.

Thus it may be concluded that the low level of conflict found in the brewing industry during technological change could be peculiar to that industry. This may be explained by the characteristics of brewery employees who are normally long serving and may therefore feel more loyalty to the company. Alternatively, it is possible that the industry's structure enables management to threaten closure if there is any employee resistance, and the above data could be seen as an indicator of managerial success in 'frightening' employees. There was no evidence from the questionnaire or interview data that management in the brewing industry were more forthcoming with employee benefits in order to achieve a smoother introduction of the new technology, although significantly fewer redundancies did occur in the brewing industry than in the more general sample.

Table 8.7: Frequency of No Union Involvement in the Eight Decision-making Areas (General Management Sample).

	No Union Involvement	
Type & Extent of Technology	13	34%
Redundancy	18	47%
Pay & Grading	7	18%
Investment Decision	18	47%
Cost/Benefit Analysis	24	63%
Selection/ Training	19	50%
Job Redesign	15	39%
Health & Safety	7	18%

n = 38

Table 8.8: Type of Management/Union Relationship Occurring in the Eight Decision-Making Areas (General Management Sample).

Area	Joint Decision- Making		Bargaining		Consultation	
Type & Extent of Technology	1	3%	1	3%	27	94%
Redundancy	2	9%	7	32%	13	59%
Pay & Grading	4	13%	16	52%	11	35%
Investment Decision	0		0		21	100%
Cost/Benefit Analysis	0		0		14	100%
Selection/ Training	2	11%	3	16%	14	73%
Job Redesign	3	13%	3	13%	17	74%
Health & Safety	9	27%	2	6%	22	67%

However, the differences could simply be differences in perception of technical and personnel management specialists, the former being the predominant respondents in the brewing study (78%) and the latter having a similar majority (78%) in the general sample.

The two sets of managers also differed significantly on whether formal negotiations occurred during technological change (chi squared = 6.56), with 62% of the general sample, compared with 32% of the brewing sample, acknowledging that such negotiations had taken place. Following on from this, significantly more managers in the general sample indicated the existence of a formal agreement covering technological change (chi squared = 4.23). In the majority of cases in both samples, (65% in the brewing study, 69% in the general survey) negotiations/discussions concerning technological change were isolated from other issues.

As regards management satisfaction with the introduction of the new technology and its consequences, 88% of the general sample and 86% of the brewery sample indicated that they were satisfied. Thus it may be concluded that management satisfaction with the conduct and outcome of microtechnological change negotiations would seem to be fairly widespread, at least in the Food, Drink & Tobacco industrial sector. The two management samples did not differ significantly on any of the subvariables relating to the cooperativeness of the working relationship with the trade unions, the communication and contact between the negotiating parties, their team strength and expertise or the power of the union.

The Relationship Between Process and Outcome in the Total Management Sample

It has already been stated that satisfaction amongst the managers was consistently high. However, no relationship was found between these feelings of satisfaction and the occurrence of either integrative bargaining or consultation between the sides (tau values -0.04 and -0.12 respectively). Interestingly, though, distributive bargaining with the union side was significantly correlated with feelings of dissatisfaction (tau = -0.21). No support was found for the hypothesis that a greater degree of integrative bargaining would lead to a greater improvement in terms and conditions of employment as a result of the new technology. Integrative bargaining was not found to be related to any of the individual trade union demands, nor to the avoidance of redundancy or deskilling.

However, a positive relationship was found between distributive bargaining and perceived improvements in terms and conditions of employment (tau = 0.19), but of the individual demands studied this type of relationship was only significantly related to improvements in health and safety (chi squared = 4.92). Important subvariables in the management data correlating with improvements in terms and conditions were – a lack of trust of the union side (tau = 0.17); inadequate technical ability (tau = 0.14); inadequate outside support (tau = 0.17); inability to change the decisions of the other side (tau = 0.19); extension of collective bargaining (tau = 0.18); informal contact (tau = 0.14); the degree of pressure exerted by the other side (tau = 0.17); an uncommitted exploration of the problems (tau = 0.15) and lack of availability of information from the union side (tau = -0.17).

Thus in the management data, distributive bargaining, with its more aggressive stance, seems to be more important than integrative bargaining in relation to improvements in employment conditions. Increases of pay are significantly related to such variables as the degree of formal contact between the two sides (chi squared = 8.02) and to an extension of collective bargaining (chi squared = 8.58), although job enrichment was closely related to the degree of informal contact (chi squared = 4.09). Finally, less redundancies were said to have occurred when employee support for the union's goals was strong (chi squared = 4.38), and also when there was less of an uncommitted exploration of the problem by both sides (tau = -0.30), a subvariable highly correlated in the management data with integrative bargaining.

THE UNION PERSPECTIVE

As with the management respondents, consultation was by far the most dominant relationship perceived by unionists in the brewing industry. As Table 8.9 shows, 55% of the sample scored 50% or over for consultation, with only 12% indicating a similar score for integrative and distributive bargaining. In fact, 50% stated that no integrative bargaining had taken place between management and unions, while 22% had stated that the relationship had consisted only of consultation. Many of the trade union respondents also indicated that they were not involved in decision-making areas such as the initial decision to invest, cost-benefit analysis, type and extent of technology and job redesign (see Table 8.10). While the number of brewery trade unionists sampled is too small to make many firm conclusions, Table 8.11 nevertheless highlights the predominance of consultation in the management/union relationship. Integrative and distributive bargaining have a significant impact only in the areas traditionally expected. However, in four cases it was indicated that some distributive bargaining had occurred over the type and extent of technology. The management data from the same companies showed no evidence of this, and in fact the most common complaint of trade unionists interviewed was that they had not been involved at an early enough stage in decision-making. As one union official stated, 'participation was just a charade, for by the time discussions started the management knew exactly what they wanted to do'.

Approximately half the unionists interviewed were satisfied with their degree of involvement during technological change, and five factors were thought to be necessary for participation or integrative bargaining to work in this situation. Firstly, adequate union power within the brewery, for then management was forced to secure union cooperation if they wanted a peaceful change. Secondly, trust and honesty between the two sides; as one official stated, the union 'had shown its worth' to the company and its members. Thirdly, a commitment from management to the idea of participation and industrial democracy. Fourthly, an adequate level of knowledge and expertise concerning new technology and finally a friendly relationship between management and unions. No procedural issues were mentioned as being of major importance.

In one company union rights to negotiate over job changes resulting from technological change had been written into the company agreement, but most unionists seemed ambivalent about the need for a technology agreement. One union official felt that such an agreement would reduce the flexibility of the union approach. While the majority of unionists interviewed complained of a lack of involvement, a few however did envisage some problems if the unions adopted or were allowed a more 'participative' role in technological change. As one unionist concluded, 'it is impossible to have full democratic rights without the responsibility that goes with it'.

Table 8.9: Analysis of the Type of Relationship Between Management and Unions During Technological Change (Brewery Trade Unionists).

Degree	Problem-Solving %		Bargaining %		Consultation %	
0	9	50	6	33	2	11
1 - 25	4	22	4	22	4	22
26 - 50	3	17	6	33	2	11
51 - 75	1	6	1	6	2	11
76 - 99	1	6	1	6	4	22
100	0		0		4	22

n = 18

Table 8.10: The Frequency of No Union Involvement in the Eight Decision-Making Areas (Brewery Trade Unionists).

Area	No Union Involvement	
Type & Extent of Technology	8	47%
Redundancy	3	18%
Pay & Grading	4	24%
Investment Decision	10	59%
Cost/Benefit Analysis	10	59%
Selection/ Training	7	41%
Job Redesign	8	47%
Health & Safety	1	6%

n = 17

Table 8.11:   Type of Management/Union Relationship
in the Eight Decision-Making Areas During Technological Change (Brewery Trade Unionists).

Area	Joint Decision-making		Bargaining		Consultation	
Type & Extent of Technology	2	22%	4	44%	3	34%
Redundancy	4	31%	4	31%	5	38%
Pay & Grading	2	17%	7	58%	3	25%
Investment Decision	0		1	12%	7	88%
Cost/Benefit Analysis	0		1	20%	4	80%
Selection/ Training	3	33%	1	11%	5	56%
Job Redesign	2	40%	1	20%	2	40%
Health & Safety	4	29%	3	21%	7	50%

From the questionnaire data, a number of subvariables were found to be significantly correlated
with   problem-solving.   Unlike   the   information
elicited in interviews, many of these related to
procedural matters, and there is some similarity
here   with   the   information   collected from   the
managers.   However,   there was a marked difference
between the management and union samples concerning
the   variables   relating to team expertise   and
strength. Within the union data these variables are
strongly and positively correlated with integrative
bargaining.   Whereas, for management these correlations had been negative.   Tau values for the
significant variables are shown in Table 8.12.   The
unionists   interviewed   recognised   the   need   for
distributive bargaining during technological change,
arguing that some issues were more conflictual and
had to be 'bargained over' rather than 'talked
about'.   There seemed to be no problems connected
with handling integrative and distributive bargaining within the same relationship. The subvariables
significantly correlated with distributive bargaining are presented in Table 8.13.

Table 8.12:   Variables Significantly Correlated with
Integrative Bargaining (Brewery Trade Unionists).

Sub-variables	*Kendall Tau Correlations
An uncommited exploration of the problem	0.391
The degree of pressure exerted on the other side	0.515
The degree of formal contact	0.331
An extension of collective bargaining	0.543
Involvement of the unions at an early stage.	0.401
Clarity of one's team objectives	0.418
Well-prepared decision approach	0.370
Adequate knowledge about the new equipment.	0.302

* Correlations are significant at the 0.05 level.

In the management data, variables relating to
team knowledge and expertise had also been negatively correlated with distributive bargaining. A large
number of subvariables relating to contact and
communication between the sides, the strength of
team expertise, and a cooperative negotiating relationship significantly correlated in a negative
direction with the degree of consultation.   As with
the management data, the consultative relationship
was perceived by the unions to be very different
from the other two. However, whereas team expertise
and a cooperative attitude towards the other side is
negatively correlated with consultation for the
unions, the correlations had been positive for
management.   These correlations in the union data
are presented in Table 8.14.

Table 8.13:   Variables Significantly Correlated with Distributive Bargaining (Brewery Trade Unionists).

Sub-variables	*Kendall Tau Correlations
An extension of collective bargaining	0.479
Outside support from colleagues	0.469
Well prepared decision approach	0.419
Adequate knowledge about the new equipment	0.349

* Correlations are significant at the 0.05 level.

Table 8.14:   Variables Significantly Correlated with Consultation (Brewery Trade Unionists).

Sub-variables	*Kendall Tau Correlations
Clarity of issues from the other side	-0.303
Uncommitted exploration of problem by both sides	-0.2867
Degree of pressure exerted on the other side	-0.313
An extension of collective bargaining	-0.597
Ability to change decisions of other side	-0.283
Early involvement of the union in decision-making	-0.373
Clarity of one's team objectives	-0.374
Well prepared decision approach	-0.435
Adequate knowledge about the new equipment	-0.492
Trust of other side	-0.298

* Correlations are significant at 0.05 level.

The General Trade Union Sample

In the general union sample, more integrative bargaining and less consultation was reported in relationships with management, although this difference between the two union samples was not statistically significant (see Table 8.15). Thirty percent of the general sample scored 50% or over for problem-solving, with 29% of the sample indicating a similar degree of consultation. For the brewery trade unionists these percentages had been 12% for problem-solving and 55% for consultation. There was very little difference between the degree of distributive bargaining for the two samples, with a very large percentage of both groups indicating that this type of relationship occurred on very few occasions. Again, a large number of the general sample of trade unionists indicated no union involvement in decisions regarding the investment, cost-benefit analysis, the type and extent of technology and job design (see Table 8.16). Also, when there was involvement the majority of these unionists indicated that it was only of a consultative nature. As Table 8.17 shows, most joint decision-making occurred in areas such as redundancy, selection and training and health and safety, and again most of the distributive bargaining was in the area of pay and grading. This was similar to the brewing industry except for the redundancy issue, where the trade unions had reported more integrative and distributive bargaining. This difference may be explained by the fact that for many respondents in the general sample decisions about redundancy were not applicable as no redundancies had taken place. However, in the areas of selection, training and job redesign a greater degree of integrative and distributive bargaining was indicated than had been by the brewery trade unionists. The majority of trade unionists in the brewing industry stated that there was either consultation or no involvement in these areas.

There was a significant difference between the two union samples concerning whether 'formal negotiations' had taken place during the introduction of new technology (chi-squared = 4.01). Seventy-eight per cent of the general sample, in contrast to 55% of the brewery sample, indicated that there had been formal negotiations. Also, significantly more formal agreements concerning technological change were indicated by the general sample than the brewery unionists (chi-squared = 4.71). In both samples there was a greater tendency for negotiations/discussions about technological change to be isolated from other issues (64% in brewing and 62% in the general survey). A greater percentage of the full-time officials indicated that they were satisfied with the introduction of the new technology and its consequences (52% of this sample, 39% of the brewery unions), but this difference was not significant.

Table 8.15: Analysis of the Type of Management/Union Relationship During Technological Change (General Union Sample).

Degree	Problem-Solving %		Bargaining %		Consultation %	
0	14	16	25	28	18	20
1 - 25	30	34	26	30	28	32
26 - 50	17	19	23	26	16	18
51 - 75	14	16	9	10	9	10
76 - 99	3	3	3	3	9	10
100	10	11	2	2	8	9

n = 90

Table 8.16: Frequency of the Occurrence of No Union Involvement in the Eight Decision-Making Areas (General Union Sample).

Area	No Union Involvement	
Type & Extent of Technology	18	22%
Redundancy	11	13%
Pay & Grading	2	2%
Investment Decision	47	57%
Cost/Benefit Analysis	44	53%
Selection/ Training	12	15%
Job Redesign	24	29%
Health & Safety	10	12%

n = 83

Table 8.17:   Type of Management/Union Relationships
Occurring in The Eight Decision-Making (General
Union Sample).

Area	Joint Decision-making		Bargaining		Consultation	
Type & Extent						
of Technology	11	17%	19	30%	34	53%
Redundancy	13	28%	17	37%	16	35%
Pay & Grading	17	22%	50	66%	9	12%
Investment						
Decision	6	19%	2	6%	24	75%
Cost/Benefit						
Analysis	4	12%	9	26%	21	62%
Selection/						
Training	22	32%	22	32%	25	36%
Job Redesign	11	20%	24	43%	21	37%
Health &						
Safety	25	35%	21	30%	25	35%

However, significant differences were found
between the two samples for five of the subvariables
relating to the behaviours and conditions underlying
the negotiating process.   Three of these related to
aspects of team strength and expertise, variables
which were significantly correlated with integrative
bargaining for the brewery unionists.   These subvariables with their chi-squared values and respective levels of significance are presented in table
8.18.

Table 8.18:   Variables Showing Significant Differences Between the Brewery and General Union
Samples.

Subvariables	chi-squared	Prob.
Well prepared		
decision approach	5.46	.05
Knowledge about		
new equipment	5.05	.05
Attendance on courses		
about new technology	8.40	.003

More than 50% of the officials interviewed believed that team knowledge and expertise were of prime importance if the unions were to be fully involved in the area of new technology. Many emphasised the importance of educating and training shop-stewards and officials and were disillusioned with the old trade union philosophy of 'by the people and for the people'. It was recognised that in some areas, including the area of new technology, there was a need for professionals and specialists working on behalf of the union.

The general sample of trade unionists seemed to show more confidence in their team's strength and capabilities, and this may account for the greater degree of integrative bargaining reported by this sample. There was a significant difference between the two samples with respect to the variable relating to decentralisation of decision-making, with a higher percentage of the general sample of unionists believing that most decisions were made at plant level (chi squared = 5.46). Such a factor has obvious importance for union involvement in decision-making. The main problem for the unions, as seen by one official interviewed, was that they were being involved in 'rear-guard' action after the main decisions had been made. It was felt that if the employer came to the unions open-minded and amenable to suggestions, then any bitterness or 'win-lose' situation could be avoided.

However, as with the brewery trade unionists, some apprehension was voiced about becoming too involved with management, such participation negating the image of the 'two sides of industry'. It was stated by one official that if there was a redundancy situation it would be important for him 'to step back and maintain some independence'. The problem of participating with management in techno-logical change and of effectively protecting (union) members was therefore one of which many union officals were aware. The solution offered by a few (and only a few unionists were in such a position) was to combine integrative and distributive bargain-ing in the same relationship. Such unionists were the ones whose team strength and expertise were well established, and they felt that because management and unions were working together an awareness of what management was doing, or could do, need not be lost.

Finally, it should be mentioned that the general sample tended to rate the management side as more unfriendly than the brewery trade unionists (chi squared = 4.28). However, whereas 72% of brewery trade unionists indicated that they distrusted management, only 48% of the full-time officials responded in this way. A similar pattern emerged for the variables related to the constructiveness of the management side, although neither chi-squared value (3.43 and 2.15) was significant at the 0.05 level. In view of these findings it could be concluded that management may be perceived as more friendly by a union team that is less prepared for decision-making and with little knowledge or expertise in the area under discussion, but that such unionists will be less trusting and may regard management proposals as less constructive than if they were more informed.

Two possible reasons may be put forward to explain these differences between the union samples. Firstly, there was a significant difference in the degree of microtechnological change which the two groups had experienced. The full-time officials were asked to complete the questionnaire in relation to the most significant technological change they had experienced, and whereas 76% of this sample perceived the change in which they were involved as fairly major, only 44% of the brewery sample responded in this way (chi squared = 7.50). This information is especially important in view of the evidence from the brewing study that major projects seem more conducive to union involvement and to improvements in employee benefits than are more limited incremental changes. However, it is notable that such projects were the exception rather than the rule, the majority of companies carrying out limited changes in a gradual manner - 'to lessen the drama of the episode and deter union involvement'.

Secondly, most of the union sample from the brewing industry were shop-stewards or convenors, whereas the general union sample was made up entirely of full-time officials. Therefore, differences found between these groups may have had little to do with the idiosyncracies of the brewing industry, but rather may simply reflect the different trade union roles. Eighty-eight per cent of the total union sample were full-time officials, and the sample is therefore different in nature to that of the brewing officials. However, both the questionnaire data and the interviews with the shop-stewards and convenors in the brewing industry indicate less integrative bargaining and less team strength and expertise than for the full-time officials. Therefore conclusions from the total union sample may be viewed as an optimistic assessment of what probably occurs in many companies at the shop-floor level.

The Relationship Between Process and Outcome in the Total Union Sample

The questionnaire data revealed a strong positive correlation between union satisfaction with the technological change and the occurrence of integrative bargaining in the management/union relationship (tau = 0.55). No relationship was found with distributive bargaining, and there was a strong negative correlation with consultation (tau = -0.45). In fact, the interviews with trade unionists highlighted a marked difference in attitudes towards the new technology between those who indicated involvement in integrative bargaining and those involved in more distributive bargaining or consultation. The former unionists fully embraced the introduction of new technology, outlining the advantages which would result rather than any of the drawbacks. One unionist stated with pride that 'my members are not luddites', and felt that 'microtechnology is the greatest invention since the steam engine'. The only regret of another was that 'the whole process of technological change did not start sooner'. In contrast, the prevalent attitude of those involved in distributive bargaining or consultative situations was that of opposing redundancies and preserving jobs, and they perceived technological change as more of a threat than a panacea. Such findings provide some evidence that resistance to change among trade unionists will be lessened if they are more involved in the decision-making. One trade unionist stated:

> The most bitter pill, if manufactured <u>with</u> the union, will be swallowed.

Interviews with unionists who were satisfied with their involvement in technological change also pointed to one other important factor which could have influenced their perceptions of participation. This will be described as an adherence by these unionists to a management ideology regarding the new technology. One such unionist emphasised the strong financial expertise within his union. Union analysts had looked closely at the cost-effectiveness of various computer technologies and it was stated that the union would always support the most efficient technology, even at the cost of some jobs. There were also strong feelings amongst many of these unionists that worksharing or the reduction of the working week would not be a cost-effective way of preserving jobs. They believed it was important to 'talk' to companies, and disliked a 'them and us' attitude.

Unlike the management sample, trade union respondents showed a significant positive correlation between perceived improvements in terms and conditions of employment and the extent of integrative bargaining between management and union (tau = 0.39). This type of relationship was also significantly related to two specific trade union demands, namely increased job satisfaction (chi-squared = 5.61); and productivity bargaining (chi-squared = 12.41), and significant relationships were also found between the occurrence of integrative bargaining and both redundancy (chi-squared = 4.14) and deskilling (chi-squared = 13.07). Relationships with more integrative bargaining seemed to result in fewer redundancies and fewer instances of deskilling.

The union data, however, also showed distributive bargaining to be significantly correlated with improvements in terms and conditions of employment resulting from technological change (tau = .19), and indeed a greater number of individual trade union demands were related to this type of relationship than to integrative bargaining. These included improvements in skill (chi-squared = 6.22); better health and safety (chi-squared = 4.08); increases in pay (chi-squared = 9.96); reduction in working hours (chi-squared = 4.17) and reduction in overtime (chi-squared = 6.61). However, distributive bargaining showed no significant relationship with a reduction in deskilling or redundancy.

With the occurrence of a predominantly consultative relationship between management and unions the outcomes of technological change were found to be very different. A strong negative correlation was found between the degree of consultation and improvements in terms and conditions of employment (tau = -0.46), and it was also shown that less consultation in the relationship was related to the achievement of union demands such as improvement in skills (chi-squared = 10.16); health and safety (chi-squared = 10.33) and productivity bargaining (chi-squared = 11.79). On the other hand more consultation in the relationship was found to be related to more deskilling (chi-squared = 6.6) and more redundancies (chi-squared = 6.5).

A COMPARISON OF THE MANAGEMENT AND UNION PERSPECTIVES

This chapter has outlined a number of differences between managers and trade unionists in their perceptions and experiences of the negotiating relationship during technological change. The statistical significance of these differences were tested using independent t-tests or chi-squared analysis, depending on whether the data was interval or nominal. Management tended to see themselves as having a more cooperative attitude towards the other side, perceiving the trade unions as more friendly (t = 8.57, sig 0.001); their goals more valid (t = 3.01, sig 0.005) and affording them greater respect (t = 11.29, sig 0.001). They also indicated greater satisfaction with the availability of information from the other side (t = 2.46, sig 0.01). They believed more strongly that the unions had been involved at an early enough stage (t = 6.23, sig 0.001), and that most of the decision-making concerning technological change was conducted at plant level (t = 2.92, sig 0.005). The unions, on the other hand, indicated significantly more pressure from the other side (t = 3.88, sig 0.001) and felt that contact with management had been more formal (t = 1.96, sig 0.05). They felt that more agreements had been signed (chi-squared = 4.25, sig 0.05) and that there had been a greater extension of collective bargaining in the negotiations (t = 4.24, sig 0.001).

Differences in the degree of team strength and expertise were also apparent. The management team showed more confidence in the clarity of their objectives (t = 2.00, sig 0.05); believed their knowledge concerning the new equipment to be more adequate (t = 2.85, sig 0.005) and had a more well planned and prepared approach to decision-making (t = 2.74, sig 0.01). On the other hand, trade union respondents seemed more convinced of their bargaining power than was reflected by the responses of the management sample. For example, 62% of trade unionists, as opposed to 33% of managers, indicated that an industrial dispute occurred or was threatened during the introduction of the new equipment. This raises the issue of the real strength of the union position, and it is significant that of the 25 breweries visited, in only 6 were there any instances or threats of industrial conflict. Such a low degree of conflict may be regarded as rather surprising, especially in view of the difference in objectives between the two sides, and the limited degree of 'participation' and union involvement which has been found. Furthermore, as shown in table 8.19, an analysis of these conflict situations showed that the union could be termed 'successful' in only 2 out of the 6. Even then only a slight increase in payment levels was achieved, and this was after substantial strike action. The unions have been unsuccessful in achieving demands such as a reduction in hours and longer holidays.

Using the techniques of factor analysis, it was found that a large percentage of the variance in the management data resulted from management's percep- tions of the cooperativeness of the relationship between the two sides, with procedural aspects of management/union cooperation being far less signifi- cant. For the trade union sample, team strength and expertise emerged as the most important factor in the data collected. However, such strength was not very prevalent in the negotiations studied, and the dominance of management in this area could be an important reason in explaining the extent of consul- tative type relationships during technological change.

Both negotiating teams were in agreement over the low level of integrative bargaining in the rela- tionship with the other side. Sixty per cent of the management sample and 54% of trade unionists indi- cated that less than 25% integrative bargaining had occurred in their relationship during negotiations concerning technological change. Indeed 18% of the former and 22% of the latter stated that there had been no integrative bargaining in their relation- ship. In relation to 'distributive bargaining' and 'consultation', significant differences were found in the assessments of the teams. Whereas an astonishing 81% of managers indicated that less than 25% distributive bargaining had taken place, the percentage was reduced to 57% for trade unionists (chi-squared = 11.31). In the case of 'consulta- tion', only 21% of the managers felt their relation- ship with the other side had contained 25% or less of this element, although 49% of trade unionists believed that this had been the case (chi-squared = 12.3).

Interesting differences were also found between the two teams in the types of relationships which were stated to have occurred in the various areas of

171

Table 8.19:   Causes and Outcomes of Disputes between
Management and Unions During Technological Change in
the Breweries Visited.

Nature of Conflict	Industrial Action	Outcome
Disagreement about amount of bonus employees should receive.	3 week strike	Bonus demand was granted
Demand for reduction in work hours from 37 to 35.	None	Hours remained the same
Demarcation problem when employees refused to do the work of those made redundant.	None	Nothing achieved
Demands for increase in pay, shorter hours, longer holidays,paternity leave etc.	7 week strike	Increase in pay achieved
Dispute over number of employees needed. Company wanted 3 (as in the old plant), the operators wanted 4, the shop-stewards 12, as production had increased 12 fold.	Start of operations delayed for 1 year	ACAS were involved and ruled that the company was right
Problem of whether the new technology resulted in a significant differ-ence to the work of elec-tricians. Management did not agree that the effect was significant enough to warrant special status.	Refusal of electricians to carry out 2nd line maintenance i.e repairs in workshops off the line	Very little effect on the company who are contracting out most of the work

decision-making connected with technological change projects. The most notable were in decisions regarding the initial investment, the cost/benefit analysis and the type and extent of the technology to be implemented. Not one manager in the sample indicated that the unions had been involved in a joint decision-making or bargaining capacity with respect to the first two of the above decisions, and only 6 indicated that such union involvement had occurred in the third decision. In fact a large percentage of these managers felt that the unions had not been involved at all in any of these decisions. This is particularly interesting in view of the finding that 73% of the managers were quite satisfied that the unions had been involved at an early enough stage. As for the trade union responses, 22% indicated involvement in joint decision-making or bargaining in the investment decision, 36% in a cost/benefit analysis and 49% in decisions concerning the type and extent of technology to be implemented. In fact, the trade union sample indicated a greater degree of involvement in all eight areas of decision making than was attributed to the union side by the managers surveyed. On the basis of the above findings, it seems that a completely different impression of trade union influence during technological change would be gained from management and trade union perceptions of the situation.

In relation to the conditions and behaviours underlying these various negotiating relationships, only the trade union responses fully support the model of integrative bargaining presented in Chapter Four. For the trade unions, perceptions of the occurrence of integrative bargaining have a strong positive relationship with the cooperativeness of their attitude towards the management side, tending to heighten feelings of trust, respect and legitimacy for the other team. Team strength and expertise were also indicated in both the questionnaire and the interviews as being important for trade union involvement in technological change. Many unionists emphasised the education and training of officers and the importance of some specialist union resource in this area. This is also supported by the fact that in situations where unionists felt that they were involved in only the most minor way, a lack of team strength or expertise was very prevalent, as was a distinctly non-cooperative working relationship between the two sides.

The most notable differences in the management data in relation to integrative bargaining were the absence of positive correlations in relation to team expertise and a cooperative attitude. Integrative bargaining for managers did not seem to be related to an improved working relationship between the two sides, and correlations with elements of union strength led one to conclude that such participation with trade unions during technological change is something endured rather than welcomed. In relation to team strength and expertise, no relationship was found between elements of this variable and the occurrence of integrative bargaining in the management responses.

The only consensus beween management and union respondents concerning the elements of integrative bargaining is to be found in relation to the importance of issues relating to communication and contact between the sides. Both parties seem to be in agreement that a strict procedural discipline, in terms of an uncommitted exploration of the problem by both sides, a large amount of formal contact, an extension of collective bargaining and the involvement of the unions at an early enough stage, is strongly related to the occurrence of integrative bargaining. However, some significant differences also occur in this category. The trade union data include some additional subvariables such as the availability of information from the other side, their ability to change managerial decisions and the occurrence of decision-making at plant level. Pressure exerted by the other side, however, seems to be important in the management data, but not for trade unionists. These findings are illustrated in Table 8.20. Similar findings for managers and trade unionists are also found when the procedural subvariables relating to communication and contact are correlated with distributive bargaining and consultation. Many of the subvariables show positive correlations with distributive bargaining for managers and trade unionists, while for consultation the correlations are negative for both teams. These findings are illustrated in tables 8.21, 8.22, 8.23 and 8.24.

Table 8.20: Correlations of Variables in the Bargaining Process with the Perceived Degree of Integrative Bargaining for Union and Management Negotiators.

Variables	Management (Tau)	Unions (Tau)	Sig. (.05)
Cooperation			
Friendliness	0.02	0.20	n.s.
Trust	0.01	0.27	sig.
Legitimacy	0.09	0.32	sig.
Respect	0.01	0.28	sig.
Constructiveness	0.12	0.25	sig.
Communication and Contact			
Clarity of other side	0.21	0.27	n.s.
Satisfaction with information	0.09	0.31	sig.
Uncommitted exploration of problems	0.30	0.33	n.s.
Pressure exerted by other side	−0.20	0.09	sig.
Informal contact	0.06	0.21	n.s.
Formal contact	0.22	0.22	n.s.
Extension of collective bargaining	0.18	0.26	n.s.
Ability to change decisions	−0.07	0.28	sig.
Involvement of unions at early stage	0.15	0.36	n.s.
Decision-making at plant level	0.10	0.34	sig.
Team Strength and Expertise			
Clarity of objectives	0.07	0.15	n.s.
Well prepared decision approach	−0.09	0.29	sig.
Knowledge about new equipment	−0.02	0.21	sig.
Adequate technical ability	−0.01	0.05	n.s.
Outside support	−0.09	0.17	sig.
Union Bargaining Power			
Employee support for unions' goals	0.19	0.17	n.s.

Table 8.21: Strength and Significance of the Relationships Between the Degree of Distributive
Bargaining and Variables Relating to Communication
and Contact (Total Management Sample).

Subvariables	Kendall tau	Prob.
Pressure exerted by other side	0.34	.001
Formal contact	0.26	.001
Extension of collective bargaining	0.26	.001

Table 8.22: Strength and Significance of the Relationships between the Degree of Distributive
Bargaining and Variables relating to Communication
and Contact (Total Union Sample).

Subvariables	Kendall tau	Prob.
Clarity of other side in stating issues	0.14	.05
Pressure exerted by other side	0.19	.004
Extension of collective bargaining	0.12	.04
Ability to change decisions of other side	0.17	.008
Involvement of trade unions at an early stage	0.13	.05

Table 8.23:   Strength and Significance of the Rela-
tionships between the Degree of Consultation and
Variables Relating to Communication and Contact
(Total Management Sample).

Subvariables	Kendall tau	Prob.
Clarity of other side in stating issues	−0.14	.05
Uncommitted exploration of problems	−0.28	.001
Pressure exerted by other side	−0.32	.001
Formal contact	−0.28	.001
Extension of collective bargaining	−0.25	.002
Involvement of union at early stage	−0.15	.03

Table 8.24:   Strength and Significance of the Rela-
tionship Between the Degree of Consultation and
Variables Relating to Communication and Contact
(Total Union Sample).

Subvariables	Kendal tau	Prob.
Clarity of other side in stating issues	−0.29	.001
Satisfaction with information from other side	−0.27	.001
Uncommitted exploration of problems	−0.32	.001
Pressure exerted by other side	−0.13	.03
Informal contact	−0.27	.001
Formal contact	−0.21	.001
Extension of collective bargaining	−0.23	.001
Ability to change decisions of other side	−0.37	.001
Involvement of union at early stage	−0.38	.001
Extent decisions were taken at plant level	−0.30	.001

177

In the management data, the variable relating to team strength and expertise was correlated with the degree of distributive bargaining and consultation in the management relationship with the union side. As Table 8.25 shows, there were strong negative correlations between three of the subvariables in this category and the degree of distributive bargaining that occurred in the relationship. This would seem to indicate that when management is involved in such a relationship during technological change, their expertise is very low and their decision-making approach not well planned. It was also found that managers admitted making more concessions to the union side when there was some distributive bargaining in the relationship (chi-squared = 10.03). It may therefore be concluded that distributive bargaining over technological change is due more to the weaknesses of management in this situation than to the strength of the trade union organisation. Further support for such a conclusion may be found in the relationship between management strength and a consultative type relationship with the unions. A significant positive relationship was found in the management data between a well prepared decision approach by their team and a mainly consultative relationship between the two sides (tau = 0.18). Again these findings would seem to indicate that when the management team is strong they will choose to involve the unions only slightly. For those cases in which distributive bargaining did occur, the management data shows high correlations with lack of trust for the union side (tau = 0.19), and with feelings that the unions are unfriendly (tau = 0.26) and not constructive (tau = 0.19).

Table 8.25: Strength and Significance of Relationship Between the Degree of Distributive Bargaining and the Expertise of the Management Team (Total Management Sample).

Subvariables	Kendall tau	Prob.
Well prepared decision approach	-0.31	.001
Adequate knowledge about new equipment	-0.31	.001
Technical ability	-0.18	.01

In conclusion, it may be suggested that both management and union respondents perceive integrative
bargaining, distributive bargaining and consultation
to be quite different relationships. For the union
sample, team strength and expertise and a cooperative attitude towards the union side were highly
correlated with the existence of an integrative
bargaining relationship between management and
unions. These variables were not significant in a
distributive bargaining relationship, and were
negatively correlated with consultation. A number
of variables relating to communication and contact,
however, were common to both integrative and distributive bargaining (e.g. extension of collective
bargaining; ability to change the decisions of the
other side; early trade union involvement), but it
is significant that more cooperative aspects of the
procedure (e.g. informal contact; uncommitted
exploration of the problem by the two sides) are
correlated only with integrative bargaining. For
consultation all these procedural subvariables are
negatively correlated. Aspects of trade union bargaining power were not positively related to any of
the three types of relationships, although employee
support for the union's goal was, surprisingly,
negatively correlated with distributive bargaining.
This could reflect the usual familiar frustration
experienced by active union officials when they
confront the apathy of the shop-floor.
   In the management sample, one of the most
interesting differences to emerge between integrative and distributive bargaining was that there was
a strong negative correlation, for the distributive
relationship only, with aspects of team strength and
expertise and a completely non-cooperative attitude
on the part of management towards the union side
(e.g. lack of trust, feelings that the other side
was not constructive). It is also significant that
a well planned team approach by management was positively correlated with a consultative relationship
between the two sides. Again a number of issues
relating to contact and communication between the
sides seemed to be common to both integrative and
distributive bargaining, but the variables indicating more cooperation again being correlated only
with integrative bargaining. It is significant
that, in the management data, aspects of union bargaining strength, such as the degree of unionisation, employee support for the union's goals, are
positively related only to integrative bargaining,
although managerial concessions to the unions show a

strong positive relationship with both integrative and distributive bargaining, and a negative relationship with consultation.

It had also been hypothesised that a greater degree of integrative bargaining in the management/union relationship would improve perceived satisfaction concerning the technological change and the achievement of a greater number of union demands. This hypothesis was well supported in the union sample, with integrative bargaining between management and unions significantly related to a perceived general improvement in terms and conditions of employment, to a number of specific benefits, and to the avoidance of redundancy and deskilling. This type of relationship was also highly correlated with union satisfaction concerning the change. For management, no such relationships with integrative bargaining were found. Only the occurrence of more distributive bargaining between the two sides was significantly correlated with an improvement in terms and conditions of employment. Managerial satisfaction concerning the technological change appeared to be consistently high, and it is therefore significant that only with the occurrence of distributive bargaining between the two sides was there any indication of managerial dissatisfaction. On the basis of these findings it would seem fair to conclude that management and unions differ in their preferred negotiating relationship during the implementation of new technologies.

Chapter Nine

STRATEGIES AND POLICY IMPLICATIONS

The research conducted in the brewing industry and
the information collected from a more general sample
of managers and trade unionists provided very little
evidence that the T.U.C. objective of 'change by
agreement' was being achieved. No instance was
found in which the technological change had been
negotiated, although some 'effects' of the change
were subject to collective bargaining. However, it
is significant that a large number of trade union
substantive demands are consistently not being
achieved. These included a reduction of working
hours, increases in holidays, earlier retirement,
and work-sharing. Such schemes have been suggested
as a means of preventing job loss during the introduction of microtechnology. It seems that management is not willing or perhaps not able to adopt
these schemes. Therefore, although the most
frequently quoted union objective in the cases
studied was to preserve as many jobs as possible,
there is little indication of the trade unions
achieving this and so avoiding redundancies.

MANAGERIAL ATTITUDES AND STRATEGIES

It is clear that management does not view technological change as a negotiable issue. Many managers
interviewed resented the bargaining stance which
they felt was prevalent in the union approach
towards technological change. They believed that
there were certain 'givens' in the situation, such
as labour reduction, which make it impossible for
trade unionists to participate or be seen to participate. There was a fear (which was usually found to
be unwarranted) of a 'negative' union reaction to
such changes, and information was therefore passed

181

to the other side with extreme caution. It is significant that much of the information collected from management by the researcher had not yet been discussed with the union side, and the fact that many managers refused access to union representatives at their plant was indicative of their strategy of excluding the unions from this potentially controversial area. Many of the managers interviewed outlined a number of reasons for their apparent success in deterring union involvement and ensuring the implementation of the new technology in the way they wished.

Firstly, the relative ease of gaining acceptance to change at a time of economic recession was fully appreciated by management, and the position of the trade union was very much weakened. In a number of instances employees were threatened with the closure of their plant if the union could not reach an agreement, and fear was easily generated amongst employees by highlighting the competition they faced in the industry from those companies with much more sophisticated technologies. Not surprisingly, therefore, many trade unionists stated that it was difficult to get support for any industrial action because employees were increasingly concerned about keeping their jobs at a time of high unemployment. Significantly, only 33% of the management sample indicated that there had been a threat or occurrence of an industrial dispute during technological change, and in 25 companies visited, only 6 instances of industrial conflict were found. These were caused mainly by grievances over substantive issues such as pay, reduction in hours or increased status, rather than procedural issues such as the exclusion of trade union representatives from decision-making.

Many managers also pointed to the usefulness of what was termed a 'softly, softly' approach to technological change, in reducing the drama of the situation and thereby deterring the necessity of union involvement. In one company the manager stated that the plan followed was to deal first with those areas which were the least contentious, i.e. those with limited manpower implications. After these so called 'innocent' changes had been implemented, more controversial changes would then be made, with the power of employees to resist obviously weakened. The implications of piecemeal changes carried out in a gradual way may be difficult to appreciate in the short-run and they do not initially appear dramatic enough for the trade union

organisation to attempt or succeed in gaining benefits for their members. In one company information
was given concerning a five year plan of separate
micro-applications, and this provided an insight
into the cumulative effect such changes could
produce. The aim of the plan was a 25% reduction in
manpower, and a movement towards the 'operator tech-
nician'.

The success of these managerial strategies is
obviously related to the strength and expertise of
the management team. The questionnaire responses
showed that the majority of managers were confident
about the clarity of their team's objectives (89%);
their preparations for decision-making (89%); the
adequacy of their knowledge about the new equipment
(78%); and their technical ability to play a meaningful role in the situation (60%). A number of
examples were also found of companies actively
involved in the setting up of managerial expertise
in this area. This involved either one person who
had been specifically employed to look at various
applications, or a 'project team' with the requisite
skills to make such decisions. In the brewing
industry, it was found that professional bodies such
as the Brewers Guild organise courses which explain
the new technology to management and help them to
cope with it. This industry also consists of a very
close and tight network of management teams, and
frequent exchange visits are organised by the
different breweries so that each may learn from the
experiences of others.

Management expertise is an often quoted objection to arguments for increased shop-floor involvement in decision making, and as pointed out by
Marchington and Loveridge (1979), 'the idea of non
useful and generally destructive contributions from
the shop-stewards would appear to exert a
particularly pervasive influence over British
management thought'. The current research indicates
that many managers felt that the trade unions lacked
the necessary knowledge and expertise in this area,
and would be unable to provide much feedback in the
conceptual stages of the introduction of new technologies. While it could be argued that such statements by management are merely rationalisations for
a desired course of action (Marchington and
Armstrong 1981), there is evidence that weaknesses
in trade union organisation and strategy in the
present situation is also partly accountable for
their failure to achieve greater involvement in
decision-making.regarding new technology.

TRADE UNION STRATEGIES AND ORGANISATION

Managerial perception of trade union influence and strategies was indicative of the weakness in the union's position. In six of the companies visited, management was surprised at the absence of a trade union reaction and at the union's apparent lack of concern about future plans and applications. For example, one manager commented that the trade union did not seem to realise the implications of production being increased by 65% to 70% with no extra jobs being created. Also, in the majority of companies visited there had been no initiative from the trade unions for formal agreements on new technology. The majority of managers felt that the union strategy had lacked expertise and preparation and that if there was a reaction it could at best be described as 'suspicious' or 'defensive'.

This was illustrated in one brewery by an incident during the annual negotiations, when the electricians' union had enquired about what the company was doing about new technology. Not surprisingly, management's reply was 'nothing special', which to the astonishment of the managers brought an end to the discussion. In only one company was it stated that certain applications had not been made because of the possibility of adverse relations with the trade union. The ignorance of many trade unionists concerning future plans for technological change resulted at times in an unwarranted complacency on their part. An example of this was found in the brewing study, where in one company the trade union official dismissed the issue of technological change as being 'of no great consequence' and as 'something which happens all the time', while his management counterpart spoke of plans to eventually 'automate everyone out of the process'.

In the brewing industry one aspect of trade union organisation militated against union involvement at an early stage in decision-making. A complete lack of coordination was found between the union representatives in the various operating companies of the same brewing group, which provided management with a major advantage in carrying out technological change in this industry. Although over the last five years many of these operating companies had become profit centres able to initiate changes as long as they were cost-effective, the decision to make a technological investment on one site, resulting in the closure of others because of

184

excess capacity, still occurred at a central level. This was found to be a prevalent trend in the brewing industry, and the union was at an obvious disadvantage because there was no representation at this level to demand involvement in decision-making. The predicament of many trade unionists was summed up by one interviewee who felt that 'my union woke up five years too late, finding themselves in a hurricane of new technology with no planning for it'.

The problems of tracing the manpower implications of technological change may also have inhibited trade union involvement. It is not difficult for management to completely dissociate technological change and manpower savings, and the present economic climate has made this task even easier. Secondly, any redundancy which occurs may be blamed on poor market performance after or before a microtechnological change has occurred. In a study by the Labour Research Department (1982) it was similarly found that in 2/3 of the cases where jobs were lost during microtechnological change, the jobs were not lost when the equipment was being introduced, but some time later. Thirdly, the more common gradual and piecemeal application of microtechnology enabled companies to reduce their labour force in a less dramatic fashion through natural wastage. Finally, there was evidence in the brewing industry that the manpower impact of technological change may not be felt only on the site where the changes had taken place, and may have even more serious implications in other companies within the same group. In at least four cases technological investments in one brewery had resulted in the closure of a number of smaller breweries within the organisation.

In view of these findings, it has to be concluded that any trade union influence on managerial discretion during microtechnological change covered by the present research must indeed have been slight. In the vast majority of cases, the trade unions have effectively been excluded from the important areas of decision-making, and when they are finally involved the scope left for discussion, and their ability to change management decisions, was obviously limited. However, when the unions were involved, especially in 'distributive bargaining', there was a strong association with an increased degree of perceived improvement in terms and conditions resulting from the change, as seen by both management and by union respondents. 'Integrative bargaining', on the other hand, only showed significant associations in the union data, and even there it did not seem to have resulted in the creative and innovative solutions to manpower problems suggested by the existing literature.

POLICY IMPLICATIONS

The trade union weaknesses outlined above raise a number of important questions concerning the adequacy of the strategy, structure, and even perhaps the underlying philosophy of the trade union movement in dealing with technological change. The traditional role of the trade union movement as an 'opposition' force in industry, reacting to managerial decisions, has been shown to have only the slightest impact when faced with well-formulated management plans, and a management team with the expertise to implement them. Management has been able to reduce the 'drama' of microtechnological change to such an extent that there is nothing the trade unions can 'react to', and as a result nothing is usually achieved from the change. This reactive trade union stance, while still in operation today, was criticised in relation to technological change almost ten years ago by Hugh Scanlon. He stated:

> It is no longer possible or desirable to wait for the end of a specific contract period to negotiate, when management's decisions are already and quite arbitrarily in the pipeline. These decisions may threaten technological unemployment, obsolescence of skills, disappearance of trades and industries and geographical displacement of the workers themselves. To protect workers adequately, we must be involved with decisions as they occur. We need an anticipatory function at the planning and implementation stages. This is getting to the kernal of our struggle for industrial democracy.

In many of the cases studied, trade union strategies, had not been clearly formulated and planned, and information was received only when management plans were fully developed and could not be changed. There was little evidence that the trade unionists put forward alternative plans and suggestions on how to handle the problems the new technology created, and they also seemed to lack awareness of probable microtechnological advancement in their industries. It is therefore not surprising that managers commented on the lack of trade union reaction during change projects and that management's proposals for the implementation of microtechnology were adopted with relative ease. Management had highly trained specialists either employed or working as consultants for them and an unprepared trade unionist therefore had little chance of success.

One of the reasons for the insufficient attention devoted to the issue of technological change could simply have been the factor of work overload described by many of the trade union officials. In dealing with a large number of companies, the amount of time which can be devoted to any particular project is obviously limited. However, many of the full-time officials interviewed also believed that they lacked sufficient knowledge and expertise to play a meaningful role in negotiations. They complained that they were not being kept adequately informed about the introduction of new technologies by shop stewards in organisations until it was too late to achieve anything. The only union demand achieved with any frequency was an increase in basic pay for operating the new equipment. Job loss and redundancy were outlined as being main problems in the future with microtechnology, and these are problems that will not be solved by unions continually battling for pay increases to the detriment of all else. Policies for reducing hours and work-sharing schemes were not well formulated, and were certainly not being achieved. In addition, very little attention was being given to job redesign schemes, and to ensuring that new forms of work are both interesting and challenging. Therefore, in a time of rapid technological change, it is becoming increasingly important for trade unions to pay more attention to issues relating to the quality of working life.

These weaknesses in trade union strategy have important implications for both the structure and philosophy of the trade union movement in this country. The old dictum of 'by the people and for the people', without recourse to any specialist knowledge, is futile when unions are faced with increasingly specialised management teams. This lack of knowledge is highlighted here as being a main weakness in trade union strategy, and the failure to recognise the importance of such expertise is a major criticism of T.U.C. recommendations in this area. Benson and Lloyd (1983) have also taken up this point, stating that if 'their (the trade unions) knowledge of the available alternative technologies is to go beyond the collective intelligence of their members and the limited speculation on future technologies which ultimately stems from their bargaining opponents, a new and independent source of economic and technological information must be available'. As early as the 1930s, Bernal (1965) effectively outlined the danger of the state's technology policy being formed in the boardrooms of monopoly companies, advocating that such danger could only be averted by first formalising the liason between scientists and organised labour, through the establishment of a permanent joint Science Advisory Committee (SAC). Although such a committee was in fact established in 1937, with the intention of providing the movement with an independent source of scientific and technical advice concerning the long term industrial trends, it failed to achieve its aims and was short-lived.

The most interesting achievements to date in this area have occurred in Norway. It was the Norwegian labour movement which pioneered the use of data agreements to regulate the introduction of new technology, and by now most of the working population of that country is covered by such an agreement. These agreements provide employees with greater powers than the new technology agreements in Britain, emphasising that information concerning systems change should be given sufficiently early to allow the unions to exercise real influence upon the decisions made, and that systems descriptions should also include information about the effects on employees. It is interesting that such agreements also enable unions to elect an additional 'data steward' with systems as their special field of responsibility and with the right to receive education for their job.

The new procedures have substantially enlarged the agenda of collective bargaining in Norway. Unions have become concerned with the impact of new systems on social contracts, job availability and the power structure at work, and have resisted attempts to increase surveillance, to increase work pressure and to deskill jobs. This has resulted in many changes in work organisation, with unions now commissioning their own research into the impact of information systems, and expanding their training programmes to disseminate knowledge on both policy and practical issues among the membership. One such union is the Norwegian Chemical Workers Union, which with the aid of the Institute for Industrial Social Research in Trondheim and the Norwegian Computing Center, attempted to acquire extra knowledge and expertise in microtechnological change (Levin 1980). The aim of the project was to build up a long term strategy at the national level. They tried to develop methods and a local knowledge base for evaluating the quality of working life consequences of proposed new technologies. One short term result of the project has been an increased awareness of the problems raised by the introduction of new technology, and it is argued that the union is now more resistant to proposals for introducing new equipment and has become more interested in the consequences of the new technology for the quality of working life. The Norwegian National Union of Iron and Metal Workers has also recognised that lack of information is a problem, and has set up its own research in this area. It now provides courses for its members, allowing them to present an informed point of view when company policy decisions on the use of this technology are being considered (Nygaard and Bergo 1975). The Norwegian Government has encouraged trade union involvement in technological change by providing the trade unions with a legal right to participate in the design of new technology.

Many of the unionists interviewed felt that some such legal provision was needed in this country. They felt that disclosure of information about investment alternatives and the consequences for work organisation and employment had not been provided by management. While formal agreements and legislation regarding workers' rights to participate in decision-making does not guarantee that such involvement will take place, it does seem that an effective educational and ideological basis for involvement is being built up in Norway.

If trade unions are to be really effective in the microtechnological debate, their influence needs to be felt beyond the shop-floor and beyond the company boardroom. It needs to be felt in the areas of design and manufacture. It has already been shown that technology need not be designed according to a set of strict criteria related only to profit maximisation and control. And once systems have been designed there is still scope to introduce new methods of production and new products. Such achievements will not be easy and will involve a greater degree of confidence and expertise than is evident within most trade unions today. The Council of Nordic Trades Union (NFS), in seeking to increase union influence, have called for research into how computer technology could be used for improving the work environment, democratising working life and developing democracy in society. The guidelines they have issued include the following:

-   giving union aims the same importance in state research as those aims which concern economic and technical factors

-   ensuring that union organisations have a large influence over research within the computer industry, computer service companies and in other institutions and companies that are today under the control of the employer

-   increasing information resources for research on the effects of computers on conditions of working life

A major contribution to such thinking in Britain was the corporate plan drawn up by the Lucas Aerospace workers. These workers questioned 'what the company made, how it was made, why they made it and in whose interest'. In opposition to the structural unemployment that was beginning to affect them, they campaigned for the right to work on 'socially useful products.' Of particular interest in relation to this campaign was the fact that the 'combine committee' which was set up linked together the highest level technologists and the semi-skilled workers on the shop-floor. As Cooley concludes, 'there was a creative cross-fertilisation between the analytical power of the scientist and the technologist on the one hand, and the direct class sense and understanding of those on the shop-floor on the other'. Such a careful linkage of knowledge and power, while preserving pre-existing ideals, may be very difficult. The research which was conducted in the brewing industry certainly found that the unionists who felt they had greater power and influence in the situation seemed to have accepted a managerial definition of technological progress and its consequences.

In conclusion, there are a number of problems and difficulties which the unions face due to the nature of microtechnological change and the way it is implemented. For any meaningful management/union participation to occur in this context, it is essential that trade unionists are fully aware of these problems. In the majority of cases studied, the union lacked such awareness, and where such problems were recognised the unions had a poor strategy for dealing with them. The obvious political implication of such limited trade union involvement is not that workers should give up the struggle, resigning themselves to a micro-technological future beyond their control, but that they should take it more seriously. The unprecedented issues raised by microtechnological change call for new strategies from workers and unions. The vast resources of management and the powerful ideology of 'technology as progress' make it imperative that this labour perspective be developed autonomously by unions in their role as adversaries, before they engage in any joint-collaboration with management (Shaiken 1980). Over the next decade, increases in the level of unemployment and the collapse of traditional areas of work will become even more important areas of debate and discussion. Unless the trade union movement reforms its organisation and improves its strategy, it will not feature as a major force in this debate.

Chapter Ten

CONCLUSIONS

The brewing industry is shown to be particularly suited to the introduction of microelectronics, with this type of investment perfectly feasible in most sized companies. The financial stability of the industry and its unusual structure have made it an especially interesting area of study and, unlike much of the rest of British industry, financial constraints and crises have not had such an influential impact on the process and direction of technological change. A nationwide survey of the brewing industry showed that 58% of companies had already adopted microtechnology in one or more of the 12 possible areas surveyed and that almost all were planning further applications. Two important scenarios emerged in relation to the process of change. Some companies introduced microtechnology in a gradual, piecemeal way, resulting in very few employee benefits and making it difficult for workers to identify the long-term negative consequences. In other companies, change was more obvious and dramatic, involving either the complete transfer of operations to a new brewery, or the installation of a major piece of equipment.

Management expressed great reluctance to 'pay' for technological change, in terms of either money or a reduction in hours and in only a few cases, mainly those involving major projects, were any of these benefits achieved. Surveys of new technology agreements have also shown a failure to secure such provisions (Mainwaring 1982; Williams and Moseley 1981) and the information presented here indicates that a similar picture is found. Seventy-four per cent of the total sample of managers and trade unionists indicated that little improvement in terms and conditions of employment had resulted from the installation of the new equipment. There were only five areas in which 50% or more of the sample indicated that improvements had been made - job evaluation, job enrichment, skills and retraining, health and safety and job satisfaction. While these findings are only 'perceptions' of what occurred, it is significant that the only major differences between the four groups sampled reflected the relatively high percentage of full-time union officials who indicated that an increase in pay resulted from microtechnological change. However, the officials who were interviewed claimed that such pay increases had been achieved at the expense of most other demands.

Management reasons for introducing the new technology seemed to follow closely the manufacturers' promises of increased control, cost-efficiency and labour reduction, and there is some evidence that this vision has become reality. A survey of the advertising literature of brewing equipment manufacturers showed that many emphasise the elimination of the human input in brewing operations, and claim that the automated systems will 'reduce the risk of error and variation in the process constants.' The managers interviewed fully realised the potential for increased control with the new technology and, as one interviewee commented, 'there is no longer a reliance on individual expertise' and 'discipline is easier when the computer dictates the orders'.

Such statements are far removed from the design principles outlined by Davis (1971) and Mumford (1977), which embodied the notion that workers should control the technology and not vice versa. Evidence was also found of the isolation of tasks and the breakdown of social relationships in work situations where microtechnology had been introduced on a large scale. In many companies, managers reported that workers complained of loneliness and it was felt that the isolation of jobs had reduced feelings of team spirit among employees. Therefore, whereas a surprising 61% of managers in the brewing industry indicated that 'job enrichment' had occurred during the technological change, the increased responsibility and initiative demanded of employees, which was the basis of such enrichment, would seem also to have had a number of negative consequences. These usually took the form of increased managerial control and of reductions in the numbers employed (c.f. Kelly 1980). Although a few managers stated that manual aspects had been purposely maintained or built into the new processes 'to prevent boredom and improve job satisfaction', it must be concluded that such considerations were not viewed as main priorities in the adoption and implementation of new technology. Very few managers indicated that improvements in working conditions or matters concerning health and safety were important reasons for changing the technology.

The failure of the trade union movement in influencing managerial discretion and in achieving many of their demands must be partly attributed to their limited involvement in many aspects of the change process. In five of the eight decision-making areas investigated the unions were not involved in any meaningful way. These were the initial decision to invest, the cost-benefit analysis, the type and extent of technology to be implemented, job redesign and the selection and training of employees. Greater union involvement, either in an integrative or distributive bargaining capacity, occurred in relation to issues such as pay and grading, redundancy and health and safety.

In each company visited, decisions concerning new technology were always finalised by management committees before they were put to employees and their unions. Even in one case where union members indicated that they were satisfied with their involvement in the project, it was found that discussions between the two sides had not begun until approximately four years after the initial management decision to invest. Such findings support a growing awareness of the relative lack of trade union influence in strategic decision-making (Hickson and Mallory 1981; Cressey et al. 1981). Although Wilson (1982) found that decisions concerning new equipment or plant constituted the second largest area of union involvement in strategic decision-making, the degree of influence in these decisions was still found to be minimal. In a decision to open a new plant in an engineering firm, departments such as manufacturing, finance and purchasing had a good deal of power, as did the managing director; and externally the supplier of the new equipment and the competitor spurred on the decision process and set its pace. The union, on the other hand, was found to be one of the least influential interest groups.

INTEGRATIVE BARGAINING OVER TECHNOLOGICAL CHANGE

It is well documented that achieving an integrative or cooperative bargaining approach is not without difficulty in a conflict based industrial relations system. The most ardent opponents of such cooperation have pointed to the danger that the union organisation may become too closely identified with management (Clegg 1960; Dahrendorf 1959), and some managers clearly fear that they might lose their power in decision-making. On the other hand, it can be argued that the achievement of more integrative agreements may be advantageous to both sides, being tantamount to achieving 'the greatest good for the greatest number'. Certain issues may be more amenable to integrative relationships than others, and it has been assumed that negotiations concerning technological change, covering a wide variety of issues, may have a special potential for the development of cooperative management/union relationships. However, in relation to this assumption, it is significant that 20% of the total sample surveyed indicated no such cooperation in the management/union relationship. In fact the majority of both managers and trade unionists stated that less than 25% integrative bargaining had occurred in their relationship with the other side.

Many of the managers interviewed felt that it was impossible for both sides to participate in this way, and they also resented any distributive bargaining which they saw as 'forced' upon them. The main reason indicated by management for the introduction of microtechnology, both in the questionnaire and in the interviews, was the reduction or avoidance of labour costs, and this 'rationalisation' was not open to debate or discussion with the trade unions. In contrast, most of the trade unionists interviewed welcomed a more participative relationship with management during the introduction of microtechnology. A commonly held view was that the new equipment and techniques would be introduced even without their involvement and that therefore only by increasing their degree of participation in the procedure could they hope to influence it.

However, a few unionists did outline the potential problems of this kind of participation, and indicated that at times, e.g. in a redundancy situation, they would not be able to cooperate with management. In keeping with these findings, the questionnaire data revealed a strong positive correlation between union satisfaction with the technological change and the occurrence of integrative bargaining between the two sides, while no such correlation was found in the management data. It may therefore be concluded that whereas increased participation and integrative bargaining was the preferred negotiating relationship of the union team, this was certainly not the case for the majority of managers surveyed.

Further support for this conclusion is available from an analysis of the conditions and behaviours found to underlie the occurrence of integrative bargaining between the two sides. In the management data, not one of the variables describing the strength and expertise of the management team was significantly correlated with the degree of integrative bargaining in the relationship. The only significant relationship found with any of the above variables was between a well prepared decision approach by the management team and a mainly consultative relationship with the other side. The team strength and expertise of the union side was, however, highly correlated with the occurrence of integrative bargaining. The fact that such strength and expertise was found to be very limited may explain why such a low degree of integrative bargaining occurred. Many variables relating to communication between the two sides seemed to be important for the occurrence of integrative bargaining in both samples, but variables relating to a cooperative relationship between the two sides were significant only within the union data. Unionists also perceived a greater degree of integrative bargaining when there were 'formal negotiations', and when new technology issues were isolated from other issues. Interestingly, these are two conditions which management attempted to avoid.

All of the unionists interviewed described the underlying conditions and behaviours of the negotiating process as being those most important for successful integrative bargaining. The factors highlighted were similar to those which had been investigated in the questionnaire, namely strength and expertise of the union side, trust and honesty between the teams, and management commitment to participative structures. The interview data therefore provided some support for identifying the antecedent conditions of integrative bargaining. Such data also show that parts of the model tested are not limited to association between the variables, but may suggest or support a causal interpretation.

It may be concluded from the above findings that the trade union data provide some further contribution of the importance of the factors which were proposed by Walton and McKersie (1965) and tested by Peterson and Tracy (1976) as being associated with integrative bargaining. This is true for most of the subvariables relating to a cooperative working relationship and to the frequency and openness of communications. Variables relating to team expertise, which were found to be important for integrative bargaining in Peterson and Tracy's work, were also significant in the trade union data. However, amongst management respondents, support for Walton and McKersie's model was only found for those variables relating to contact and communication between the sides. Generally, in this context, management lacked the motivational orientation for integrative bargaining. Therefore, it may be argued that if such a relationship did occur it was not because both sides wanted it, an assumption of Walton and McKersie, but rather because the union side had enough expertise or procedural advantage to demand it.

The union respondents in the survey seemed firmly convinced of the effectiveness of a joint management/union approach to the problem of change, and believed that the attainment of improved terms and conditions would be met as a result of their increased involvement. In fact an analysis of the questionnaire responses showed that an increased amount of integrative bargaining in the management/union relationship was highly correlated with less redundancy and deskilling, and improvements in bonus payments, productivity bargaining and retraining. The interview information tended to support the conclusion that there is a causal link between them.

However, this 'influential nature' of integrative bargaining was not evident in the management data. It is certainly the case that very little integrative bargaining was perceived by managers, and they could hardly be expected therefore to see much of an effect. But the difference between the responses of management and union negotiators in relation to integrative bargaining raises an important question concerning the 'reality' of the influence as perceived by the unions. The lack of union involvement in the important areas of decision-making has already been discussed, and it is therefore quite probable that the influence of 'integrative bargaining' which was reported to have

occurred was largely 'subjective'. There is much
evidence in the literature to show the ease with
which people can be made to feel that they have
participated (Wall and Lischeron 1977) and the
influence that such 'subjective participation' has
on people's perceptions of events.

In addition, it is interesting and perhaps
somewhat alarming that unionists who felt they had
participated in an integrative way with management
also showed different attitudes towards new technology compared with those who had been less involved.
These unionists fully embraced the introduction of
microtechnology, outlining the advantages rather
than any drawbacks. The findings suggest that the
unionists who felt involved in an integrative
relationship with management adhered strongly to
what could be described as the 'managerial rationalisation' of the situation, and as such did not pose
a threat to management's 'way of thinking'. There
were similar findings in the study by Wilson et al.
(1982), and these authors concluded that unions
involved in strategic decision-making get their own
way only when this is congruent with 'management's
way'. Such findings raise some problems concerning
integrative bargaining, especially when the union
movement is weak, and when management is able to
manipulate the information which the unions receive.
This was illustrated in one company where the aim
was to get people 'into the right frame of mind', so
that information presented to employees could be
tailored in such a way that the right questions were
asked. Evidence of the influence of specialists in
controlling decision-making in this way is well
documented in the literature by authors such as
Pettigrew (1973) and Winkler (1974).

INTEGRATIVE VS. DISTRIBUTIVE BARGAINING

The distinction between integrative and distributive
bargaining was proposed by Walton and McKersie
(1965). They characterised distributive bargaining
as a process of resolving pure conflicts of
interests between the parties, analogous to the most
competitive type of bargaining, with one person's
gain resulting in a loss to the other. Integrative
bargaining, on the other hand, referred to a system
in which the objectives of the two parties are not
assumed to be in conflict. The processes are viewed
as antithetical – the latter emphasises the free
exchange of accurate and believable information,

whereas the former will involve a certain amount of suspicion and withholding of information. Peterson and Tracy (1976) found that respondents had difficulty in distinguishing between 'issues' and 'problems' (Walton and McKersie's terms for referring to more and less conflictual areas), with many unionists maintaining that nothing was non-distributive.

In the case study of the brewing industry both management and union respondents perceived integrative and distributive bargaining as quite separate processes and they expressed no difficulty in handling both processes within the same relationship. While many managers resented what they saw as the dominance of the latter process in the union approach, the majority of unionists interviewed felt that such a win-lose situation could be avoided if the union was involved at an earlier stage in decision-making. However, only few examples were found where these two processes had been effectively combined in a negotiating relationship, and where this did occur it was felt to have been very useful. One manager stated that 'problem-solving' had helped representatives of both sides to overcome the pressures of their respective interest groups during a job evaluation exercise. A few unionists believed that a combination of integrative and distributive bargaining in the negotiating relationship had helped them to overcome the problem of participating with management in technological change while at the same time successfully protecting the interests of their members.

The most notable differences between the two processes related to the variables describing a cooperative relationship between the parties and those describing team strength and expertise. For the union sample, such variables were highly correlated with the degree of integrative bargaining but were not significantly related to distributive bargaining. In the management sample, no significant relationship was found between integrative bargaining and either variable, while distributive bargaining was negatively correlated with aspects of team strength and expertise, and with a completely non-cooperative relationship towards the union side. While Peterson and Tracy (1976) found fewer conflicts than in the present research, it is significant that the pattern of similarities in the correlations for the two sides were related more to 'intra-team' than to 'inter-team' variables. It was these latter variables that provided the main focus in this research. A further explanation for differences between the studies may lie in the fact that the previous authors, in studying the 'success' of both these processes rather than simply the degree of their occurrence, were simply indicating a general satisfaction with the negotiations when either process was successful. It is argued that their research did not therefore adequately discriminate between the different relationships. In the brewing industry, distributive bargaining was found to be negatively correlated with feelings of satisfaction regarding the process and outcome of change, while integrative bargaining was positively correlated with this variable.

However, as with Peterson and Tracy's study, the two processes shared some similarity with regard to a number of variables relating to communication and contact between the sides. However, the more cooperative aspects of these procedures (e.g. the uncommitted exploration of the problems by the two sides and informal contact) were correlated only with integrative bargaining. Union bargaining power was not strongly associated with either integrative or distributive bargaining in the union data, with the degree of unionisation and employee support for the union's goals positively related only to integrative bargaining in only the management data. These findings would seem to indicate that while showing some similarity, the two processes are less alike than has recently been suggested by Peterson and Tracy and by Turkington and Smith. On the other hand they may not be as divergent as assumed by Walton and McKersie.

Unlike integrative bargaining, distributive bargaining was found to be correlated with improvements in terms and conditions of employment in both management and union data. Peterson and Tracy, and Turkington and Smith, found a significant difference between management and union correlations concerning the equitability of the contract to both sides, and in the latter study the correlation was significant only for union respondents. It may be argued that distributive bargaining is less prone to managerial control and manipulation, and is therefore more likely to show results in both sets of data. Some support was also found for the proposition that these two processes were appropriate for dealing with different types of issues. Bonus payments, productivity bargaining and retraining, for example, were found to be associated with a greater degree of integrative bargaining, while more 'conflictual' demands such as increases in pay and reduction in hours were significantly related only to the degree of distributive bargaining in the relationship.

MANAGEMENT VS. UNION RESPONDENTS

Significant differences have been reported between management and union perceptions and experiences of the negotiating relationship during change. A far greater number of differences have been suggested than in previous studies. Management during these negotiations tended to show a more cooperative attitude towards the other side, believing them to be more friendly and demonstrating attitudes of legitimacy and respect for the other team. It may be argued that such feelings are connected to the greater confidence they feel in their team strength and expertise, the clarity of their team objectives, their knowledge concerning the new equipment, and their plans and preparation regarding decision-making.

In relation to bargaining procedures, management respondents were significantly more satisfied than trade unionists with the availability of information from the other side. They also believed more strongly that the unions had been involved at an early enough stage and that most of the decision-making concerning technological change had been conducted at plant level. The union respondents, on the other hand, felt that there had been a greater formality in their relationship with management, and indicated that there had been a wider agenda for discussion. They also seemed more convinced of their bargaining power than was reflected in the opinions of the managers sampled.

A large percentage of the variance in the management data was accounted for by management's perception of the cooperativeness of the relationship between the two sides, while for the union respondents the most influential factor was team strength and expertise, with management-union cooperation being far less significant. It may be argued that such findings reveal basic inequalities between the two sides when negotiating technological change, with team strength and expertise being a crucial factor in the union data, but not featuring as a factor for management. While in the 'general' samples it may be argued that such differences could be attributed to the fact that respondents are referring to different situations, similar findings occurred in the brewing study where management and union representatives were referring to the same situation. There are some interesting differences between these results and similar variables in the work of Peterson and Tracy (1976) and Turkington and Smith (1980). Peterson and Tracy found that union representatives accorded greater legitimacy and respect to the management side than management did to the unions, and Turkington and Smith found that managers reported that negotiations had come closer to precipitating a work stoppage than did their union counterparts. In the present study significant differences were found between the correlations of management and union respondents in relation to variables describing the cooperative relationship between the teams, and the strength and expertise of one's own team. Analyses of similar variables in other studies has not revealed such differences. In Peterson and Tracy's study only the variable relating to the legitimacy of the goals of the other side showed a significant difference in the correlations of the management and the union teams. There was no significant difference between the correlations relating the effectiveness of work organisation and decision procedures between the teams. In Turkington and Smith's study a significant difference was found only for the correlation relating respect for the other team and success in problem solving, and this correlation was found for managers but not for unions. Both these studies found a high level of similarity between the union and management responses, and Turkington and Smith concluded that the parties do not seem to approach integrative bargaining from diametrically opposed standpoints. On the basis of the findings presented here, such a conclusion cannot be justified and the differences between the two sides should not be underestimated.

THE WAY FORWARD

In reviewing the literature surrounding the technological debate, it was argued that 'choices' exist
in both the design and implementation of new technology. It may be concluded from the evidence
presented in this book that new microelectronic
equipment is being designed and implemented in a
very 'determined' way. In the brewing industry,
principles of control were prominent in the designs
of new equipment, and cost-efficiency and labour
reduction emerged as the main reasons for implementation. It is true that some decision-makers did
wander from this 'determined way', introducing job
enrichment schemes and attempting to make work with
microtechnology more satisfying. However, more
innovative manpower adjustment policies such as the
reduction in hours, job sharing and increased
holidays are consistently not being adopted.
Managers have to a large extent attempted and
succeeded in dissociating improvements in terms and
conditions of employment from the introduction of
new equipment, and have prevented technological
change from becoming a negotiable issue. Nevertheless, to conclude that there has been an 'unfettered
triumph of capital over labour' would also not be
justified. There was some evidence of conflict,
dispute, and struggle as well as participation
between the sides, all of which have had some impact
on the outcome of technological change. However,
what is questioned here is the degree of union
influence and the size of its impact.
The design and choice of technology are still
unquestionably managerial prerogatives, and no
instance was found where discussions with the trade
unions had started before management had made these
decisions. By that time the scope for union
influence had been severely narrowed, and the main
achievement during the process of implementation was
generally slight pay increases, usually at the
expense of everything else. The imbalance of power
between management and union negotiators was very
evident in many of the cases studied, and confidence
in their own team's strength and expertise was found
to be much higher among the managers surveyed.
While the impact of the recession cannot be
dismissed as a causal factor in the trade union
weaknesses identified, the research raises a number
of important issues in need of further investigation.

Firstly, there is a potential problem regarding the 'reality' of the trade union perception of the bargaining process in this context. Many trade unionists indicated a greater degree of involvement and participation in the change project than was ever attributed to them by the managers surveyed. Also, those unionists who were shown to be satisfied with their involvement adhered closely to what could be termed a management appreciation of the change. Conclusions from the present research are limited by the fact that it dealt with perceptions of events rather than a more objective analysis of what actually occurred. While perceptions have obvious importance, a further examination of the factors which affect such perceptions, and the extent to which they may have been manipulated by management, needs to be undertaken. The predictive model of integrative bargaining, and of the effects it may have on the outcome of change, received considerable support in the union sample, therefore justifying further testing by means of a more detailed case study approach. The position of management in consistently rejecting union involvement in this area also deserves closer scrutiny, and there is a need to examine the factors which may change managerial attitudes regarding participation.

Secondly, the disclosure of information and the aquisition of knowledge have been outlined as major problems for the trade unions in dealing with new technology. A large number of the trade unionists surveyed were dissatisfied with the information they received from the other side, and there was certainly a lack of knowledge and information on their part concerning the technology. This situation persisted despite the fact that 87% of the trade unionists indicated that courses about the new technology had been organised by their side. It has been a common complaint in experiments on participative management that employees or their representatives have insufficient information to participate in the decision-making process in a meaningful way (Ahlin and Svensson 1980; Carnall 1979; Brannen et al. 1976). It seems to be the case that disclosure of information to trade unions and union involvement in the introduction of microelectronics are inextricably linked as major industrial relations issues. Apart from the degree, the quality and timing of such disclosure, it is suggested that there may be major organisational constraints and problems in terms of the time, resources and expertise available to the trade unions. Such problems may make the use of company information almost as significant a problem as the lack of disclosure. The difficulties surrounding the disclosure of information are so serious that this should be a priority of further research in the area of microtechnological change. A similar conclusion was reached in a recent study based at Ruskin College (Levie and Moore 1981).

Thirdly, this study has provided empirical evidence that issues of technological redundancy and unemployment need to be confronted and given greater attention. Fresh initiatives are necessary to stimulate employment and to improve the quality of working life. Research into the feasibility of worksharing schemes and the employment policies to match such schemes should therefore proceed apace as a possible means of preventing the well documented financial and social costs of increasing unemployment.

It is often stated that 'war is too important to be left to the generals'. Similarly, the main concern in the present volume is that the issues and implications of microtechnological change are largely being left to the discretion of profit seeking companies. While the trade union movement is falling far short of what it may potentially achieve from a technological change project, it nevertheless needs to be recognised that there are limits to what trade unions can do in isolation. It is no coincidence that in Norway, for most of the post-war period, the third party to the negotiating process has been a Labour government promoting pro-labour legislation, opening up areas of management decision-making to local unions and giving them access to the state's research resources. Perhaps it is naive to believe that any trade union movement, no matter how well organised and informed, is in a position to solve what are essentially the political problems of technological change. Our experience of this technology is still in its infancy. The debate needs to be widened considerably.

APPENDIX A

CASE STUDY 1

The new brewery of this company combined a move to a 'greenfield site' with the introduction of a high technology production process. The new development comprised the production centre for one of the four regional areas of this large Brewing group. It replaced an old brewery and canning plant which were very labour intensive, with the brewing operation similar to that used about 150 years ago. The new plant was planned to meet the predicted growth in beer sales forecast in the mid-70s and the rapid rise in demand for lager beers. It was estimated that the new brewery would have a capacity of $1\frac{1}{2}$ million barrels a year, which was approximately three times the capacity of the old brewery.

Manpower Requirements

The technological change led to about a 30% reduction in manpower numbers. All employees were invited to transfer but those who did not wish to could opt for redundancy. Under an agreement negotiated with the unions, compensation was based on 150% of the relevant state payments. Early retirement was also available to staff aged over 50 and pensions were not offset against redundancy payments. As is traditional in this industry, many of the employees had long service with the company and decided to take the options which were being offered. Eventually 40% of the people employed at the new brewery had to be recruited. A survey carried out by the company of employee reasons for accepting the voluntary package highlighted fears of insecurity both in terms of changes in the type of work with the new technology and the new three shift system which was to be operated.

The company philosophy in carrying out the change was that machines should be used to do the 'heavy labouring work' and people should retain their decision-making capacity. Fuller automation could have been achieved but management recognised that some manual aspects should be maintained to prevent boredom and improve job satisfaction. Nevertheless, the changes in job content and skills required were quite substantial. The company aimed for a 'flexible worker' who could be moved from one job to another as needs arose. There was a complete abolition of many supervisory grades resulting in only about three levels from the lowest labourer to management. No evaluative study has yet been carried out to determine whether the job is more satisfying for the worker as a result. In order to achieve objectives such as flexibility of working and an elimination of traditional demarcations, moves were made to harmonise staff and manual terms and conditions of employment.

A New Pay and Grading System

It was believed by both management and unions that the old
payment system failed for three main reasons:

1) There were too many grades.
2) The differentials between the grades had become distort-
   ed.
3) The nine grade structure did not fit the new technology
   as grades were too rigidly defined and both sides
   anticipated enormous change over the next few years.

Management and unions decided on a new system of job
evaluation which would provide the framework for the new
structure.   The system choosen was Paterson's decision-
banding technique under which grades are based not just on
job content but also on the individual's ability and merit in
that job.   The difference between one grade and another is
based on the level of decision-making required in jobs.   In
a particular job this will depend on the type of work done;
the nature of the decisions made i.e. whether the job demands
the employee to make the same or different decisions on a
recurring or occasional basis;   the level of discretion
allowed;   the amount of training or experience required and
the consequences of the various decisions.   It was decided
for each of the factors there should be four 'degrees' or
'levels' of decision-making and at each level there should be
two skill bands.   These skill differentials were payable
when an employee became more proficient in a particular job
and more versatile by acquiring job-related skills.   It was
believed that the major advantage of this system is that all
jobs could theoretically be evaluated in terms of just one
factor, resulting in less complex wage bargaining with fewer
areas open to conflict and dispute.   In fitting in with this
scheme of things the company also felt that everyone working
shifts should receive the same payments for the inconvenience
regardless of grade or type of work done.

The Process of Change
The company set up what was termed a 'Humanities Committee'
to consider a whole range of people aspects relted to the new
site.   Twelve major tasks were identified for consideration
and these ranged from security, catering, manpower, terms and
conditions of employment to the initial occupation stage and
early brewing trials.   Through this committee the personnel
department of the company was fully involved in the
commissioning of the new brewery.

This committee was set up approximately four years after
the initial decision to invest was made and at about the same
time also a series of discussions was begun with the

divisional officers and convenors of the three unions involved. As a result of these discussions, a consultative document prepared by management was presented to the unions for review before formal negotiations started. These negotiations concentrated on six areas:

1) A procedural agreement.
2) A new code of conduct to replace the former book of rules.
3) A revised package of terms and conditions of service.
4) The introduction of a new sick pay benefit scheme.
5) The development of a payment structure.
6) A suitable redundancy agreement.

Apart from these formal negotiations, a communications structure was agreed with the three major unions to ensure that all employees affected by the change were consulted. This was achieved through departmental consultative groups, coordinated by a central consultative committee. It was the responsibility of these groups to pass on views and recommendations to the central consultative committee. No formal joint union/management decision-making committees were set up. However, the company did organise joint visits to other breweries which had recently carried out technological changes, in order to gauge the necessary changes in job design for the new brewery. The managers interviewed stated that there had been few problems with the commissioning of the new brewery and it was thought that one of the main reasons for this was the good relationship between management and unions. However, it cannot be overlooked that the change was made easier due to the fact that the company had moved the whole operation to a new 'greenfield site', rather than altering existing technology on the same site.

Case Study 2

The new brewery of this company was a highly capital intensive plant utilising very sophisticated technology. Most operations were process-controlled and handled largely by operators at centralised control panels. The new plant produced up to two million barrels of beer a year which was achieved with only half of the labour force that was employed at the old medium sized plant. In addition, as a result of this charge the company had closed a number of its smaller breweries.

Manpower Requirements

There had been a major effect on manpower levels, particularly in the brewery's fermentation and process departments. In 1974, the old brewery employed a total of 83 operators on these functions while in the new plant only 36 were needed. In addition to this reduction in jobs available, the nature of the work had also been changed. The technology placed new pressures on employees, such as the ability to work without direct supervision and to take quick decisions on a continuing basis for eight hours at a time. These requirements had led to a decline in the number of semi-skilled and unskilled brewing and processing grades, and an increse in the numbers of skilled operators had been necessary.

In order to achieve these changes in manning levels the company had adopted a policy of natural wastage, voluntary redundancy and redeployment. When the new plant was under construction in 1973, the management planned to freeze all recruitment at the old brewery and to recruit only temporary employees. Initially employees were recruited on this basis for 18 months but the length of possible employment shortened as the date for commissioning the new plant and the changeover approached. As the temporary workers became familiar with the semi-skilled tasks involved, the permanent operatives selected for future employment were in turn released for intensive training and familiarisation with the new plant.

While all permanent employees were invited to apply for positions in the new plant, the selection procedures were very rigorous. The company stated that appointment would depend largely on ability rather than on length of service. In addition to more usual selection processes all applicants for the senior operators' posts were expected to take a '16 P.F. test', which yield scores on 16 personality factors such as shyness, submissiveness, boldness etc. The answers were analysed by a consultant psychologist, and then the decision was made as to the suitability for the given job. All other operators were also subjected to rigorous selection and recruitment procedures, and the company believed that they were an important feature in explaining the successful operation of the new plant. The company estimated that more than 70% of its appointments to the new plant were in fact drawn from its existing employees with the remaining proportion drawn from outside applicants, including some of the temporaries who were offered full time employment.

At the new plant supervision has become much more technically qualified. The company recruited technical graduates for these posts rather than the old style supervisor who worked himself up from the lowest ranks. The operating groups on the line have become much smaller due to decreased manning levels and this has resulted in a more participative style of management. The highly qualified line management have taken on much of what was regarded as the traditional personnel role in terms of industrial relations, formulation of job descriptions, recruitment and training.

The Pay and Grading System
In the new brewery the chargehand grade was abolished and the chargehand's rate was paid to the operators concerned. Also two maintenance-of-earnings agreements were signed. These aggreements identified four groups of individuals affected by the change:

1) Those earning more on transfer.
2) Those temporarily moving from shift to day work.
3) Individuals working less overtime hours with a
    corresponding drop in earnings.
4) Those required to work more hours but receiving less
    gross earnings on transfer to the new site.

There was no problem with the first group. The second, it was agreed, would continue to be paid shift premium for up to ten months and would adopt a flexible approach to working hours during the commissioning of the new plant. The third group was compensated with an immediate cash payment of 50% of the shortfall occurring within the future year, and the fourth group was to be compensated in full for any shortfall.

The Process of Change
    The driving force in the whole change process was a specialist management team set up by the site manager at the outset. It was this team which had total responsibility for the decision-making regarding the manpower implications of the technological change. The specialist team comprised mainly of technical and production management and the only representative for the personnel department was the training manager. The involvement of the personnel function in the

process was minimal which owes much to the company philosophy that line managers should be responsible for all personnel issues.

One of the main tasks of the specialist team was to devise a new training programme. The team were able to familiarise themselves with the new technology by testing similar equipment already in use by other companies of the group. Visits were also arranged to observe similar processes at work in breweries outside the group, and to major suppliers of equipment and brewing materials. Members of the management team then started producing training manuals for operators and during this process certain features of the plant's design were altered in line with what were found to be the practical problems of operating it. Formal training courses and sessions at the company's residential training centre were supplemented by working visits to other plants and suppliers to see the technology working in practice. Manual tasks were intentionally built-in during this job-design process in order to give the operators a specific degree of responsibility for the smooth operation of the plant and to enhance job satisfaction.

No formal joint union/management committee was at any stage established to deal with any issues concerning the introduction of the new technology. Formal negotiations were held with the unions concerning various selection, training and payment issues. On matters outside the collective bargaining sphere the workforce was kept informed by management by means of posted notices. No consultative machinery was set up to deal with problems and whatever consultation occurred was on an ad hoc basis as needs arose and as the workforce requested more information.

APPENDIX B

QUESTIONNAIRE GIVEN TO MANAGERS AND TRADE UNIONISTS INVOLVED
IN TECHNOLOGICAL CHANGE NEGOTIATIONS

1. Which team are you a member of?

    Management ____ Union ____

2. What role do you have in this team?

    If Management   If Union
    Technical Specialist ____   Full Time Official ____
    Personnel Specialist ____   Convenor ____
                                 Shop Steward ____

3. How many people are employed at your plant at this time?

    _____ (approx)

4. In which of the following areas in your plant has
    micro-computer technology been adopted? Tick both if
    applicable.

        In the Control of Physical Elements
          of Production
        In the Provision of Information For   ____
          Administrative and Financial Purposes etc. ____

5. What has been the extent of micro-computer application
    at your plant to date?

        Very minor _____ Very major

6. What were the reasons for installing advanced equipment into your plant? Plese tick those reasons which apply.

    a) To replace wornout machines and equipment   ____
    b) To reduce the workload of employees   ____
    c) To expand production   ____
    d) to improve working conditions   ____
    e) To reduce labour costs per unit of output   ____
    f) To reduce capital costs per unit of output   ____
    g) To make work places safer   ____
    h) To improve the quality of the product   ____
    i) To meet competition and survive economically ____

7. Were there any redundancies due to the introduction of new equipment? If yes, please indicate an approximate %.

    No   ____
    Voluntary only   ____   ___%
    Voluntary and compulsory   ____   ___%

8. What % of your workforce has been retrained as a result of this new equipment?

    _____%

9. What %, if any, accepted early retirement?

    _____%

10. What % of employees affected by changes in technology were unionised?

    25% or less   ____
    26% - 50%   ____
    51% - 75%   ____
    76% - 100%   ____

11. To what extent have terms and conditions of employment improved at your plant as a result of this new equipment?

    Not at all _____ Very much

12. Which of the following have resulted from the
introduction of new equipment? Please tick all those
which apply.

a)	An increase in pay	Yes	____	No	____
b)	Changes in job evaluation	Yes	____	No	____
c)	Improved bonus payments	Yes	____	No	____
d)	Improved productivity bargaining	Yes	____	No	____
e)	Increased/reduced* working hours	Yes	____	No	____
f)	More/less* overtime	Yes	____	No	____
g)	More/less* shiftwork	Yes	____	No	____
h)	Earlier retirement	Yes	____	No	____
i)	Longer holidays	Yes	____	No	____
j)	Work-sharing	Yes	____	No	____
k)	Job enrichment	Yes	____	No	____
l)	Improved skills and retraining	Yes	____	No	____
m)	De-skilling	Yes	____	No	____
n)	Better health and safety	Yes	____	No	____
o)	Increased/decreased* job satisfaction	Yes	____	No	____

* PLEASE DELETE AS APPLICABLE.

13. At the time of implementation of new equipment was there
any official or unofficial industrial action by
employees?

Yes   ____
No   ____

If NO, was there ever any threat of a disruption of work?

Yes   ____
No   ____

14. Please indicate the type of relationship between
management and unions in introducing this new
equipment?

a) Formal negotiations   ____
b) Some discussion of issues ____
c) Some contacts   ____

214

15. Were the discussions/negotiations concerning the new technology

    a) Isolated from other issues   ____
    b) Included in other negotiations/discussions
           (e.g. annual pay negotiations)   ____

16. Indicate the degree of union involvement in the following areas during the introduction of new technology?

	Joint Decision -making	Bargaining	Consult -ation	No Involvement
Type and extent of technology	____	____	____	____
Redundancy	____	____	____	____
Pay & grading	____	____	____	____
Investment in new machinery	____	____	____	____
Cost/benefit analysis	____	____	____	____
Selection/ training	____	____	____	____
Job redesign	____	____	____	____
Health & safety	____	____	____	____

PLEASE ANSWER THE REMAINING QUESTIONS IN RELATION TO ANY CONTACT YOU HAVE HAD WITH THE OTHER TEAM CONCERNING THE INTRODUCTION OF NEW EQUIPMENT.

17. How clear or vague was the other side in stating issues concerning the implementation of the new equipment?

    Very vague _____ Very clear

18. How satisfied were you with the information you received from the other side?

        Dissatisfied _____ Satisfied

19. To what extent did management and unions explore various problems together in an uncommitted way before presenting solutions?

   Very little _____ Very much

20. How much pressure was exerted on your team by the other side?

   Very little _____ Very much

21. How much did representatives of both sides get together outside regular sessions to explore issues/problems off the record?

   Very little _____ Very much

22. Were formal management/union groups set up to investigate various issues?

   For all issues _____ For none at all

23. Was there a formal agreement concerning technological change which regulated management/union relationships?

   Yes _____   No _____

24. Was there an extension of collective bargaining between management and unions in this situation?

   Not at all _____ Very much

25. Was your team able to change the decisions of the other side?

   Not at all _____ Very much

26. Do you believe the unions were involved at an early enough stage in management decision-making?

   Not at all _____ Very much

27. To what extent were the decisions concerning new equipment taken at plant level?

    Not at all _____ Very much

28. How clearly had your team formulated its objectives in relation to the introduction of new equipment before any contact with the other side?

    Not clearly _____ Very clearly

29. Were any concessions made by your team?

    Yes ____   No ____

30. How adequately prepared was your team for the decisions which had to be made?

    Unprepared _____ Prepared

31. How supportive were employees to the union's goals?

    Unsupportive _____ Supportive

32. How much support did your team receive from colleagues at head office or others, who were not directly involved in the situation?

    Very little _____ Very much

33. To what extent do you believe the knowledge of your team concerning the new equipment was adequate?

    Inadequate _____ Adequate

34. Did you feel your ability to play a meaningful role in this situation was limited by a lack of technical knowledge?

    Not at all _____ Quite a lot

35. Have any courses concerning new technology been organised by your team?

    Yes _____   No _____

36. Were joint union/management courses or visits concerning the new equipment arranged by your company?

    Yes _____   No _____

37. In general, how friendly were the people on the other side with members of your team?

    Unfriendly _____ Friendly

38. How much did you trust the members of the other team?

    Very little _____ Very much

39. How valid in your opinion were the goals of the other side?

    Invalid _____ Valid

40. How much respect did you have for the people on the other side?

    Very little _____ Very much

41. How constructive was the other side in its proposals concerning the implementation of the new equipment?

    Not constructive _____ Very constructive

42. How satisfied is your team with the introduction of the new equipment and its consequences?

    Dissatisfied _____ Satisfied

In the final question I want you to analyse the type of relationship you had with the other side during the implementation of this new technology along the following three dimensions:

A) This is a process which is distinguished by the 'participation' between management and unions in dealing with issues/problems (such as new technology), in searching for alternative solutions and arriving at a mutually satisfactory agreement.

B) In this process management and unions find it easier to adopt adversay positions, and agreement is reached less by participation and the discussion of alternatives, than by compromise between the opposing demands of the two parties.

C) Here most of the decision-making has been carried out by management and the unions are kept informed.

Your relationship may have contained elements of each of these processes so I would like you to place a percentage beside each (The three totalling 100%). which you believe reflects the part it played in your relationship.   If you feel the relationship was totally A, totally B, or totally C, please place a 100% beside the relevant one.

43. Please analyse your management/union relationship in introducing the new equipment along the defined dimensions?

A	_____ %
B	_____ %
C	_____ %
Total	100%

INTERVIEW SCHEDULE FOR MANAGERS

1) What is the type and extent of micro-applications in your company?

2) What were the reasons for the introduction?

3) What were the manpower implications of these changes?

4) How did the unions react?

5) To what extent did management and unions participate in the introduction of this new technology?

6) What issues caused most problems?

7) Were there any industrial disputes - what were the reasons and outcomes?

8) What factors helped management/union relationships at this time?

9) Was a new technology agreement asked for and signed?

10) To what extent were decisions regarding the new technology taken at plant level?

INTERVIEW SCHEDULE FOR TRADE UNIONISTS

1) What were your union's main concerns during the change?

2) What were the union's demands?

3) What concessions were made by the union – which of your demands were not satisfied?

4) What impact did union involvement have on management – i.e. what concessions were made by management?

5) What were the most conflictual issues and was there a dispute at this time?

6) To what extent were there <u>problems</u> that management and unions solved jointly? What were these problems?

7) To what extent were <u>issues</u> more distributive – i.e. a gain for one side meaning a loss for the other? Can you give examples?

8) How easy or difficult was it to work with these two different types of relationship?

9) What factors do you believe helped participation between management and unions?

10) To what extent was there cooperation between the different unions at the plant. Were there any problems?

11) Did your union or any of the others in the company make any initiative for a new technology agreement to be signed? Are there any other plant agreements relevant to this issue?

12) What lessons, if any, did you learn from the experience?

REFERENCES

Abbott, L.F. (1976), Social Aspects of Innovation and Industrial Technology, HMSO, London

Ahlin, J.E. and Svenson, L.J.P. (Royal Institute of Technology, Stockholm) (1980), New Technology in Mechanical Engineering Industry: How Can Workers Gain Control, Economic and Industrial Democracy, Vol. 1, November, pp. 12-26

Almond, G.A. and Verba, S. (1965), The Civic Culture, Little Brown, Boston

Anthony, P. (1977), The Ideology of Work, Tavistock Publications, London

Argyris, C. (1957), Personality and Organization, Harper and Row, New York

Argyris, C. (1964), Integrating the Individual and the Organisation, Wiley, New York

Ashenfelter, O. and Johnson, G.E. (1969), Bargaining Theory, Trade Unions and Industrial Strike Activity, Vol. 59, p. 36

Asplund, C., (1981), Redesigning Jobs: Western European Experiences, European Trade Union Institute, Brussels

Baldamus, W. (1961), Efficiency and Effort, Tavistock, London

Balke, W.M., Hammond, K.R. and Meyer, G.D. (1972), Application of Judgement Theory and Interactive Computer Graphics Technology to Labour-Management Negotiation: An Example, Report No. 145, Program of Research on Human Judgement and Social Interaction, Boulder, Institute of Behavioural Science, University of Colorado

Bamber, G. (1980), 'Microchips and Industrial Relations', Industrial Relations Journal, Nov/Dec. pp. 7-19

Bartos, O.J. (1970), Determinants and Consequences of Toughness, In Swingle, P. (ed.), The Structure of Conflict, Academic Press, New York, pp. 45-68

Becker, H. (1973), 'Whose side are we on? discussed in The Sociologist as Partisan: Sociology and the Welfare State', in Gouldner, A.W., For Sociology, Penguin, London

Bendix, R. (ed.) (1974), Work and Authority in Industry, Harper, New York

Benson, I. and Lloyd, J. (1983), New Technology and Industrial Change, Kogan Page, London

Bernal, J.D. (1965) Science in History, 3rd Edn, (1965), C.A. Watts & Co., London

Bessant, J.R. et al, (1981), The Impact of Microelectronics: A Review of the Literature, Pinter, London

Beynon, H. (1973), Working for Ford, Allen Lane, London

Blackler, F. and Brown, C. (1978), Job Redesign and Management Control, Saxon House, Farnborough

Blake, R.R. and Mouton, J.S. (1961), Group Dynamics: Key to Decision-Making, Gulf Publishing Co., Houston

Blauner, R. (1964), Alienation and Freedom, The University of Chicage Press, Chicago

Blumberg, P. (1968), Industrial Democracy - The Sociology of Participation, Constable, London

Blyton, P. and Hill, S. (1981) 'The Economics of Worksharing', National Westminster Bank Quarterly Review, November, pp. 37-45

Bowey, A.M. (1976), The Sociology of Organisations, Hodder and Straughton, London

Braverman, H. (1974) Labour and Monopoly Capital: the degradation of work in the twentieth century, Monthly Review Press, New York

Brannen, P., Batstone, E., Fatchett, D. and White, P. (1976), The Worker Directors: A Sociology of Participation, Hutchinson, London

Brewing Sector Working Part (1980), Microelectronics and the Brewing Industry, NEDO Report

Bright, J.R. (1958), Automation and Management, Harvard Business School, Boston

Broekmeyer, M.J. (1968), De Avberdsvaad in Zuidslavie, Meppel: Boom

Burawoy, M. (1979), Manufacturing Consent: Changes in the Labour Process under Monopoly Capitalism, University of Chicago Press, Chicago

Burns, T. and Stalker, G.M. (1960), The Management of Innovation, Tavistock Publications, London

Butteriss, M. and Murdoch, R. (1975), Work Restructuring Projects and Experiments in the UK, Department of Employment Research Unit, London

Cain, J.T. (1977), 'Microprocessors and education', Computer, 10 (1), pp. 9-10

Carnall, C.A. (1979), 'The Social Context of Work Organisation Change', Personnel Review, Vol. 8, No. 4, Autumn

Carnall, C.A. (1980), 'The Evaluation of Work Organisation Change', Human Relations, Vol. 33, No. 12

Carnall, C.A. (1982), 'Semi-Autonomous Work Groups and the Social Structure of the Organisation, Journal of Management Studies, Vol. 19, No. 3, pp. 277-294

Chamberlain, N.W. and Kuhn, J.W. (1965), Collective Bargaining, McGraw-Hill, New York

Cherns, A.B. (1976), 'The Principles of Organizational Design', Human Relations, 29, 8, pp. 783-792

Child, J. (1972), 'Organizational Structure, Environment and Performance: the role of strategic choice', Sociology, 6, pp. 1-22

Child, J. (ed.) (1975), Man and Organization: The Search for Explanation and Relevance, Allen and Unwin, London

Clarke, R.O., Fatchett, D.J. and Roberts, B.C., (1972), Workers' Participation in Management in Britain, Heinemann, London

Clegg, H.A. (1960), A New Approach to Industrial Democracy, Blackwell, Oxford

Coch, L. and French, J.R.P. (1948), 'Overcoming Resistance to Change', Human Relations, II: 512-32

Cockerill, A. (1979), 'Technical Change and Economic Performance in the Brewing Industry', in Pearson, A.W. (ed.), Research and Development Management, 10th Anniversary Conference, Manchester Business School

Cole, G.D.H. (1972), Self-government in Industry, Hutchinson, London

Confederation of British Industry (1980), Jobs - facing the future, DBI Staff discussion document

Cooley, M. (1979), New Technologies: whose right to choose. in Pro. Information Systems, Organisational Choice and Social Values, EEC Conference, Pisa, Italy

Cooper, R. (1972), 'Man, Task and Technology', Human Relations, 25, pp. 131-157

Cornwall, J. (1977), Modern Capitalism, Its Growth and Transformation, Martin Robertson, Oxford

Counter Information Services Report (1980), The New Technology, Pluto Press, London

Cressey, P., Eldridge, J., MacInnes, J. and Norris, G. (1981), Industrial Democracy and Participation: A Scottish Survey, Research Paper No. 28, Department of Employment, November

Cressey P. and McInnes, J. (1980), 'Voting for Ford: Industrial Democracy and Control of Labour', Capital and Class, II, pp. 5-33

Cross, J.G. (1969), The Economics of Bargaining, Basic Books, New York

Crozier, M. (1964), The Bureaucratic Phenomenon, Tavistock, London

Curnow, R. (1979), 'Where is Microelectronics Taking Us?', Personnel Management, September, pp. 40–42

Cutler, T. (1978), 'The Romance of 'Labour'', Economy and Society, Vol. 7, No. 1, pp. 74–9

Dahrendorf, R. (1959), Class and Class Conflict in Industrial Society, English Edition, Routledge and Kegan Paul, London

Daniel, W.W. and Stilgoe, E. (1978), The Impact of Employment Protection Laws, Policy Studies Institute, London

Davies, L.E. (1966), 'The Coming Crisis for Production Management: Technology and Organisation', International Journal for Production Research, 9, 65–82

Davis, L.E. and Cherns, A.B. (1975), The Quality of Work Life, Vols I and II, Free Press, New York

Davis, L.E. (1971) 'Job Satisfaction Research: The Post Industrial View', Industrial Relations, Vol. 10, No. 2, May, pp. 176–193

Davis, L.E. and Taylor, J.C. (eds.), The Design of Jobs, (1972), Harmondsworth

Department of Employment (1979), The Manpower Implications of Micro-Electronic Technology, HMSO, London

Department of Scientific and Industrial Research (1956), Automation, HMSO

Dey, I. (1980), 'Making Redundancy Redundant — Or How to Save Jobs Without Really Trying', International Journal of Manpower, 1, 2, pp.15–20

Dickson, D. (1974), Alternative Technology: and the politics of technical change, Fontana

Dowling, M., Goodman, J.F.B., Gotting, D. and Hyman, J. (1981), Employee Participation: Practice and Attitudes in North-West Manufacturing Industry, Research Paper No. 27, Department of Employment, November

Downing, H. (1980), Word Processors and the Oppression of Women, in Forester, T, the Microelectronics Revolution, Blackwell, Oxford

Drexler, J.A. and Lawler, E.E. (1977), A Union-Management Co-operative Project to Improve the Quality of Work Life, Vol. 13, No. 3, pp. 373-399

Druckman, D. (1968), 'Pre-negotiation experience and dyadic conflict resolution in a bargaining situation', Journal of Experimental Social Psychology, 4, pp. 367-83

Dubin, R. (1965), 'Supervision and productivity: Empirical findings and theoretical considerations', in Dubin, R., Homans, G.C., Mann, F.C., and Miller, D.C. (eds.), Leadership and Productivity, Chandler, San Francisco

Dyer, L., Lipsky, D.B. and Kochan, T.A. (1977), 'Union Attitudes Toward Management Cooperation', Industrial Relations, Vol. 16, No. 2, pp. 163-172

Edwards, C. (1978), 'Measuring Union Power: A Comparison of two methods applied to the study of local union power in the coal industry', British Journal of Industrial Relations, 16, 1-15

Elbaum, B. and Wilkinson, F. (1979), 'Industrial Relations and Uneven Development: a comparative studyt of American and British steel industries', Cambridge Journal of Economics, Vol. 3, No. 3, September, pp. 275-304

Emery, F.E., (1964), Report on the Hunsfoss Report, Tavistock Documents Series, London

Emery, F.E. (1978), The Emergence of a New Paradigm of Work, Centre for Continuing Education, ANU, Canberra

Evans, C. (1979), The Mighty Micro, Coronet, London

Fatchett, D. (1978), 'Time to Take Stock', Personnel Review, Vol. 7, No. 2, Spring, pp. 50-54

Follett, M.P. (1947), see Metcalf, H.C. and Urwick, L.

Forester, T. (ed.) (1980), The Microelectronics Revolution, Blackwell, Oxford

Forslin, J., Sarapata, A. and Whitehill, A.M. (eds.) (1979), Automation and Industrial Workers: A 15 Nation Study, Vol. 1, Part 1, Pergamon Press, London

Fox, A. (1971), A Sociology of Work In Industry, Collier-Macmillan, London

Francis, A. and Willman, P (1980), 'Microprocessors: Impact and Response', Personnel Review, Vol. 9, No.2, Spring, pp. 9-16

Francis, A., Snell, M., Wilkinson, P. and Winch, G.W. (1982), 'The Impact of Information Technology at Work: The Case of CAD/CAM and MIS in Engineering Plants', in Bannon, L., Barry, U. and Holz, O. Information Technology: Impact on the Way of Life, Conference Proceedings, Tycooly International

Freeman, C. (1980), 'Unemployment and Government', in Forester, T., The Microelectronic Revolution, Blackwell, Oxford

French, F.R.P. (1964), 'Laboratory and Field Studies of Power', in Kahn, R.L. and Boulding, E., Power and Conflict in Organisations, Tavistock, London

Frey, R.L. and Adams, J.S. (1972), 'The Negotiator's Dilemma, Simultaneous In-Group and Out-Group Conflict', Journal of Experimental Social Psychology, Vol. 8, pp. 331-346

Friedman, A. (1977), Industry and Labour, Macmillan, London

Friedman, A. (1978), Worker Resistance and Marxian Analysis of the Capitalist Labour Process, BAS Conference Paper, Mimeo

Gallie, D. (1978), In Search of the New Working Class, Cambridge University Press

Gergen, K.J. (1969), The Psychology of Behaviour Exchange, Addison-Wesley, London

Gevers, P. (1977), Works Councils in Belgium, Catholic University of Louvain, Sociology Department Working Paper, (Mimeo)

Giddens, A. (1979), Central Problems in Social Theory, London

Goldthorpe, J.H., Lockwood, D., Bechhofer, F. and Platt, J. (1968), The Affluent Worker: Industrial Attitudes and Behaviour, Cambridge University Press

Gospel, H. (1978), 'The Disclosure of Information to Trade Unions: approaches and problems', Industrial Relations Journal, Vol. 9, No. 3, pp. 18-26

Gottschalk, A.W (1973), A Behavioural Analysis of Bargaining, in Warner, M. (ed.), The Sociology of the Workplace, Halstead, New York

Green, K., Coombs, R. and Holroyd, K. (1980), The Effects of Microelectronic Technologies on Employment Prospects: A Case Study of Tameside, Gower, London

Greiner, L.E. (1967), Patterns of Organisational Change, Harvard Business Review, May/June, pp. 119-130

Guest, D.E. and Fatchett, D. (1974), Worker Participation: Individual Control and Performance, IPM, London

Gustavsen, B. (1973), Environmental Requirements and the Democratization of Industrial Relations, In Pucis, E. (ed.), Participation and Self-Management, Vol. 4, Zagreb Institute for Social Research

Hackman, J. and Lawler, E. (1971), 'Employee Reactions to Job Characteristics', Journal of Applied Psychology, Monograph 55, 259-286

Hazelhurst, R.J., Bradbury, R.J. and Corlett, E.N. (1969), 'A Comparison of the Skills of Machinists on Numerically-Controlled and Conventional Machines', Occupational Psychology, 43, 169-182

Healy, J.J. (ed.) (1965), Creative Collective Bargaining, Prentice-Hall Inc., Englewood Cliffs, New Jersey

Herrick, Q. and Maccoby, M. (1975) Humanizing Work: A priority goal of the 1970's, in Davis, L.E. and Cherns, A.B. (eds.), The Quality of Working Life, Vol.1, New York

Herzberg, F. et al, (1959), The Motivation to Work, Wiley, New York

Hespe, G. and Little, A., (1959), The Motivation to Work, Wiley, New York

Hicks, J.R. (1963), The Theory of Wages, St Martins Press, New York

Hickson, D. and Mallory, G. (1981), 'Scope for Choice in Strategic Decision-Making and the Trade Union Role', in Thomson, A. and Warner, W., The Behavioural Sciences and Industrial Relations, Gower, London

Hickson, D.J., Pugh, D.S., Hinings, C.R. and Turner, C. (1969), 'The Context of Organisation Structures', Administrative Science Quarterly, 14, 1, pp. 91-114

Hickson, D.J., Pugh, D.S. and Pheysey, D.C. (1969), 'Operations Technology and Organisation Structure: An Empirical Appraisal, Administrative Science Quarterly, Vol. 14, pp. 378-97

Hobsbawn, E.J. (1968), 'Custom, Wages and Work-Load in Nineteenth-Century Industry', in Briggs, A. and Smith J. (eds.), Essays in Labour History, Macmillan, London, pp. 113-139

Holter, H. (1965), 'Attitudes towards employee participation in company decision-making processes', Human Relations, Vol. 18, No. 4, pp. 297-321

Hull, D. (1978), The Shop Steward's Guide to Work Organisation, Spokesman, pp. 23-4

Hyman, R. and Brough, I. (1975), Social Values and Industrial Relations, Blackwell, Oxford

ILO (1972), Labour and Social Implications of Automation and Other Technological Developments, Geneva, ILO

Jacobs, E. (1980), 'Open Letter to Management', Industrial Society, January/February, pp. 9-10

Jacobs, E., Orwell, S., Paterson, P. and Weltz, F. (1978), The Approach to Industrial Change in Britain and Germany, Anglo-German Foundation

Janowitz, M. (1959), 'Changing Patterns of Organisational Authority: the Military Establishment', Administrative Science Quarterly, 3, 473-493

Jefferys, J.B. (1946), The Story of the Engineers, Lawrence and Wishart

Jenkins, C. and Sherman, B. (1979), The Collapse of Work, Eyre Methuen, London

Johnson, D.W. (1971), 'Effects of Warmth of Interaction, Accuracy of Understanding, and Proposed Compromises of Listener's Behaviour', Journal of Counselling Psychology, pp. 307-16

Jones, B. (1982), Destruction or redistribution of engineering skills? The case of numerical control, in Wood, S., The Degradation of Work Skill, Deskilling and the Labour Process, Hutchinson, London

Kahn, R.L. (1974), 'Organization development: some problems and proposals', Journal of Applied Behavioural Science, 10 pp. 485-502

Kassalow, E.M. (1977), 'White Collar Unions and the Work Humanisation Movement', Monthly Labour Review, May, Vol. 100, No. 5, pp. 485-502

Katz, D. and Kahn, R.L. (1966), The Social Psychology of Organizations, Wiley, New York

Keeley, M. (1978), A Social Justice Approach to Organizational Evaluation, ASQ, 23, pp. 272-292

Kelly, J. (1980), 'The costs of job redesign: a preliminary analysis', Industrial Relations Journal, Vol. II, No. 3, July/August, pp. 22-34

Kendall, M.G. (1955), Rank Correlation Methods, Griffin and Co, (2nd ed.), London

Kerr, C. (1964), Labour and Management in Industrial Society, Doubleday, New York

King, P. (1975), 'Strategic Control of Capital Investment', Journal of General Management, Vol. 2, No. 4, pp. 16-24

Klimoski, R.J. (1972), 'The Effects of intra-group forces on intergroup conflict resolution', Organisational Behaviour and Human Performance, 8, 363-83

Kochan, T.A. and Dyer, L. (1976), 'A Model of Organisational Change in the Context of Union-Management Relations', The Journal of Applied Behavioural Science, 12, pp. 57-80

Kochan, T.A., Lipsky, D.B. and Dyer, L.D. (1975), Collective bargaining and the quality of work: The views of local union achivists, Proceedings of the 27th Annual Winter Meeting of the Industrial Relations Research Association, Madison, Wisconsin, IRA, pp. 150-162

Kolaja, J. (1965), Workers' Councils, Tavistock, London

Kornhauser, H.R., Durkin, R. and Ross, A.M. (1954), Industrial Conflict, McGraw-Hill, New York

Labour Research Department (1982), 'Survey of New Technology', Bargaining Report, 22

Lamborghini, B. and Antonelli, C. (1981), The Impact of Electronics on Industrial Structures and Firm's Strategies, in Microelectronics, Productivity and Employment, OECD, Paris, pp. 77-121

Lawrence, P.R. (1969), 'How to Deal with Resistance to Change', Harvard Business Review, January/February, pp. 4-15

Lazonick, W. (1979), 'Industrial Relations and Technical Change: the case of the self-acting mule', Cambridge Journal of Economics, Vol. 3, No. 3, September, 231-262

Leavitt, H.J. (1965), 'Applied organizational change in industry: structural technological and humanistic approaches', in James, G. March (ed.), Handbook of Organizations, Rand-McNally, Chicago, pp. 1144-70

Legge, K. (1978), 'Power, Innovation and Problem-Solving in Personnel Management', McGraw-Hill, London

Levie, H. and Moore, R. (1981), The Impact of New Technology on Trade Union Organization, Trade Union Research Unit, Ruskin College, Oxford

Levin, M. (1980), 'A Trade Union and The Case of Automation', Human Futures, Vol III, No. 3, Autumn, pp. 209-215

Lewicki, R.J. and Alderfer, C.P. (1973), 'The tentions between research and intervention in intergroup conflict', Journal of Applied Behavioural Sciences, 9, pp. 424-449

Lewin, K., Lippitt, R. and White, R.K. (1939), 'Patterns of agressive behaviour in experimentally created social climates', Journal of Social Psychology, 10, pp. 271-299

Littler, C.R. and Salaman, G. (1982), Braverman and Beyond. 'Recent Theories of the Labour Process', Sociology, Vol. 16, No. 2, May, pp. 251-269

Lorsch, J.W. (1976), 'Managing Change', in Lawrence, P.M., Barnes, L.B., Lorsch, J.W. and Homewood III, I. Organizational Behaviour and Administration: cases and readings, pp. 668-680

Loveridge, R. (1980), 'What is Participation? A Review of the Literature and Some Methodological Problems', British Journal of Industrial Relations, November, pp. 297-317

Lucas Aerospace Combine Shop Steward Committee, (1976), Corporate Plan: A contingency strategy as a positive alternative to recession and redundancies, Unpublished

Lupton, T. (1975) ''Best Fit' in the Design of Organizations Personnel Review, Vol. 4, No. 1, pp. 15-31

Maddock, I. (1978), 'The Future of Work' in Technology Choice and the Future of Work, British Association for the Advancement of Science, pp. 8-27

Mainwaring, T. (1981), 'The Trade Union Response to New Technology', Industrial Relations Journal, July/August, pp. 7-25

Mann, F.C. and Hoffman, L.R. (1960), Automation and the Worker, Henry Holt & Co, New York

March, J.G. and Simon, H.A. (1958), Organisations, Wiley, London

Marchington, M. and Armstrong, R. (1981), 'Employee Participation: Problems for the Shop Steward', Industrial Relations Journal, January/February, Vol. 12, No. 1, pp. 46-61

Marchington, M. and Loveridge, R. (1979), 'Non-Participation: The Management View?', Journal of Management Studies, May, Vol. 16 (2), pp. 171-184

Marsh, P. (1982), The Robot Age, Abacus, London

Marrow, A.J., Bowers, D.G. and Seashore, S.E. (1967), Management by Participation, Harper and Row, New York

Martin, R. (1977), The Sociology of Power, Routledge and Kegan Paul, London

Marx, K. (1967), Capital, Vol. 1, International, New York

Maslow, A.H. (1943), 'A Theory of Motivation', Pyschological Review, 50, pp. 370-396

Mayo, E. (1933), The Human Problems of an Industrial Civilization, Macmillan, New York

McCarthy, W.E.J. and Ellis, W.D. (1973), Management by Agreement: An Alternative to the Industrial Relations Act, Hutchinson, London

McKechnie, S. (1981), The Trade Union Demands, The Changing Pattern, Paper presented at a one day conference 'Health Hazards of VDUs', July, HUSAT, Loughborough University of Technology, pp. 13-39

Melman, S. (1958), Decision-Making and Productivity, Blackwell, Oxford

Metcalf, H.C. and Urwick, L. (eds.) (1941), 'Dynamic Administration', The Collected Papers of Mary Parker Follet, Pitman

Miles, R.E. (1965), 'Human Relations or Human Resources', Harvard Business Review, July, pp. 150-165

Morley, I.E. and Stephenson, G.M. (1970), 'Formality in experimental negotiations, a validation study', British Journal of Psychology, 61, 383-4

Morse, N.C. and Reimer, E. (1956), 'The Experimental Change of a Major Organizational Variable', Journal of Abnormal and Social Pyschology, 52, 120-9

Mulder, M. (1958), 'Group Structure: Motivation and Group Performance', The Hague: Commissie voor Opvoering van Productiviteit and Moulton

Mulder M. (1971), 'Power Equalization through Participation', Administrative Science Quarterly, Vol. 16, March, pp. 31-38

Mulder, M. and Wilke, H. (1970), 'Participation and Power equalization', Organizational Behaviour and Human Performance, 5, 430-448

Mumford, E. (1977), The Design of Work: New Approaches and New Needs, in Rijnsdorp, J. (ed.) Case Studies in Automation Related to the Humanisation of Work, Proceeding of the IFAC Workshop, Netherlands, Pergamon Press, pp. 9-17

Mumford, E. and Banks, O. (1967), The Computer and the Clerk, Routledge and Kegan Paul, London

Mumford, E. and Pettigrew, A. (1975), Implementing Strategic Decisions, Longman

Musson, A.E. (1980), 'Technological Change and Manpower: An Historical Perspective', International Journal of Manpower, 1, 3, pp. 2-5

Nadler, D.A., Hanlan, M. and Lawler, E.E. (1980), 'Factors influencing the success of laobur-management quality of work life projects', Journal of Occupational Behaviour, Vol. 1, 53-67

Nash, J.F. Jnr. (1950), 'The Bargaining Problem', Econometrica, April, pp. 155-62

Noble, D.F. (1977), America by Design, Alfred A Knope, New York

Noble, D.F. (1979), 'Social Choice in Machine Design, in the Case of Automatically Controlled Machine Tools', in Zimbalist, A. (ed.) Case Studies on the Labor Process, Monthly Review Press, New York, pp. 18-50

Nygaard, K. and Bergo, O.T. (1975), 'The Trade Unions - New Users of Research', Personnel Review, Vol. 4, No. 2, Spring, pp. 5-10

Offe, C. (1976), Industry and Inequality, Edward Arnold, London

Oldham, G.R. and Hackman, J.R. (1978), 'Development of the Job Diagnostic Survey', Journal of Applied Psychology, 60, pp. 161

Oldham, W.G. (1980), The Fabrication of Microelectronic Circuits, in Forester, T. The Microelectronics Revolution, Blackwell, Oxford, pp. 42-62

Pahl, R. and Winkler, J. (1974), 'The Economic Elite: Theory and Practice' in Stanworth, P. and Giddens, A. (eds.) Elites and Power in British Society, CUP, Cambridge

Parkin, F. (1972), Class Inequality and Political Order, Paladin, London

Pateman, C. (1970), Participation and Democratic Theory, Cambridge University Press

Paul, W. and Robertson, R. (1969), Learning from Job Enrichment, ICI Ltd, London

Pavitt, K. and Soete, L. (1980), 'Innovation Activities and Export Shares: some comparisons between industries and countries', in Pavitt, K. (ed.) Technical Innovation and British Economic Performance, Macmillan Press Ltd., London

Pen, J. (1952), 'A General Theory of Bargaining', *American Economic Review*, March, pp. 24-42

Perrow, C. (1970), *Organisational Analysis: A Sociological View*, Tavistock Publications, London

Peterson, R.B. and Tracy, L.W. (1976), 'A Behavioural Model of Problem Solving in Labour Negotiations', *British Journal of Industrial Relations*, Vol. XIV, No. 2, pp. 159-173

Peterson, R.B. and Tracy, L.W. (1977/8), 'Differences in reactions of union and management negotiations to the problem-solving process', *Industrial Relations Journal*, Vol. 8, No. 4, Winter, pp. 43-53

Pettigrew, A.M. (1972), 'Information Control as a Power Resource', *Sociology*, Vol. 6

Pettigrew, A.M. (1973), *The Politics of Organizational Decision-Making*, Tavistock Publications, London

Poole, M. (1975), *Workers' Participation in Industry*, Routledge and Kegan Paul, London

Price Commission (1977), 'Beer Prices and Margins', Report No. 31, HMSO, London

Pruitt, D.G. and Lewis, S.A. (1975), *Journal of Personality and Social Psychology*, Vol. 31, No. 4, pp. 621-633

Qvale, T.U. (1979), *Industrial Democracy in Europe*, Work Research Institute, Norway

Rapaport, A. (1970), 'Conflict resolution in the right of game theory and beyond, in Swingle, P. (ed.), *The Structure of Conflict*, Academic Press, New York, pp. 1-43

Reynaud, J.D. (1972), *Industrial Relations and the Negotiation of Change*, Bulletin, International Institute of Labour Studies, No. 9, ILO, pp. 3-16

Reynolds, L.G. (1960), *Labour Economics and Labour Relations*, Prentice-Hall, Englewood Cliffs, New Jersey

Roethlisberger, F.J. and Dickson, W.J. (1939), *Management and the Worker*, Harvard University Press, Cambridge, Mass.

Rothwell, R. (1979), *Technical Change and Competitiveness in Agricultural Engineering. The Performance of the UK*, SPRU Occasional Paper, No. 9

Rowthorn, S. and Ward, T. (1979), 'How to run a company and run down an economy: the effect of closing down steel making in Corby', Cambridge Journal of Economics, Vol. 3, No. 4, December, pp. 327-40

Sayles, L.R. (1958), The Behaviour of Industrial Work Groups, John Wiley and Sons, New York

Schon, D. (1971), Beyond the Stable State, Basic Books, New York

Sciberras, E. (1979), 'Television and Related Products Sector', Final Reprint for the OECD, SPRU

Sciberras, E., Swords-Isherwood, N. and Senker, P. (1978), Competition, Technical Change and Manpower in Electronic Capital Equipment, A Study of the UK Minicomputer Industry, Occasional Paper Series, No. 8, September

Scott, W.H., Halsey, A.H., Banks, J.A. and Lupton, T. (1956), Technical Change and Industrial Relations, Liverpool University Press, Liverpool

Senker, P. (1980), 'Manpower and Skill Implications of Technical Change in the Engineering Industry', International Journal of Management, 1, 3, pp. 13-20

Shaiken, H. (1979), 'Numerical Contol of Work: Workers and Automation in the Computer Age', Radical America, Vol. 13, No. 6, November-December

Shaiken, H. (1980), Computer Technology and the Relations of Power in the Workplace, International Institute for Comparative Social Research, Berlin

Siegel, S. and Fouraker, L.E. (1960), Bargaining and Group Decision-Making, McGraw-Hill, New York

Simon, H.A. (1965), 'Administrative Decision-Making', Public Administration Review, March, 31-37

Smith, A. (1937), Wealth of Nations, Modern Library Edition, New York

Sorge, A. (1976), 'The Evolution of Industrial Democracy in the Countries of the European Community', British Journal of Industrial Relations, Vol. XIV, No. 3, November, pp. 274-294

Stark, D. (1978), 'Class Structure', Class Struggle and the Labour Process, Harvard University, Mimeo

Stewart, R. (1971), How Computers affect Management, Macmillan, London

Swingle, P. and Gillis, J.S. (1968), 'Effects of Emotional Relationship Between Protagonists in the Prisoner's Dilemma, Journal of Personality and Social Psychology, Vol. 8, pp. 160-5

Swords-Isherwood, W. and Senker, P. (1980), 'Management Resistance to the New Technology', in Forester, T. (ed.), The Microelectronics Revolution, Blackwell, Oxford

Tabb, J.Y. and Goldfarb, A. (1970), Workers' Participation in Management, Pergamon, Oxford

Tannenbaum, A., Kavcic, B., Rosner, M., Vianello, M. and Wieser, G. (1974), Hierarchy in Organizations, Pergamon Press, Oxford

Taylor, F.W. (1911), The Principles of Scientific Management, Harper and Bros.

Taylor, J.C. (1975), 'The Human Side of Work', Personnel Review, Summer, Vol. 4, No. 3, pp. 17-22

Taylor, R. (1980), The Fifth Estate, British Unions in the Modern World, Pan, London

Thomas, J.M. and Bennis, Warren, G. (eds.) (1972), Management of Change and Conflict, Penguin, London

Thornton, P. and Routledge, C. (1980), 'Managing the Manpower Aspect of Applying Micro-Electronic Technology', International Journal of Manpower, Vol. 1, No. 1, pp. 7-10

Tipton, B. (1982), 'The Quality of Training and the Design of Work', Industrial Relations Journal, Vol. 13, No. 1, Spring, pp. 27-41

Trade Union Council (1955), Congress Report

Trade Union Council (1956), 'Trade Unions and Automation', Trade Union Congress Report, pp. 512-525

Trade Union Council (1965), Congress Report

Trades Unions Council (1979), Employment and Technology, Report by the TUC General Council

Trist, E. (1981), The Evolution of Socio-Technical Systems, Occasional Paper No. 2, June, Ontario University of Labour

Trist, E.L. (1953), 'Area Organisation in the National Coal Board', Tavistock Document Series, London

Trist, E. et al, (1963), Organisational Choice, Tavistock, London

Trist, E. and Bamforth, K. (1959), 'Some Social and Psychological Consequences of the Longwall Method of Coal-getting, Human Relations, IV, February, pp. 3-39

Tucker, J. (1957), Instructions for Travellers, London

Turkington, D. and Smith, D. (1981), 'Testing a Behavioural Theory of Bargaining: An International Comparative Study', British Journal of Industrial Relations, Vol. XIX, No. 3, pp. 361-369

Ure, A (1935), The Philosophy of Manufacturers, Knight, London

Ursell, G. et al, (1978), 'Managers' attitudes towards Industrial Democracy', Industrial Relations Journal, Vol. 9, No. 3, pp. 4-17

Ursell, G. et al, (1979/80), 'Shop Stewards attitudes towards industrial democracy', Industrial Relations Journal, Vol. 10, No. 4, pp. 22-30

Van der Velden, H.A. (1965) 'Feitelijk funktianeren van viev under nemingsvade, Utrecht: Institute of Social Psychology, University at Utrecht

Vroom, V. (1960), Some Personality Determinants of the Effects of Participation, Prentice-Hall, New Jersey

Walker, K.F. (1970), Workers' Participation in Management: Concepts and Reality, in Barrett, B. et al, (eds.), Industrial Relations and the Wider Society, Macmillan, London

Wall, T.D. and Lischeron, J.A. (1977), Worker Participation, MacGraw-Hill, London

Walton, R.E. (1975), 'The diffusion of new work structures: explaining why success didn't fade', Organizational Dynamics, Winter, pp. 3-22

Walton, R. and McKersie, R. (1965), A Behavioural Theory of Labour Negotiations, MacGraw-Hill, New York

Warner, M. (1982), 'Worker Participation and Employee Influence: A Study of Managers and Shop Stewards', Industrial Relations Journal, Vol. 13, No. 4, Winter

Warner, M., Heller, F., Wilders, M. and Abell, P. (1979), What do the British Want From Participation and Industrial Democracy, Anglo-German Foundation, London

Warr, P. (1973), Psychology and Collective Bargaining, Hutchinson, London

Webb, S. and Webb, B. (1932), Methods of Social Study, Longmans Green, London

Wedderburn, D. and Crompton, R. (1972), Workers' Attitudes and Technology, University Press, Cambridge

Whisler, T.L. (1970), Information Technology and Organizational Change, Wadsworth Belmont, California

Wilkinson, B. (1981), Technical Change and Work Organisation, Ph.D thesis, University of Aston

Williams, R. and Moseley, R. (1982), Technology Agreements: Consensus, Control and Technical Change in the Workplace, Paper presented to EEC/FAST Conference

Williams, R. and Pearce, B. (1982), Design, New Technology and Trade Unions: A Case Study, Paper presented at Design Policy Conference, Royal College of Art, July, London

Wilson, D.C., Butler, R.J., Cray, D., Hickson, D.J. and Mallory, G.R. (1982), 'Union Participation in Strategic Decision-Making', British Journal of Industrial Relations, 20, 322-341

Winkler, J.T. (1974), 'The Ghost at the Bargaining Table: Directors and Industrial Relations', British Journal of Industrial Relations, 12, 191-212

Wood, S. (1979), 'A Reappraisal of the Contingency Approach to Organizations', Journal of Management Studies, October

Wood, S. (1982), The Degradation of Work: The Deskilling Debate, Hutchinsons, London

Wood, S. and Kelly, J. (1982), 'Taylorism, responsible autonomy and management strategy', in Wood, S. (ed.), The Degradation of Work, Skill, Deskilling and the Labour Process, Hutchinson, London

Woodward, J. (1965), Industrial Organisation Theory and Practice, University Press, Oxford

Wright, E.O. (1975), 'Alternative Perspectives in Marxist Theory of Accumulation of Crisis', Insurgent Sociologist, vol. 6, 1, pp. 5-39

Zeuthen, F. (1930), Problems of Monopoly and Economic Welfare, Routledge, London

AUTHOR INDEX

Clark, R.O., 82
Clegg, C., 93
Clegg, H.A., 85, 92, 93, 94, 195
Coch, L., 66
Cockerill, A., 119
Cole, G.D.H., 76
Confederation of British Industry (CBI), 10
Cooley, M., 14, 36, 190
Coombs, R., 10
Cooper, R., 17
Corlett, E.N., 17
Cornwall, J., 52
Council of Nordic Trades Union (NFS), 190
Counter Information Services, 12
Cray, D., 198
Cressey, P., 43, 83, 93, 94, 194
Crompton, R., 17
Cross, J.G., 95, 96
Crozier, M., 86
Curnow, R., 10, 15
Cutler, T., 43

Dahrendorf, R., 85, 86, 92, 195
Daniel, W.W., 24, 82
Davis, L.E., 17-19, 20, 193
Department of Employment, 10, 11, 13, 24, 26, 69
Department of Scientific and Industrial Research, 9
Dey, I., 24, 27
Dickson, K., 28-30
Dickson, D., 49
Dickson, W.J., 46
Dowling, M., 91, 94
Downing, H., 13
Drexler, J.A., 101
Druckman, D., 113
Dubin, R., 71
Dyer, L., 4, 34, 71, 101

Edwards, C., 29, 42
Elbaum, B., 41

Eldridge, J., 83, 93, 94, 194
Electrical, Electronic, Technical and Plumbing Union (EETPU), 54, 92
Ellis, W.D., 95
Emery, F.E., 16, 20
Fatchett, D., 80, 82, 85, 86, 88, 89, 93, 204
Follet, M.P., 96, 99, 115
Forester, T., 9
Forslin, J., 29
Fouraker, L.E., 95, 112
Fox, A., 44, 71
Francis, A., 14, 47
Freeman, C., 13
French, J.R.P., 66
Frey, R.L., 100, 111
Friedman, A., 42-44, 49, 50

Gallie, D., 66-68
General and Municipal Workers Union (GMWU), 73, 92
Gergen, K. J., 111
Gevers, P., 80
Giddens, A., 58
Gillis, J.S., 111
Goldfarb, A., 80
Goldthorpe, J.H., 90
Goodman, J.F.B., 91, 94
Gospel,H., 114, 115
Gotting, D., 91, 94
Gottschalk, A.W., 117
Green, K., 10
Greiner, L.E., 70
Guest, D.E., 86, 88
Gustavsen, B., 86
Hackman, J., 21
Hackman, J.R., 21
Halsey, A.H., 45, 47, 69
Hammond, K.R., 114
Hanlon, M., 101
Hazelhurst, R.J., 17
Healy, J.J., 100, 111, 113, 114

244

Trist, E., 16, 21-23, 31, 32
Turkington, D., 103, 104, 117, 200, 202

Ure, A., 34, 35
Ursell, G., 91, 93

Van der Velden, H.A., 80
Verba, S., 76
Vianello, M., 74
Vroom, V., 76

Walker, K.F., 76, 77, 79, 83, 86
Wall, T.D., 80, 87, 88, 93, 198
Walton, R., 4, 97, 98-103, 109, 110-113, 197-199
Walton, R.E., 21
Ward, T., 27
Warner, M., 47, 79, 92
Warr, P., 97
Webb, B., 75

Webb, S., 75
Wedderburn, D., 17
Weltz, F., 25, 68
Whitehill, A.M., 29
White, P., 80, 85, 93, 204
White, R.K., 76
Wieser, G., 74
Wilders, M., 79, 92
Wilke, H., 82, 115
Wilkinson P., 47
Wilkinson, B., 18
Wilkinson, F., 41
Williams, R., 56-61, 63, 64, 65, 192
Willman, P., 14
Wilson, D.C., 194, 198
Winch, G.W., 47
Winkler, J., 81, 115, 198
Wood, S., 41, 43
Woodward, J., 117
Wright, E.O., 42

Zeuthen, F., 95

SUBJECT INDEX

managerial objectives, 34
managerial prerogative, 203
managerial strategies, 181-183
manpower adjustment difficulty of, 15
manpower implications, 2
manpower planning characteristics of, 24, 25
manpower policies, 23
manpower problems, 12, 13
microapplications impact of size, 125 126-128
micro revolution, 1
monopoly capitalism, 37
mutuality clauses, 61

needs at work, 20, 21
new technology agreements, 54, 59, 60, 192
health and safety, 64
pay, 65
redundancy, 63
trade union involvement, 61
work design, 64
working hours, 65
National Graphical Association (NGA), 54
Norwegian data agreements, 188
numerically controlled machines, 50

organisational choice, 16, 17
overtime, 25, 27

participation attitudes to, 90-94
ideologies and, 74-76
productivity and, 88
satisfaction and, 88

workers' ability and, 81
workers' desire for, 79, 80
participation and change, 66, 67, 69
participation research, 78
weaknesses of, 89, 90
participative structures, 68, 83-87
piecemeal microapplications, 128, 129, 142, 143, 182
political factors, 30
problem-solving see integrative bargaining

quality of working Life, 17
and new technology, 52
factors contributing to, 17, 18

reasons for change, 117
reduction of hours, 25
redundancy, 23, 24, 27, 185, 205
research methodology, 107, 118-120
resistance, 42, 46-48
responsible autonomy, 50
retraining, 14

satisfaction with change, 4
Science Advisory Committee, 188
scientific management, 36, 41
skills, 14, 15
shortages, 29
socio-economic constraints, 28, 29
socio-technical theory, 2, 16, 17, 33
spinning industry, 50